ABG0760

$11.95

973.04 Prpic, George J.
PRP
        South Slavic
        immigration in
        America

DATE		

2TR
2005   80 5973   2109

The Immigrant Heritage of America Series

Cecyle S. Neidle, *Editor*

Ivan Meštrović's statue of the "Immigrant Mother" in Cathedral Square,
Milwaukee, Wisconsin

SOUTH SLAVIC IMMIGRATION IN AMERICA

By GEORGE J. PRPIC

John Carroll University

TWAYNE PUBLISHERS

A DIVISION OF G. K. HALL & CO., BOSTON

Library of Congress Cataloging in Publication Data

Prpic, George J
    South Slavic Immigration in America.

    (The Immigrant Heritage of America Series)
    Bibliography: pp. 281–97
    Includes index.
    1. Slavic Americans—History.   I. Title.
E184.S6P73   973′.04′918   77–17041
ISBN 0–8057–8413–6

MANUFACTURED IN THE UNITED STATES OF AMERICA

For Hilda, Francis and Maya

Contents

About the Author

George J. Prpic was born in 1920 in Banat, grew up and was educated in Croatia (both parts of Yugoslavia). He graduated from the Real Gymnasium in Požega (1939) and received Diploma of the Faculty of Jurisprudence, Croatian University, Zagreb (1944). After living as a refugee in Austria and studying History at the University of Graz he immigrated to the United States in May 1950 under Truman's DP Act. For some five years he worked in Cleveland's factories. In 1956 he became a U.S. citizen and got his M.A. in History at John Carroll University. Three years later he earned his Ph.D. in History at Georgetown University, Washington, D.C.

He has taught at John Carroll U. since 1958. He is Professor of History and a member of the Institute for Soviet and East European Studies. His specialties are U.S. immigration, ethnic problems and East European history. He has published in English, Croatian, German and Spanish: books, chapters, articles and studies dealing with South Slavic immigrants and their historical background. He is the author of *The Croatian Immigrants in America* (1971); *A Century of World Communism* (1974); two books dealing with Croatian publications abroad; and co-author of *Selected Communities of Cleveland* (1974). His favorite theme is the role of the anonymous immigrants, especially Slavic women.

Preface

Living in the Balkans, an area in southeast Europe so marked by political unrest that it was characterized as the "Powder Keg of Europe" in the nineteenth century, the South Slavs comprise the Bulgarians, Croatians, Macedonians, Montenegrins, Serbs and Slovenians. They had a turbulent history. While Slovenians enjoyed independence for only a short period—and during the Middle Ages were incorporated by the Germans into the Holy Roman Empire—the Bulgarians, Croatians, Montenegrins, and Serbs established independent states that endured for centuries. Between the late 1300s and early 1500s all of these states were subjugated by foreign invaders: Hungarians, Venetians, Austrian-Germans, and especially the Ottoman Turks.

Today, the six nationalities inhabit two states: Yugoslavia (which means "the country of South Slavs") and Bulgaria, both countries being ruled by Communist governments.

Until the advent of industrialization in the late 1940s, the great majority of South Slavs were peasants, people of the soil. They were mostly small farmers engaged in agriculture, animal husbandry, forestry, and fishing. By the early 1900s many of these peasants had little or no land. Large sections of the Adriatic hinterland, Montenegro and Macedonia had little arable land. In northern Croatia many peasants were fairly prosperous. In most of Serbia and Bulgaria the lot of peasants, all living in villages, was fairly good. In other sections of the Balkans the villagers were poor, especially in the southern mountainous areas stretching from Slovenia into Macedonia. They were neglected, illiterate and without hope for the future. Before 1914 industrialization affected only parts of Slovenia and Croatia. The middle class was small in all the Balkan countries before the 1920s.

During the centuries of conquest, the South Slavs assimilated many non-Slavic groups and inherited from oppressive foreign rulers a taste for violence. To survive they had to fight and after overthrowing the foreigners they fought each other. Separated by differences in religion, culture, historical development and the rise of fierce nationalism, the South Slavs are still torn apart by controversies and disputes over territories.

The Croatians, who lived along the Adriatic Sea, were the first to migrate overseas. During the Turkish wars, from the late 1300s until the late 1800s, all South Slavs were involved in a mass exodus to various parts of Europe. Slovenian and Croatian emigrants arrived in the United States long before the era of the "New Immigration." However, the largest group of Slovenians and Croatians, along with their Balkan neighbors, arrived in the United States between 1890 and 1920. The immigrants who arrived during the high tide of immigration were less successful than their predecessors. The new immigrants who settled in the industrial centers of the East and Midwest were people of the soil, mountaineers, shepherds and farm laborers. Although some were successful, most eked out a bare existence in the mills, factories and mines of a booming, industrialized America. Many failed miserably and returned home, sick and disappointed. In the course of time those who stayed improved their lot and the news of their success meant that the lure of "Amerika" continued undiminished for those remaining in the homeland. Immigration was an escape from wars and insecurity, from conscription and oppressive regimes, from poverty and landlessness. The flight to America depopulated whole regions along the Adriatic; today every fifth Slovenian and Croatian lives in the United States.

After 1945 a different breed of immigrant came to America. Unlike their predecessors they are in general well-educated and skilled professional people. Most adapted quickly to their new homeland and quite a few became very prosperous. In the continual exodus from Yugoslavia an average of six thousand immigrants reaches the United States every year. Because of modern transportation and communication, the ties between homeland and immigrant are much closer than before. Many new immigrants are political refugees who observe developments in the homeland with keen interest. Being politically active, they sometimes make dramatic headlines in U.S. newspapers as demonstrated in the September 1976 airplane hijacking by Croatian nationalists.

This book attempts to cover the fascinating story of the life and contribution of the South Slavs in America from the earliest arrivals to the 1970s. Although outstanding figures in many fields have been included, the primary emphasis of this book is on the role of the average, anonymous immigrant whose hard work, ingenuity and drive, rich cultural heritage and love of freedom contributed to this nation. There are names and stories which deserve to be told, but it is not possible in a single volume to chronicle all the worthy contributions of six ethnic groups. And, it is hoped that this introductory study will encourage detailed studies of the accomplishments of the South Slavic communities in the United States. There is a great need in this era of ethnicity and ethnic studies for additional works since the South Slavs, in spite of their large numbers and significant contributions, are little known to the American public.

After providing the historical background of the South Slavic peoples and their migrations in the first two chapters, I divided the book into four parts. Croatians are dealt with in the first section since they were the first to arrive. Today they comprise the largest majority of South Slavs in America. The second part is devoted to the Slovenians; the third deals with the Serbs and Montenegrins; and the fourth discusses the Bulgarians and Macedonians. Each part chronologically follows the life and settlement of the different groups with one last chapter dwelling on the contributions and the future of the South Slavs in the United States. A short conclusion sums up the role and significance of the nationalities.

Finally, I would like to say that I grew up in a society where America was very popular. In Croatia, I lived among the returned "Amerikanci." We knew a great deal about America, not realizing then that some day fate would bring us here. Like thousands of my countrymen I have found a new homeland where I am happy and content. My years of residence in this country have given me a great appreciation of the earlier generations of South Slavic immigrants who paved the way for us. I feel that we owe them a great debt. I hope I have succeeded in repaying that debt by depicting their lives, and the lives of us who came much later, but that I leave for the reader to decide.

GEORGE J. PRPIC

John Carroll University
June 1977

Foreword

As editor of a series intended to bring to the fore all the ethnic groups of which the American population is composed, I am aware that to single out one particular national group for comment might be misjudged as partiality. I am not of Slavic descent; the closest I have come to the Balkans is through the study of European history and through reading—Emily Greene Balch's *Our Slavic Fellow Citizens* and Rebecca West's *Black Lamb and Grey Falcon*—and through my travels in the Balkans— the unforgettably beautiful Bay of Kotor, the craggy peaks of Montenegro, the walled city of Dubrovnik, surrounded by the fabulous Adriatic, all of which Professor Prpic speaks of in his book. But I must admit that I've always had a "soft spot" for these tall, handsome, stalwart, uncomplaining, hard-working Balkan Slavs who gave to America's industries countless workers, two of the greatest scientific wizards, Serbs Nikola Tesla and Michael Pupin, and the great Croatian sculptor, Ivan Meštrović, who created among other works the hauntingly beautiful, larger-than-life statue of an immigrant mother whose expression clearly betrays the anguish of her existence. And there were the Slovenians: Frederick Baraga, the missionary and Louis Adamic, the writer. These were not the only South Slavs who were stamped with the mark of genius; Milovan Djilas—whose many books were printed in America—is also the possessor of unusual talent and so was Franz von Suppé, but unlike the first five they did not contribute to America's greatness.

It is especially for the South Slavic women, peasant women mostly, that I feel the greatest sympathy. In my estimation they were the most martyred of America's immigrant women.

Two axioms underlie the subject of immigrants and their relationship to America. One: that the "seasoning process" was for all, whether they came from Western Europe, or from the South and East, a time of terrible stress. A European education did not help unless it was in English. America wanted brawn not brain, and it was infinitely harder for the educated to wield a pickaxe and shovel than it was for those accustomed to hard sweaty labor. Even Tesla, the inventor of alternating current, was for a time compelled to fall back upon digging in the streets to keep alive. Of how little use a university education or knowledge of languages was in the 1880s, one can gather from reading Edward Steiner's autobiography, *From Alien to Citizen*. Intellectual talents were of no help.

Two: each nationality, barring none, made its distinct and significant contribution to the development of our nation, both through the labor of all and through individual effort and accomplishment.

Professor Prpic traces in detail the spread of South Slavic settlers throughout the breadth and width of America from the early days when these Slavs came in sailing ships to become oyster fishermen in the Gulf states and the later years when they participated in the Civil War and the Gold Rush, to the present. Dedicated priests served heroically as missionaries to the Indians, as spiritual leaders of early communities, and later helped to erect churches and fraternal organizations. As industrial workers these Slavs gave their toil and too often their lives to the steel mills, mines and stockyards where they were miserably exploited as industrial laborers and miners.

No group of workers were more inhumanely treated than striking miners. In addition to the bitter labor conflicts of the late nineteenth and twentieth centuries in which Slavs participated, there were the regularly occurring accidents in the coal mines. In some mine accidents women lost not only their husbands, but young sons at the same time. These were not the days when one could at least hope for fair compensation.

That brings us back to their women, those peasant women of incredible physical stamina and a capacity for endurance exceeded by no other group of immigrant women. They were slaves not only to their families, cooking, baking bread, washing and ironing for them, but also taking care of other men who lived with the family, for the Slavic woman was also a "boarding missus," providing homes for gangs of single men who paid a

Foreword

pittance for the food these women cooked and the clothes they washed for them.

To the present descendants of the Croatians, Slovenians, Serbs, Montenegrins, and Bulgarians, the experience of their forefathers in America must seem as unbelievable as the stories of the Turkish atrocities to which many of these peoples had been subjected. Professor Prpic treats the story of these South Slavs— their hopes, struggles, and their concerns with historical objectivity and with love.

CECYLE S. NEIDLE

Brooklyn, 1977

Acknowledgments

I am forever grateful to Dr. Cecyle S. Neidle, the editor of Twayne Publishers' "The Immigrant Heritage of America" series. Without her advice, patience, and encouragement I would have never finished this book. Her work as editor went beyond the call of duty during some five years of preparing this work.

I am also thankful to Professor Michael Novak and to the Rockefeller Foundation whose grant in Humanities, awarded in the summer of 1974, enabled me to complete the manuscript.

As so many authors have done, I, too, give due credit to my wife Hilda, for her sound criticism and help, especially in the first part of the book. To her and our children I dedicate this book which has deprived them of many hours of the more enjoyable aspects of life.

Over the years my school, John Carroll University (which is located in University Heights, a suburb of the very cosmopolitan city of Cleveland) has granted me a reduced teaching load for research and writing. My thanks go to Dr. Arthur J. Noetzel, Academic Vice President, and to Dr. William J. Ulrich, my colleague and chairman of the Department of History, as well as to Dr. Michael S. Pap, director of the Institute for Soviet and East European Studies for direct and indirect support; to Dr. Joseph S. Kelly of JCU's Department of Religious Studies and to his wife Ellen for editing and typing the long manuscript (earlier version); to Mrs. Mary K. Sweeny, the reference librarian at our Grasselli Library; to Mrs. Florence H. Krueger of the same library for all the efficient and friendly help. I am also indebted to Dr. Edward G. Gobetz, Professor of Sociology at Kent State University for loaning me the rare and invaluable book on American Slovenians by J. Trunk, *Amerika in Amerikanci*, and for additional information on his countrymen, the Slovenians. Other authors and individuals from whose pioneering works my study benefited, I quote in my references. Due credit must go especially to Dr. G. G. Govorchin and to Adam S. Eterovich.

For the typing of the last version of this manuscript I am indebted to our faculty secretaries: Marilyn F. Collins, Mary T. Talarico, Vlasta Vrana, and Margie P. Wasdowich. Their services were generously provided by John Carroll University.

The fact that the publishers patiently waited for the completion of this manuscript is gratefully acknowledged. That it took me this long to finish it is perhaps best explained by the fact that it deals with six different nationalities whose past presents an intricate part of East European and Balkan history.

CHAPTER 1

Who Are the South Slavs?

AFTER the launching of the Soviet Sputnik in October 1957, more interest in the Slavic immigrants coming to the United States from the Balkans and East Europe became evident. Historians had over the years called attention to those "Who [had] Built America." On the whole, only a few scholars, some national leaders, and a few journalists concerned themselves with the state of nationality groups.

The passage of the new U.S. immigration law in October 1965 intensified the study in ethnic backgrounds. While Greater Cleveland, for example, was always aware of its composition of some fifty different nationalities—a majority of them East Europeans—many parts of the nation only recently "rediscovered" the immigrant.[1]

Now the search for identity is on. Grumbling voices of discontent are heard from the Poles and other Slavs. Loud protests are being raised by the Italians. Many scholars agree that the "ethnic vote" is a reality, as proven in all elections during the 1970s.

During the last ten years newspapers, magazines, periodicals, and hundreds of books have discussed the ethnics and their problems much more extensively than they did during the four previous decades. This interest and the ethnic revival itself were partly due to the Civil Rights movement of Blacks and Spanish-speaking people. This nation, indeed, has become aware of the presence of discontented ethnic groups. In 1976 Bicentennial and important election year, the candidates of both parties accepted the fact that the East Europeans, Slavic, and South Slavic ethnic groups want to be recognized, just as do other groups, for instance the Spanish-speaking and Blacks. President Ford even had appointed an adviser on ethnic affairs who was of Ukrainian origin.

After the passage of the Ethnic Heritage Studies Bill on June 8, 1972, the main proponent of the bill, U.S. Senator Richard S. Schweiker of Pennsylvania, called it "an important new Federal commitment to ethnicity and pluralism as positive forces in America." By this law special Ethnic Heritage Centers are to be established, ethnic and immigration studies, language programs, and various other ethnic activities in culture and arts are to be supported. The Bicentennial observances called attention of the nation especially to the *contribution* of all ethnic groups.[2]

I   *The Literature on the South Slavs*

The South Slavs were almost unknown to the Americans until they were introduced to them in 1910 by Emily Greene Balch in her excellent book *Our Slavic Fellow Citizens*. She had collected material for this during her visit in the Slavic lands of the Habsburg Empire. She wrote with understanding and objectivity. Hers was the first book that discussed extensively the Slovenians, Croatians, Montenegrins, Serbians, and Bulgarians. But, in spite of their large numbers, the South Slavs remained fairly unknown among our scholars and the community. During World War I the interest in them increased as President Woodrow Wilson became a champion of self-determination for all Slavic peoples. Then in the 1930s and 1940s, Louis Adamic, an American writer of Slovenian birth, continued Miss Balch's pioneering work. Among his numerous books and articles on general problems of immigration and immigrants were numerous writings on the South Slavs. No one ever wrote more about them than Adamic did. Several of his books have been reprinted in this upsurge of ethnic interest.

With the influx of immigrants from the South Slavic lands after World War II a number of Croatian and Slovenian scholars have written and published on the subject. They were joined by some American-born and non-Slav writers and scholars. Books, studies, doctoral dissertations, Master's theses, articles, surveys, symposia, and encyclopedic works have discussed the South Slavs and their background.[3]

II *Historical Background of South Slavic Emigration*

Human migrations are as old as mankind. Europe, like ancient America, was peopled by migrations, predominantly from Asia. All European peoples are a mixture of various ethnic and racial components. There are three major linguistic and racial families of peoples in Europe belonging to the so-called Indo-European stock: the Slavic, the Germanic, and the Romance or Latin.

The Slavic nations have developed during the past fifteen-odd centuries. The ancient Slavs absorbed and assimilated many non-Slavic tribes and peoples. What distinguishes the Slavs from other families of nations is first of all their language. Throughout their turbulent past, their spoken and written word has remained the strongest bond among them. Until about ten centuries ago the Slavs used a more or less common language, the Old Slavic or Slavonic. Gradually, distinct languages developed among them. Only in the course of the past five centuries were these tongues refined to the point of becoming *literary* languages, differing from each other in various degrees.

This closeness in speech and the ability to understand each other have created emotional and spiritual links between the Slavic nations in their homeland and the new settlements in foreign lands. The idea of Pan-Slavism originated as an expression of Slavic solidarity. But the attempts of idealistic individuals to promote Slavic unity over recent centuries did not take root. Although the language tends to unite the Slavs, the forces that divide them have prevailed.

There are three Slavic groups of nations: the Eastern Slavs, the Western Slavs, and the Southern Slavs. The Eastern Slavs are: the Russians, Bielorussians (or White Ruthenians), and the Ukrainians. They are the most numerous of the three Slavic groups, numbering over one hundred and fifty million people. Most of them live in the Soviet Union. A great majority belong to the Eastern Orthodox Church and use the Cyrillic alphabet.

The Western Slavs include the Poles, Czechs, Slovaks, and Lusatian Sorbs, with a combined population of over forty-five million. They are located in the very heart of Europe. The Poles—numbering some thirty-three million—are the strongest among them. The rest are their southern neighbors, the Czechs and Slovaks. These three nations are well represented by millions of their kinsmen in America. In Saxony (now East Germany) there are some 150,000 Lusatian Sorbs. Over ninety percent of Poles are Roman Catholic. The Czechs and Slovaks are predominantly Catholic; some twenty percent of them adhere to Protestantism.[4]

The South Slavs are located in southeastern Europe, mostly in the Balkan peninsula. From the West to the East they are: the Slovenians, Croatians, Montenegrins, Serbs, Macedonians, and Bulgarians. Slovenia and the northern parts of Croatia belong geographically in the Alpine region and partly in the Pannonian plains of east central Europe. While the Slovenians have only a narrow access to the Adriatic Sea, the Croatians occupy some five hundred miles of its shores. Through this sea the Croatians are connected with the Mediterranean, the Near East, and the world.

III   *The Balkan Peninsula*

For good reason historians have designated the Balkans as the "Tragic Peninsula."[5] As the interests of several great powers clashed there, it was named more recently "the powder keg of Europe." The first of the modern holocausts, World War I, was triggered in the Balkans. Some of the most vicious phases of the last war, between 1939 and 1945, were fought there. Revolts and uprisings have raged over the peninsula for many centuries.

The word "Balkan" is of Turkish origin, meaning "mountain." A range of mountains called Balkans extends south of the Danube River in Bulgaria. Like a huge irregular triangle the peninsula stretches south deep into the Mediterranean Sea. Nineteen centuries ago this sea "in the middle of the earth" was completely surrounded by the powerful Roman Empire. It was basically a Mediterranean empire, a world in itself.

In 285 A.D. Emperor Diocletian—a native of Dalmatia, divided the Roman Empire into two parts. Right on the shores of the blue Adriatic, near ancient Salona, he built a splendid huge palace where he spent his last days. Later the town of Split started its existence within and around the walls of this palace.

Many towns and cities in these regions had their start in old Roman or Greek settlements.

Emperor Constantine, founder of Constantinople in the early fourth century, temporarily united the empire. In 395 it was finally divided. The city of Rome remained the center of the Western Roman Empire until it finally succumbed to the invasions of Germanic tribes in the late 400s. The city of Constantine—at the crossroads of Europe and Asia—grew to great prominence as the center of the Eastern Byzantine Empire. After the 600s it gradually became a new Greek Empire. At its height it also controlled the entire Balkans.

The historic dividing line between the former Western and Eastern Roman Empires ran from what is now northern Albania northward following the Drina River to the Sava River.[6] The Drina is a swift and curving mountain river, flowing through the gorges until in its final course it reaches the Sava, which at this point makes its way through the southern fringes of the Pannonian Plain. In its entire course of some two hundred-odd miles the Drina River constitutes a natural borderline between two worlds, the Latin and the Byzantine, the Western and the Eastern cultural and religious spheres. In the last century and until 1918, the Drina was the frontier first between the Turkish-controlled, and (after 1878) the Austrian-controlled, province of Bosnia on its west shore and Serbia on its east shore. Its waters were bloodied in two world wars.

The Balkan peninsula is surrounded on its eastern flank by the Black Sea, the Sea of Marmora, and the Aegean Sea. The western shores of the rugged peninsula face the Ionian and Adriatic Seas, and to the south there is the Mediterranean. All these waters are either connected with, or are parts of the Mediterranean Sea, which separates the continents of Africa and Europe. Through the Straits of Gibraltar the Mediterranean connects the Balkan area with the Atlantic Ocean and thus with the western hemisphere. Through the Suez Canal it links these regions with the Indian Ocean, the Pacific, the Middle and Far East, in fact with the major part of the globe. In the history of the Balkan peoples the seas have been of vital importance. They have shaped their destinies, linked them with the rest of the world. Indeed, for centuries they have caused their migrations to all parts of the world.

IV *The Two South Slav States*

The Balkan countries of today include: Rumania, Bulgaria, Yugoslavia, Albania, and Greece. All of them are republics. With the exception of Greece, they are ruled by Communist parties and are officially called Socialist Republics. Our story concerns only the two states inhabited by the South Slavs, namely, Yugoslavia and Bulgaria. These countries extend from Trieste in Italy and the western Slovenian Alps, eastward to the sandy beaches of the Black Sea and the hinterlands of Istanbul (formerly Constantinople).[7]

The Socialist Federal Republic of Yugoslavia comprises a territory of 99,000 square miles. It consists of six republics: Slovenia, Croatia, Bosnia-Herzegovina, Serbia, Montenegro, and Macedonia. Serbia also includes two autonomous provinces: Vojvodina in the north and Kosmet in the south. The latter is predominantly Albanian.

In South Slav languages the term "Jug" is a geographic one, denoting the "South." Thus "Jugoslavia," or most commonly called "Yugoslavia," designates an area where the South Slavs live, rather than their distinct nationality. Historically the term also included the Bulgarians.

It is interesting to note that in 1962 only 317,000 and in 1971 only 265,000 persons in Yugoslavia were listed in the official Yugoslav census as "Yugoslavs." According to the last census of 1971, Yugoslavia's population was 20.5 million. The inhabitants were listed as follows:

Serbs	8,137,000
Croatians	4,519,000
Slovenians	1,704,000
Macedonians	1,195,000
Moslems	1,727,000
Montenegrins	508,000

All these peoples are South Slavs. They use four different languages and three alphabets (one of them, Arabic, is used by Moslems in their religious texts) and they belong to three major religions. Traditionally the South Slavs have been influenced by the Western, Byzantine, and Islamic civilizations.

Among the national non-Slav minorities the strongest are the Albanians totaling 1,309,000, followed by the Hungarians— 479,000—and several others.[8]

The Moslems (Muslimani) are the only group listed in the census by their religious affiliation rather than by nationality. The better part of them are Croatians from the republic of Bosnia-Herzegovina who wished to avoid being lumped together with Yugoslavs. They also objected to being counted as Serbs, and due to pressure were discouraged from declaring themselves Croatians.[9]

Yugoslavia is the only Communist country in the world that for a number of years, until recently, permitted free emigration. Over a million people—mostly with passports—work in West Germany and other western European countries. A large number of accomplished professional and skilled young people have emigrated to the West and even as far as Australia. Of all European nationalities the Croatians have the highest rate of emigration. *No country in Europe today is as affected by the problem of emigration as is Yugoslavia.*[10]

The People's Republic of Bulgaria, the eastern neighbor of Yugoslavia, occupies a territory of 43,000 square miles with a population of nine million people, almost all pure ethnic Bulgarians. The remnants of ethnic Turks were permitted to leave the country after World War II. All Bulgarian scholars and present political leaders claim that Yugoslav Macedonia is part of the Bulgarian nation and the Macedonian language is merely a Bulgarian dialect. American scholars in the field of immigration have also regarded the Macedonians as closely related to the Bulgarians.[11]

The long-lasting Macedonian problem was caused by the partition of Macedonia at the end of the Balkan Wars (involving Serbia, Greece, and Bulgaria) in 1913 between the three Balkan countries. In the complex reality of Balkan politics this question is as alive today as it was decades ago.

In spite of the close affiliation of the Macedonians to the

Bulgarian nationality the Macedonian immigrants are treated in this book as a distinct group by the country of their origin—as Bulgarians from Macedonia.

CHAPTER 2

The Past of the South Slavs

IN order to understand the immigrants, one has to know their past in the old country. Even in his transplanted home in America an immigrant remains influenced by his past and the nostalgic memories of his youth. A Macedonian immigrant who as a young guerrilla fought the Turks and Greeks in Macedonia will never forget it, and he can hardly be expected to love his Greek or Turkish neighbors in America.

Let us now discuss briefly the history of the individual South Slav nations, making our historical journey from the extreme West to the extreme East: from the Slovenians to the Bulgarians. As all these nations experienced separate historical developments, we are going to discuss the individual South Slav immigrant groups in several separate parts.

I The Slovenians

The very name of the Slovenians, "Slovenec," is derived from the common name of ancient Slavs: *Sloveni, Slovinci,* or *Slavjani.* Before and after the 600s their forefathers settled all the way from the Danube River southward to the upper Drava and Sava rivers. Sava has its source in the Slovenian Alps around which the core of permanent Slovenian settlements was established. The earlier Slovenian past has not yet been recorded in its definitive form.

The Slovenians were part of the large Slavic Empire of Samo, during 627–658, before coming under Frankish domination. Then and during the time of Charlemagne (early 800s) the Slovenians became Christians. They have always remained a part of the Western Christian world, and of all the South Slavs they are the most Western-oriented people. In fact they detest being called a Balkan people!

Like the ancient Slavs, the Slovenians were peaceful and freedom-loving. They enjoyed independence for a short period during the ninth century. In Carinthia, the native dukes were installed in a democratic peasant ceremony, on a throne hewn out of rock in a field. Allegedly Thomas Jefferson read about this unique ceremony in the *Republic* by Jean Bodin and was influenced by the idea of the ruler's responsibility to the people, a principle which he used for his draft of the Declaration of Independence.[1]

Overpowered by their strong German neighbors from Bavaria and Ostmark (later Austria), the Slovenian people and their lands became part of the Holy Roman Empire. In the course of time even large sections of the rural population succumbed to Germanization. Slovenian lands shrank in size.

Throughout the centuries of Turkish warfare, Slovenian lands were devastated and depopulated by attacks and invasions by way of Croatia, Hungary, and Austria. Feudal landlords, mostly Germans, exploited the native peasants, but failed to protect them against Turkish raids. In desperation—lacking protection against the Turks and suffering feudal oppression—the peasants revolted on several occasions. In 1573 the Slovenian peasants made common cause with the Croatian peasants under the leadership of Matija Gubec, who is still popularly remembered as the "Peasant King."[2]

The Protestant Revolt of the 1500s, which coincided with Turkish wars and peasant rebellions, found many supporters among the Slovenian burghers and nobles. Primož Trubar, an eminent Slovenian contributor to the Reformation, in 1555 translated the New Testament into Slovenian. This and other Protestant editions inaugurated the Slovenian national literature; the first grammar of the Slovenian language was printed in 1584.

As most of the Protestants were German burghers and nobles, the Slovenian peasants would not follow them. The Habsburg Counter-Reformation suppressed Protestantism in Slovenia. Thousands of Protestants left the homeland and migrated to Germany and other countries. This movement and the flight of peasants—who were threatened by the Turks—was the first migration from Slovenian lands in modern history.

The Protestant literature in native Slovenian contributed to the rise of the Slovenian national consciousness. But the masses of the people remained loyal to the Catholic Church whose priests and monks were mostly sons of peasants. They remained close to the people, spread education, resisted Germanization, and provided national leadership.[3]

Industries, crafts, and trades developed and flourished in Slovenia earlier and to a much greater extent than in any other South Slavic country. In the late nineteenth and early twentieth centuries the Slovenians had proportionally more industrial workers, miners, lumbermen, tradesmen, businessmen, and artisans than any other South Slav people.

The Napoleonic era with the liberalizing tendencies of the French Revolution increased the Slovenian national revival. Napoleon's troops entered Slovenia first in 1797 during campaigns against Austria. It was during the brief French rule that the poet Valentin Vodnik (1758–1819) and other Slovenian writers and patriots engaged in literary and journalistic activities that would leave a permanent effect on the rise of modern Slovenian nationalism.[4]

In 1809 the French under Napoleon created the Illyrian Provinces with the capital in Ljubljana. The region was composed of almost all the Slovenian-inhabited Habsburg area, parts of Croatia, the Croatian Littoral, Trieste, and Dalmatia. The French respected the local customs, founded newspapers, stimulated education, built roads, and undertook many public works. The liberal French ideas were conducive to the rise of both Slovenian and Croatian patriotism and democracy. However, with the downfall of Napoleon in 1815, the reestablished Habsburg authorities crushed the liberal reforms. Slovenian lands were again divided into six different Austrian provinces.[5]

The memory of the Illyrian Provinces lingered. In 1848, when revolutions rocked the Habsburg Empire, the Slovenian leaders proclaimed as their national goal a united and autonomous Slovenia composed of all predominantly Slovenian-speaking regions. This goal was achieved seventy years later, at the end of 1918, with the destruction of Austria-Hungary. A great majority of the Slovenians then entered a union with the Croatians, Serbians, Montenegrins, and Macedonians. This was the first, the royal, Yugoslavia.[6] After four years of German and Italian occupation during World War II the Slovenian people joined the second, the Communist Yugoslavia.

II   *The Croatians*

Of Iranian descent, the Croatians settled first after 375 A.D. in the region north of the Carpathian Mountains in parts of southern Poland and northern Bohemia. This then became White Croatia. They became Slavs. In 626 A.D. some three hundred thousand of them migrated to the western parts of the Balkans, the former Roman provinces of Pannonia, Dalmatia, and Illyricum then under Byzantine supremacy. Here they defeated the Avars (invaders of Mongolian descent) and mixed with numerous peoples: Slavic settlers, the ancient native Illyrians, remnants of Celtic tribes, Romans, Greeks, and others. They formed several loosely connected states between the Drava River in the north and the Adriatic Sea in the south, from the Istrian peninsula in the west to the Drina River in the east.

The main state, White (or Western) Croatia, stretched along the larger part of the eastern Adriatic shores. Red (or Southern) Croatia was located between the Neretva River and Lake Scutari. Around ancient Dioclea in Red Croatia, a new state, Zeta, was to arise, later to be known as Montenegro.

Between the second half of the seventh and ninth centuries Western Christianity was solidly established among the Croatians. However, for some time Byzantine influences also remained. Croatia was a country at the crossroads of the two worlds, the East and the West.[7]

Following a period of Frankish and Byzantine control over some parts of Croatia during the ninth and tenth centuries, the Croatians enjoyed complete independence under their native princes. Under their first king, Tomislav (around 925 A.D.), the Croatians had a powerful army and a strong navy. Of all Slavic nations, the Croatians became the first and the most maritime people. Their destiny is tied to the Adriatic; they control its eastern shores, a beautiful rugged coast of inlets, bays, and islands with high mountains rising above the blue waters.

Bosnia in the hinterland was for centuries ruled by a Ban (viceroy, or chief) who recognized the supremacy of the Croatian king whose residence and estates were in central parts of the Dalmatian coast in the vicinity of Split. Bosnia became an independent kingdom in the fourteenth century.

It was in the eleventh century that Croatia reached the zenith of its power under Kings Krešimir and Zvonimir. Then the Croatian state started to decline. In 1102 it joined Hungary in a personal union; the king of Hungary was also the king of Croatia, and because Bosnia used to be a part of the Croatian kingdom, he also insisted on his claims to this mountainous region. Croatia proper retained its separate status. It had a parliament called the Sabor and a Ban who represented the foreign ruler. In 1527 Croatia joined Habsburg-ruled Austria. This relationship with some modifications lasted until October 1918.[8]

III   *The Turkish Era*

The advent of the Ottoman Turks was a turning point in the history of the Balkans. After defeating the Bulgarians, the fierce Moslem warriors invaded and crushed Serbia in 1389. Bosnia was the next victim. Weakened by religious strife between the Bogomils (Christian "heretics") and the Catholic Church, Bosnia fell to the Turks in 1463. Its conqueror was the same Mehmed II, the sultan who in 1453 took Constantinople. Renamed Istanbul, this city became the capital of the huge empire that for centuries influenced the destinies of the Balkans and Europe.

In 1483 Herzegovina between Bosnia and the Adriatic was captured by the Turks. In Bosnia and Herzegovina many Bogomils and Catholics were converted to Islam and as loyal Turkish soldiers fought for the expansion of the Ottoman Empire. Of the Croatian lands only the most western regions adjacent to Slovenia, between the Drava River and the sea, remained under Habsburg rule while the Turks overran all Croatian lands, Montenegro, Albania, and in the north most of Hungary.

This was the most tragic era in the history of Croatia and all her Balkan neighbors. At the time when ambitious Spaniards were expanding in the New World, Croatian lands were divided between the Turks, Venetians, and Habsburgs. The political center now shifted from the Adriatic regions to Zagreb and northern Croatia. For many decades the Croatians under the leadership of their nobles and the Church led a frontier existence under constant Turkish threat.

They fought the Turks at a terrible cost. During the late 1400s and in the 1500s alone, over seven hundred thousand natives of Croatia and Slovenia were carried off as slaves by the Turks and sold on slave markets of the eastern Balkans and Asia Minor. Croati·n and neighboring lands were bled white.[9]

During these tragic times thousands of Croatian converts to Islam fought loyally on the Ottoman side, and many became famous grand viziers, statesmen, or military leaders. The mass flight of the people from war-torn regions depopulated the country. Many Croatian settlements were established in Lower Austria, western and southern Hungary, Slovakia, and even in southern Italy.

At the same time thousands of Croatians fought as Habsburg soldiers. Some were mercenaries in the French army before the French Revolution. The name they bore was immortalized by the word "cravat" meaning a necktie, derived from the French word "les Cravates" (the Croatians); they wore it as a scarf with their uniform. Thousands died fighting under Napoleon; other thousands served as sailors in Venetian and later Austrian navies. Forced by war to leave their ancestral lands, they emigrated to foreign countries, even across the sea. They fought and worked, lived and died under many foreign flags.[10]

To their vacated homes and lands came refugees from Turkish occupied lands. The Turks also brought thousands of Vlachs and other Orthodox settlers.[11] They kept coming after the wars of 1683–1699, when large parts of Hungary and Croatia were liberated from the Turks. Many eminent Croatians in modern history were of the Orthodox faith. Under the influence of the Serbian Orthodox Church which regarded every Orthodox as Serbian, many Orthodox people in Croatia proper, in Bosnia-Herzegovina, and in Dalmatia embraced Serbian nationality.

Oriental influences imported by the Turks have survived in the Balkans. The ethnic composition of large sections of the Balkans, including the Croatian lands, was radically changed during the Ottoman period. This fact contributed to many problems and struggles in modern Balkan history.

Demographic experts and historians are agreed that the population of Croatia (and of neighboring lands) would have tripled had it not been for the centuries of Turkish wars and occupation. In spite of all these losses and immense suffering the Croatian people never gave up hope that some day all their lands would be reunited and free.

IV *The Serbs*

Unlike the Slovenians and Croatians, the Serbs are by location and mentality a completely Balkan nation with traditionally strong ties to the East. They accepted Christianity from the Byzantine Empire, in the Orthodox rite, eventually progressing toward their own national Orthodox Church. They were influenced by the Eastern cultural sphere, their rulers having had only occasional relations with the Roman Church and the West.

Some thirteen hundred years ago, ancestors of the Serbian people lived in the region around the rivers Elbe and Saale, in what is now East Germany. Around 636 A.D., some eight thousand Slavic Serbs migrated to the province of Thessaly, northwest of Salonica in Macedonia (now northern Greece). They finally settled in the mountainous region between the Drina and Ibar rivers, then a part of the Byzantine Empire. The country became known as Raša.

In the course of history, the Serbs succeeded, at their neighbors' expense, in expanding their little country considerably. Bulgaria, then Serbia's most powerful neighbor, held the territory where present-day Belgrade and Serbia proper are located.

The greatest Serbian ruler, Stefan Dušan (1331–1355), popularly called Tsar Dušan, was a member of the Nemanjić dynasty. Constantly at war with his neighbors, Dušan made Serbia into a real power. Defeating both the Bulgarians and Byzantines, Dušan created an empire stretching from Belgrade in the north to Salonica and the Aegean Sea in the south. Dušan's empire which included Zeta (later Montenegro), Serbia, Macedonia, and Albania, fostered Serbian pride and later a fierce national consciousness.

After Dušan's death the Serbian state weakened and lost much territory. On a tragic day, June 28, 1389, Serbia was crushed by Sultan Murad I, at Kossovo. Then, and until 1878, Serbia, or parts of it, was ruled by the Turks. The Serbs were the first Balkan people to revolt against the Turks, fighting for and obtaining autonomy first. In 1878 they achieved complete independence for their country.

Of the two rival dynasties fighting each other over the rule of Serbia—the Karageorgevich and the Obrenovich—by 1903 the former had prevailed. But violence remained the rule in Balkan politics. Four Serbian rulers were assassinated within a century. The Karageorgevich dynasty was finally eliminated by the Communists in 1945.

During the long Turkish rule in the eastern Balkans, and Habsburg rule in the western Balkans, the oppressed Slavs looked to Moscow for help and protection. For many years the Russian Empire fought Austria for the control of the Balkans, and when in 1878, by the decision of the Congress of Berlin, Austria-Hungary occupied the Turkish provinces of Bosnia-Herzegovina, there was violent Serbian and Russian opposition. The Serbs wanted to incorporate those provinces into their own little state.

To understand the nationalistic mentality of the Serbs, one must examine the history of independent national Orthodox churches in the Balkans. Their establishment was not only a religious matter but was politically significant. Religion and the state, or religion and nationality, were considered identical in the Balkans. During the long Ottoman occupation of Serbian lands, for example, thousands of Serbs fled to neighboring countries and settled there. Serbian diasporas were created in Hungary and in Croatia. These settlers, though they became partly assimilated in their new provinces, were nevertheless always claimed by the Serbs as their own nationals on account of their Orthodox faith. As such they were members of the Serbian Orthodox Patriarchate, with its see in Peć and later in Karlovci and Belgrade. The existence of this patriarchate stimulated the rise of Serbian patriotism and nurtured dreams of a greater Serbia, including non-Serb peoples. Dušan's Empire did not come about a second time, and such aspirations by Serb nationalists caused bitter struggles with their neighbors: the Macedonians, Albanians, Bulgarians, and others.

During World War I, which was ignited by the assassination of Archduke Francis Ferdinand by a Serbian nationalist, Serbia and Montenegro were occupied by Austrian troops. Then in December 1918, after valiant efforts to liberate their country once more, the Serbs established the Kingdom of Serbs, Croats, and Slovenes, headed by a Karageorgevich. Macedonia was occupied and Montenegro simply annexed to the new state, Yugoslavia. This imposed union, torn by antagonisms and weakened by incessant internal strife, disintegrated in April 1941.[12]

V *The Montenegrins*

Almost a century ago Alfred Lord Tennyson paid tribute to the little country of Montenegro and her people in his sonnet "Montenegro." The conclusion expresses beautifully the heroic sense of their history:

> "O smallest among peoples! rough rock-throne
> Of Freedom! Warriors beating back the swarm
> Of Turkish Islam for five hundred years,
> Great Tzernagora! never since thine own
> Black ridges drew the cloud and brake the storm
> Has breathed a race of mightier mountaineers."[13]

These people have always been a freedom-loving people of warriors and mountaineers in a country so poor that it could only feed a few. They were divided into clans who occasionally fought one another.

The country's origins go back to the old state of Dioclea. After centuries of struggle the independence of the country was restored. Under the rule of the Crnojević family it maintained ties with Rome as late as the 1490s. There were then numerous Catholics there. The country became known as Zeta. The Turks subdued parts of the country in 1499, but they could never completely overpower the mountain clans. Gradually the natives established a stronghold against the Turks, an asylum for thousands of Albanians, Serbs, and others.

In 1664 the Turkish writer and traveler Evly Chelebi still found there numerous Croatian Catholics and Moslems. However, modern Montenegro became a predominantly Orthodox country with only a few thousand Catholics left in its coastal regions. Until 1851 it was a theocratic state, ruled by a prince-bishop from the Petrović family. One of the best known was Petar II Petrović Njegoš (1830–1851), the poet and philosopher who wrote his famous epic *The Mountain Wreath* (Gorski Vijenac) in his native tongue. It is the greatest work of the Montenegrin and one of the greatest among the literatures of the South Slavs. In constant warfare against the Turks the Montenegrins displayed heroic courage, a fanatical hatred of all Moslems, and slowly expanded their rocky territory. In 1878 they doubled it and by the Treaty of Berlin (July 1878) won international recognition of their independence.[14]

The last ruler of the country was Nikola Petrović. His capital was at Cetinje. He proclaimed himself king in 1910. Able, intelligent, and shrewd, he was a true and loyal friend of Russia which had always supported the poor and backward country. One of his daughters became the wife of King Victor Emmanuel of Italy. Two were married to members of the Russian imperial family. Another was married to Peter Karageorgevich, who in 1903 became king of Serbia, and the first king of Yugoslavia in 1918. This son-in-law deprived Nikola of his throne. Against the will of the people Montenegro was in 1918 occupied by Serbian troops. King Nikola died after World War I, a sad man in exile in France.

The greatest Montenegrin poet Njegoš is buried on top of Lovćen. His new mausoleum is adorned by Ivan Meštrović's sculpture of the Prince-Bishop. It was sculptured while Meštrović was living in South Bend, Indiana. Some fifty thousand Montenegrins are scattered overseas. Wherever they live they carry the memory of their holy mountain, Lovćen, the rock of freedom.

As William Jovanovich, the American son of a Montenegrin immigrant father, appropriately writes: "The legend of Montenegro rests on history. One who values a man's courage and a nation's freedom will recognize that the history of Montenegro, in the daring and the suffering of its people, generation after generation, is unequaled in Europe."[15]

VI *The Bulgarians and Macedonians*

The ancient Bulgarians were a Turco-Ugrian people (of remote Mongolian origin). In the sixth century they resided around the Don River in what is now southern Russia. In the early 600s they established a strong Bulgarian state which was soon destroyed by the Khazars, a people of mixed Turkish, Iranian, and other tribes. A part of the Bulgarians settled in the central Volga region from which their name later was derived: Volgar, Bolgar, and Bulgar. A section of them—perhaps forty thousand strong—migrated around 680 southward to the lower Danube in the Balkans, then a Byzantine territory.

In their new homeland they were gradually assimilated by the more numerous Slavs who had settled there earlier. They gave their name to all the peoples they could absorb in the large areas from the Black Sea westward across Macedonia, to the Drina River and to the ancient fortress of Belgrade on the confluence of the Sava and Danube Rivers.

Originally ruled by khans, they were later reigned by kings. One of the greatest was Simeon (893–927) who proclaimed himself the emperor of the Romans and Bulgarians. Tsar Samuel (976–1014) ruled from Ohrid on Lake Ohrid in Macedonia In 1018 the Byzantines overpowered their rival, Bulgaria.

After 885 the disciples of St. Methodius, expelled from Moravia, established themselves at Ohrid. They gave the Bulgarians the Cyrillic alphabet and the Old Slavonic as the language of the Church and state administration. Ohrid remained over the centuries the center of the Bulgarian Church and culture.

A second Bulgarian Empire—including large sections of Macedonia—was reestablished in 1185. By 1389 most of Macedonia and Bulgaria was overrun by the Turks. For over five centuries they ruled the Bulgarians, longer than any other South Slav nation. Numerous Bulgarians accepted Islam and became important dignitaries, statesmen, and military leaders of the Ottoman Empire. The country and the people were profoundly affected by the long Turkish rule.

Thousands of Bulgarians were deported to all parts of the Ottoman Empire. A great many perished in constant warfare or were sold as captives and slaves. Thousands emigrated to southern Russia and to various cities of the Habsburg Empire, where many became successful merchants and artisans. Others settled in Constantinople and the Near East. A few sailed across the sea to faraway lands. Thus long before Bulgaria became independent a great number of Bulgarians had emigrated to foreign countries.

The Bulgarian Orthodox Church came under full control of the Greek patriarch in Constantinople and the Greek hierarchy. The Slavic Bulgarians detested the harsh control by the Greek Church which enjoyed autonomy under the Sultan. The patriarch was the Sultan's official. At the time when the Ottoman Empire was the "Sick Man of Europe" and the foreign powers struggled for control of Turkey, the Bulgarians and Greeks were furiously fighting for control of the church and education in Bulgaria and Macedonia.

During the 1800s the Bulgarians slowly underwent a national awakening. After long feuds, the Turks finally agreed in 1872 to let the Bulgarians have their own Exarchate, their independent church in territories populated predominantly by Bulgarians. This was a great national victory for the Bulgarians. It aroused fierce opposition by the Greeks and Serbs who contested with them the control of Macedonia.

Macedonia became a battleground between these three nations and during the past hundred years in the nineteenth and twentieth centuries more Christians than Turks were killed in the mutual struggle. This rugged, beautiful land was in the pre-Slavic time the cradle of Alexander the Great. It lies in the geographic center of the Tragic Peninsula. Its people belong to the Orthodox, Moslem, and Jewish faith. A majority of its inhabitants were Slavic Macedonians who spoke a Bulgarian dialect. Under the Turks the city of Salonica was for centuries home to thousands of Jews who had been expelled from Spain and had found themselves well received by the Turks. The beautiful city on the Aegean—later sending thousands of emigrants to America—was for a long time a famous center of Jewish learning and culture.[16]

The great importance of Macedonia lies in its geopolitical and strategic location. The Vardar River flows through the country from the north to the south into the Aegean at Salonica. One who controlled its valley could also control the most important part of the Balkans. Old Macedonia had a territory of some 25,000 square miles. In 1912 its population numbered some 2,500,000.[17]

In May of 1876 the Bulgarians arose against the Turks who responded with an indiscriminate massacre of thousands of innocent people. It aroused cries of protest in Western Europe. W. E. Gladstone, the leader of the Liberal opposition in the British parliament, spoke and wrote vehemently against Turkish atrocities. His pamphlet, *Bulgarian Horrors*, as well as his slogan "Macedonia to the Macedonians" have been widely quoted.

Tsarist Russia, the traditional protector of the Balkan Slavs, declared war on Turkey, invaded Bulgaria, and by March 1878, the Russian troops were at the gates of Constantinople. Bulgaria was liberated. By the Treaty of San Stefano between Russia and defeated Turkey, a Great Bulgaria, including Macedonia, was created under the Russian protectorship. In July of the same year the great powers, determined to stop the Russian expansion in the Balkans, revoked the San Stefano Treaty by a new one in Berlin. Macedonia was returned to the Turks. Only Bulgaria proper was granted autonomy. In 1885 East Rumelia was united with it. After the rule of Alexander Battenberg as the first prince, Ferdinand of Saxe-Coburg took over. King Ferdinand proclaimed complete independence of Bulgaria in 1908. But the Great Bulgaria of San Stefano remained a dream of all Bulgarian patriots.

The contest for Macedonia—still under Turkish rule—went on between the Bulgarians, Serbs, and Greeks. In 1893 the Macedonian patriots founded the Internal Macedonian Revolutionary Organization, better known as IMRO. Its purpose was to wage the struggle for a free and united Macedonia. Its slogans were: "Liberty or Death" and "Macedonia for the Macedonians." In August of 1903 on the day of St. Elijah, after long preparations, IMRO started its heroic "Ilinden Uprising" against the Turks. After fierce fighting lasting several months the revolt was crushed by Turkish troops. They burned hundreds of villages, killed and imprisoned thousands of people. The Macedonian Question remained a concern of all great powers, including the United States.

During the Balkan Wars of 1912 and 1913, Macedonia was finally delivered from the Turkish yoke by Greek, Montenegrin,

Serbian, and Bulgarian troops. By the Treaty of Bucharest in 1913, Bulgaria—defeated in a new war by her former allies—was awarded only a small section of Macedonia.

The Bulgarians remained bitter and awaited a new chance to get their cherished western land. During World War I Bulgaria joined the Central Powers and was again defeated in 1918. King Ferdinand was forced to resign. His son Boris succeeded him. The struggle of the Macedonian guerrillas continued after 1918 for several years against the government of Belgrade which mercilessly suppressed any sign of Macedonian nationality. Macedonia was regarded as Southern Serbia. The IMRO was supported by many Bulgarian and Macedonian emigrants, notably those in the United States and Canada.

In 1941 Bulgaria joined the Germans in their attack on Yugoslavia. From spring of 1941 until the end of 1944 all Macedonian and Bulgarian territories were under the control of the Bulgarian troops. During the war King Boris died and was succeeded by his young son Simeon. Meanwhile Tito's partisans—joined by Macedonian Communists—were very active in Yugoslav Macedonia. In September 1944, the Soviet government declared war on pro-Axis Bulgaria and occupied it within a few days. Macedonia was lost again. A Popular Front government established itself in Sofia. In September 1946, it expelled King Simeon and declared Bulgaria a "People's Republic," making it a loyal Soviet satellite.

In present Yugoslavia Macedonia is one of the six republics. Its capital is Skopje. The Yugoslav Constitution recognizes a separate Macedonian nationality and language. Over a million and a quarter Macedonians and a sizeable number of ethnic Bulgarians are now within Yugoslavia. In most recent years the old Macedonian Question has flared up again. The present Bulgarian government still claims Yugoslav Macedonia, as evident in frequent controversies between the media and governments in both Sofia and Belgrade. Its echoes can be plainly felt in the press and politics of the Macedonian, Serbian, and Greek emigrant groups in North America.[18]

CHAPTER 3

Early Migrations

BECAUSE the Croatians were the first of all South Slavic immigrants and also the most numerous of all, they are discussed first. Born sailors, the Adriatic Croatians are basically a Mediterranean people. In the southern part of the beautiful coast, Dubrovnik (Ragusa in Latin) was for many centuries the home of mariners. For about a thousand years, until Napoleon abolished it in 1808, Dubrovnik was a free, flourishing commercial republic whose history has fascinated historians and writers.

Founded during the 600s near ancient Epidaurus, Dubrovnik exchanged Byzantine for Venetian supremacy in 1205. It lasted until 1358. As a free patrician state it saved its independence by paying tribute to the Turks who granted its merchants extensive trade and business privileges in their Balkan and Near Eastern parts. In the beginning of the 1400s the population of the little republic was forty thousand. Its government was a mixture of aristocracy and democracy. In 1416 it abolished slavery and later on introduced many progressive measures for the benefit of all the people. The inhabitants were Catholic Croatians. During the Renaissance it developed a literature that is still the pride of the Croatian people.[1]

Several nations have tried to prove that their countrymen were on Columbus' ships as sailors when he discovered America in 1492. Croatian historians, some of them in Dubrovnik, also claimed that their sailors had been among Columbus' crew. Such statements are based on tradition rather than on solid evidence.[2]

I The First Emigrants to America

As a real maritime power, Dubrovnik obtained by a special agreement in 1494 the concession to send her ships in the service

41

of Spain along the new routes to the Spanish colonies in America. Soon afterward the first emigrants from the republic left for America "to settle there, to acquire wealth and return home again."[3] They were among the first Europeans to emigrate to the western hemisphere.

Several merchants from Dubrovnik left for Spanish America before the mid-1500s. Some stayed, while some returned as wealthy men. The government of the little republic in a letter dated March 4, 1600, to its Madrid representative, mentions "many Ragusans" who were in America, and some who died there. Subsequently, Dubrovnik obtained from the Spanish government regulations concerning the estates of the deceased emigrants.[4]

The golden era of Dubrovnik was shattered by the earthquake of 1667. Even after the disaster, however, its merchant marine rallied and matched that of its old rival the Venetian Republic. As smart businessmen, the Ragusans were also engaged in the lucrative trade with the English, Spain's old enemies. It should be noted, however, that these "Slavs, Croats, calling themselves Ragusans (Dubrovčani)," were willing to sacrifice tremendous profits by refusing to ship the slaves from Africa to the American colonies.[5]

A considerable colony of Ragusans existed in England for a long period. The word "argosy" used by Shakespeare, is a derivation from the corrupted word "Ragosy" meaning "Ragusa." An English traveler to Dalmatia more than a century ago wrote: "The reputation of Ragusan merchantmen for wealthy cargoes had been stereotyped in the word Argosy (quasi Ragosy)— synonymous to the richest kind of carack." And to the writer Rebecca West, who was enchanted by the regions of Dubrovnik and Dalmatia, the entire past of Dubrovnik was best illuminated by one single word "ragosy," which simply means "a vessel from Ragusa."[6] In her enthusiasm for the romantic history of Dubrovnik she also mentioned that the little republic sent its mariners with the conquistadorial expeditions to the New World.

However, not all these early Croatian emigrants were merchants and businessmen. One young native of the island of Korčula, which is located near the coast of the Dubrovnik

Republic,[7] heard about the New World and moved to Spain to join one of his compatriots who was employed at the court of Charles V. In 1530 he sailed for San Domingo and then made his way to the Yucatan peninsula in Mexico. During his ten years there he became a Dominican monk. Returning to Korčula he built a monastery during the 1570s and died there as its prior. In Latin he was called Vincentius Paletinus.

According to evidence, he was the first Croatian and South Slav priest in America. It is not known whether he was active as a missionary among the native Indians at Yucatan. However, he advocated the Christianization of these people in his extensive writings. His most important work was *De iure belli contra infideles Indiae Occidentalis-ad Phillipum II Hispaniae regem.* In it he argued in favor of "the right of war against the infidels of West Indies" by the government of Philip II, the ruler of the Spanish Empire. Published in 1564, Vincentius' work was considered the best treatise on the subject at that time. Valuable to the Spaniards in their American expansion was another study of his (in Spanish) of the Yucatan and its people.

In his writings Paletin maintained that it was a duty of the Pope and of Spanish kings to liberate the Indians from their ignorance and wild customs, to make them good Christians and subjects of Spain. However, the Indians should be treated as human beings and as children of God. He disagreed with the printed views of the Peruvian Bishop Las Casas who was most critical of Spanish treatment of the Indians and argued that they should be left alone. He regarded Bishop Las Casas' views as too unrealistic. Las Casas was accused of having contributed to the outbreak of hostilities between the Indians and the Spaniards. In the ensuing massacre some five thousand Spaniards and fifty thousand Indians were killed. Pope Paul III then rebuked the bishop and approved the arguments of Paletin.[8]

The archives of Dubrovnik and other Adriatic cities are now being explored by native and foreign historians. New books and studies are being written in the English language. Slowly new light is being shed on the periods of the early Croatian migrations and the veil of mystery is being lifted from some of these episodes.

II *The Mystery of the Croatans*

An episode of early American history concerns the Croatan Indians and evolves around the "Lost Colony" of Roanoke Island off the shores of North Carolina. There are persistent claims by some writers in Yugoslavia and in the United States that the name of the Croatan Indians is to be linked to the Latin form "Croata" for "Croat" or "Croatian."

A Dalmatian legend has it that ships from Dubrovnik sailed westward across the Atlantic with a cargo of refugees from Turkish territory around 1540. One or more of these vessels sank off the coast of what is now North Carolina. The survivors mixed with the native Indians, who acquired the name "Croatan." According to this legend these voyagers preceded by about four decades Sir Walter Raleigh's ill-fated attempt to establish an Anglo-Saxon colony on Roanoke Island.[9]

An American writer maintains that "a Croatian ship called at the first permanent settlement in America" (at Roanoke) and subsequently "salvaged the entire settlement from the destruction that was taking place."[10]

When the English settlers arrived at Roanoke Island in July 1584, they found among the friendly Hatteras Indians children with non-Indian racial features: "very fine auburn and chestnut colored hair." The Indians told them of the wrecked ships manned by white sailors.

Governor White, who had been sent by the British crown to lead the settlers, left a colony of over 120 people at Roanoke Island in 1587. Upon his return in 1590 he found the colony deserted and two inscriptions in the bark of a live oak tree: "Croatoan" and "Cro." Some people believe that according to their promise to White before he left for England, the settlers indicated through these signs that they had gone to live with the Indians on Croatan Island. Prevented by stormy weather from searching for the vanished colonists, White returned to England and the group left on Roanoke Island thus passed forever out of history. Was the Lost Colony absorbed by the Croatans whose descendants live today in Robeson County, North Carolina? As American historians Hawks and McMillan stated "... what may have been the origin of the tribe, known to us through the English colonists as Croatan, can only be a matter of conjecture."[11]

It is not certain that the terms "Croatoan" or "Croatan" are Indian words. If, however, the word "Croatan" is of English origin, it would indicate the Croatian descent of those white sailors. On the other hand, the similarity of the name "Croatan" (assuming that it is Indian) and "Croata" may have been coincidental. The origin of the Croatan Indians thus remains an unsolved mystery shrouded in hearsay and legend.

On several occasions a few writers in Zabreb and in the United States asserted that "the first Croatian settlement in America was founded in the sixteenth century." This happened allegedly after the large peasant revolt in 1573; when it was crushed, numerous defeated peasants—both Croatian and Slovenian—left the country moving north "as far as Prussia and the shores of the North Sea from where they traveled to America as sailors or emigrants."[12]

Several American authors claim that around 1715 some twelve hundred Croatian and Slovenian Protestants who had been living as refugees in Prussia (a Protestant country) arrived in the English American colony of Georgia in search of freedom of worship. Many of them were descendants of the refugees from peasant revolts. The defeat of Protestantism in Slovenian and Croatian Habsburg lands caused these immigrants to move to the place where the creek they named Ebenezer flows into the Savannah River. Until the time of the Civil War this religious community prospered. During the war it was mostly destroyed and soon afterward abandoned by those who had survived. Only a cemetery remained, with inscriptions of Slovenian and Croatian names on the tombstones.[13]

Again, the above statements are assertions without solid historical proof. Some people who in recent years went to the Ebenezer cemetery claim they found no Slavic names there, others insist that among the so-called Salzburgers coming to Ebenezer during the 1700s were Slovenian and Croatian Protestants.[14]

The slow trickle of individual adventurers, merchants, missionaries, and mariners in foreign service continued to flow to the Americas, both north and south of the Rio Grande. From

Trieste in the north to the Bay of Kotor in the south, the sturdy and enterprising sailors were leaving their windswept shores to navigate all the known seas. During the 1700s America was a fairly well known continent among the people of Istria, the Croatian Littoral, Dalmatia, and Dubrovnik. Of the ships that left many never returned. Those who did brought stories of faraway lands, of stormy Atlantic voyages, strange foreign peoples, and gold and silver for which Spaniards and Englishmen were constantly fighting.

It is possible that "a Dalmatian ship sailed to America by way of India at the beginning of the eighteenth century."[15] The ships of Dubrovnik continued their transatlantic voyages, more Ragusans were joining their kinsmen in the Americas. Since the early 1700s Ragusan ships sailed regularly to Cuba, San Domingo, Philadelphia, and New York. Dalmatian sailors were coming to the English American colonies on foreign ships also in the course of the eighteenth century. More and more of these Adriatic Croatians were settling along the coast between Boston and the Gulf of Mexico.[16]

CHAPTER 4

Missionaries, Sailors, and Early Pioneers

AMONG the Roman Catholic priests of different nationalities who came to the American continent from the Habsburg lands were several Croatians. They came from the interior of Croatia between the 1680s and the mid-1800s, from a country that was relatively poor, recovering from centuries of Turkish wars and itself in need of priests.

I Rev. Juan M. Ratkay, S.J.

In his native land he was known as Ivan Ratkaj. He was born on May 22, 1647, in the castle of Veliki Tabor, north of Zagreb. The Ratkajs had come from parts of Slovakia (then under Hungary) and in Croatia became counts with large estates. To Croatia they contributed military men, scholars, and priests of distinction. One of Ivan's uncles died as a missionary in India and Tibet. Ivan had a thorough education, served as page to Emperor Leopold in Vienna, became a member of the Jesuit order, and was ordained as a priest in Graz, Austria, in 1675. After a prolonged sojourn in Spain, he left Cádiz for Mexico with a group of Jesuit missionaries on July 17, 1680.[1]

He landed at Vera Cruz on September 25, 1680. After arriving in Mexico City, the capital of New Spain, he wrote a lengthy letter to his provincial in Vienna. A very interesting description of his transatlantic sailing and one of the earliest accounts of such voyages to America, it has been widely quoted by scholars.[2]

In a later letter, Ratkay described his activities, the organization of missions, and the natives. Only a few Spanish military outposts controlled large areas with hostile Indian tribes. Having reached his mission in the Tarahumara region (northwest Mexico) after a long and perilous trip, he learned the native tongue of the Tarahumara Indians. He served at several posts. In

1683 he wrote a lengthy description of the region in Latin. It is now in the Jesuit archives in Rome.

His wish to go either to California or to New Mexico was not fulfilled. The Indians poisoned him on December 26, 1683 at the mission of Carichic because he forbade their drinking orgies.

Several historians, including H. E. Bolton and P. M. Dunne, consider Ratkay's work significant. They point out that without missions in Tarahumara, Pimería, Soñora, and Baja California, the development of California and adjacent states would have been considerably delayed.[3]

II   Rev. Fernando Consag, S.J.

Ferdinand Konšćak—as he is known in his homeland—was born on December 3, 1703 in Varaždin, only a few miles distance from Ratkay's birthplace. After going through the prescribed Jesuit education and ordination as a priest in Graz, he arrived in Vera Cruz in 1730. In 1733 he came to San Ignacio mission in Lower California. It was the most northerly of fifteen missions in that desertlike land. The first mission had been established here in 1697.[4]

In June and July of 1746 Consag—as he is known in Spanish sources—with a party of soldiers and Indians undertook a long and arduous trip sailing up the Gulf of California to the Colorado River. During this exploration he drew a map which definitely confirmed the previous findings of missionaries Juan de Ugarte and Francisco Kino: that lower California was not an island as previously believed, but a peninsula. It was thus possible to go north to what is now American California and the West. The historian H. H. Bancroft calls Consag's feat the most important event of that period.[5]

Consag's diary of the expedition and map were later reprinted in many works on California. In 1748, after years of hard work, he was appointed visitator in charge of all missions in California. He continued exploring the area, collected geographic and climatic data, and in 1751 founded the Santa Gertrudis mission. In 1753 he explored the western coast of the peninsula, founded the mining village of San Antonio Real, and laid foundations for the future San Francisco de Borja mission.[6]

In Mexican history Consag is known as "Gran Apostol." He was an expert engineer, mathematician, builder of dams, roads, and mines. He was "a man of prayer, of sacrifice . . . and of charity or brotherly love."[7] A true friend of the Indians, he baptized a thousand of them. When he died in San Ignacio on September 10, 1759, hundreds of them came from very far to see their beloved Padre before the burial.

Recently a scholar called attention to this forgotten man. He considers him "the most distinguished but little appreciated missionary" who has "the unique distinction [of] being the only Croatian Jesuit to labor in this mission field." He calls him also "the greatest Jesuit explorer in the peninsula—rivaling the renowned and overpopularized Padre on Horseback, . . .Kino." This American scholar felt that Consag had received "the least recognition by California historians."[8]

The mission and church of San Ignacio still stand, a testimonial to their founders' vision. They are now an attraction for tourists who only in recent years have penetrated the isolated and wild Lower California. Consag Rocks, looming over the blue waters in the northern part of the Gulf, memorialize his name and explorations.

III *Joseph Kundek in Indiana*

Very important for missionary activities in the United States was an organization in Vienna, Leopoldinen Stiftung (Leopoldine Society). It was founded by a German priest, Rev. Frederick Résé, in 1828 under the sponsorship of Emperor Francis I. Résé was then visiting in Austria after four years of missionary activity in the diocese of Cincinnati. The new society was named after St. Leopold, an ancient margrave of Austria, and in memory of the emperor's daughter Leopoldine, who died as Empress of Brazil in 1826. Most of the needed funds were collected from private contributions. By 1861 they amounted to some $436,000, a large sum for that time. The many missionaries sent by the Leopoldine Society were all fluent in German and were concerned primarily with the German-speaking immigrants in America.[9]

Among the priests supported by the Leopoldine Society was

Joseph Kundek. He was born in January 1809, in Ivanić near Zagreb. As a young priest of the Zagreb Diocese he became a fairly well known poet and writer in the romantic national and literary revival of his people. Inspired by the letters of American missionaries printed in the *Berichte* (Reports) of the Leopoldine Society, Kundek decided to go as a missionary to America. After receiving the required training in Vienna, he sailed from Southampton, England, in June 1838 and arrived at Vincennes, Indiana, after a voyage of over forty days. Bishop Brute sent him to Jasper, the seat of Dubois County in southern Indiana. Over the years Kundek helped some seven thousand immigrants from Germany to found homes in and around Jasper.

By the end of 1839 he founded a new town, Ferdinand, named after the emperor of Austria, a great benefactor of the Leopoldine Society. Kundek worked hard, traveled on horseback virtually thousands of miles. In the fall of 1843 he established a new settlement, Celestine, and three years later Fulda. During the fall of 1851 and spring of 1852 he visited Europe and spent a few days in Zagreb.

Only one Croatian priest followed Kundek to America. Rev. Edward Martinović became the German pastor in Madison, Indiana. Fifteen German priests accompanied him. Two Benedictine priests joined them from the famous Swiss Abbey at Einsiedeln. These two founded after June 1853 a priory near the town of Jasper from which the present magnificent St. Meinrad Archabbey developed. These newly arrived priests expanded and continued Kundek's work. He succumbed to overwork and illness and died at Jasper on December 7, 1857.

Jasper still cherishes the memory of Kundek. A statue of Kundek stands near St. Joseph Church, and one of the streets is named after him. In 1954 the Archabbey of St. Meinrad celebrated its centenary. In 1957 Jasper and Indiana commemorated the centennial of Kundek's death referring to him as "a great missionary, pioneer and citizen who left Croatia, the land he loved, to come and colonize the wilderness of this great state," for which the people "owe him a huge debt of gratitude." The words are from the official proclamation of "Father Kundek Day" by the Governor of Indiana.[10]

IV   *Early Settlers in the South*

Quite unlike the black-robed priests were numerous sailors, sea captains, and fishermen who made their early appearance along the Atlantic coast and in the South and West of the United States. Some Croatian settlers who entered California during Spanish rule came from the western shores of South America. The Adriatic Croatians saw in California a resemblance to their native land. During the 1700s and early 1800s it seemed to them a "New Dalmatia." Some compatriots joined them, emigrating directly from the Adriatic in their own sailing vessels. In the West and South, before and after the fall of the Venetian Republic (1797), these people were listed by Spanish and American authorities as Venetians, Italians, or Austrians.

A few made their way to the regions around the Gulf of Mexico. One of them, Jerome Matulich, who prospered during the 1760s, engaged in selling guns and whiskey to the Indians and was arrested in Texas by Spanish authorities. Several Dalmatians were landowners in Louisiana in the 1780s. A few fishermen and small shipbuilders from the Adriatic appeared at Tampa Bay, Florida; Mobile Bay, Alabama; and in Brownsville and Galveston, Texas. For a long time these men were the only Slavs who had come to the American shores in their own windjammers.[11]

According to the burial records of Mobile County, Alabama, a certain Dalmatian fisherman died in 1822 at the age of eighty. He and his countrymen were old settlers in colonial America.

During the struggle for American independence the republic of Dubrovnik maintained friendly relations with the American delegates through its representative in Paris, Frano Favi. During the peace negotiations in 1783, Favi paid a courtesy call on the American delegation in Paris, conveyed the good wishes of his republic, and asked for courtesy and American protection for the boats of Dubrovnik, which was granted. Dubrovnik, therefore, has the distinction of being the first South Slav state to establish official relations with the United States. We may assume that some of the "Venetians" living before and after 1783 in the Gulf region under American, French, and Spanish sovereignty were subjects of the Dubrovnik Republic.[12]

After 1815, when Austria obtained from the Congress of Vienna the control of all eastern Adriatic shores (from Trieste to the Albanian border), many Adriatic Croatians emigrated to America under the Austrian flag. Many perished at sea. Some stayed in America; some returned home. Many recrossed the ocean several times. These people, rough, sun-tanned captains and sailors, could be seen in ever-increasing numbers in all major ports between Matamoras and Vera Cruz in the south and New York City and Boston in the north.

The mild climate of New Orleans and adjacent regions, the big wide river—the Mississippi—as well as the cosmopolitan atmosphere of the city appealed to the Adriatic sailors. Jobs were available for them, as fishermen, artisans, and traders. Many simply left their ships and stayed, quite a few of them unregistered, a practice that has survived in our ports to these days. Around 1830 these men were finding their way up the Mississippi River. Some transferred to vessels from Louisiana. Some married in New Orleans and settled there. A few scattered along the seacoast on both sides of the Delta. Some moved inland. A few sailed to Saint Louis and settled there.[13]

From 1815 into the 1870s many Dalmatians, sailors and others, entered the port of New Orleans as regular passengers on English and French boats. They came to join their relatives, husbands, friends, and countrymen who had preceded them. Some Dalmatian-owned ships hired themselves to American merchants and carried goods to and from Havana, Matamoras, Vera Cruz, and even Europe. Some remained, others returned to Dalmatia, and several continued to sail from Europe to Louisiana.[14]

One, Marko Maranovich, settled in the north-central part of Louisiana where he became a plantation owner and during the 1820s built a beautiful mansion, named Marko House. His last name was too difficult for his French neighbors and black slaves, so they simply called him and the residence by his first name. Today a thriving community is located on the plantation site on the Cane River, a few miles north of Alexandria. It is called Marco in memory of the immigrant planter who amassed a fortune and died a bachelor.[15]

Among the Croatian pioneers in Alabama in the 1830s and

1840s were a number of husbands with wives and children who became permanent settlers. They made their living as sailors, fishermen, stevedores, barkeepers, restaurant owners, planters, and laborers. Many of them died young. Hard work, the humid climate (unknown in the homeland), and tuberculosis—a widespread disease among the Croatians—took a large toll.

By 1850 a considerable number of Adriatic settlers were established in New Orleans. In the Plaquemine Parish, Louisiana, almost all newcomers were Dalmatian fishermen, their last names usually ending with an "ich." Some acquired French wives and numerous children. In 1850, the U.S. Census counted a large number of Croatians, tradesmen and businessmen, in the city. In the nearby Delta many made a living as fishermen, tried shrimping and gathering oysters; the Delta gradually became a booming center for growing shellfish.

The Croatians lived with utter contempt for the elements in small primitive cabins raised on stilts, above the oyster beds. Lonely, quiet men with handlebar mustaches, they perplexed the native French by their strange speech and the constant question "Kako ste?" (How are you?) and "tako" and "tolko." This earned them the nickname "Tockos." They devised a special low-hung and wide-beamed lugger, with a deep hold for large hauls. Regularly they sailed up the Delta to New Orleans to sell their catch and expanded their business. Some crossed to the state of Mississippi to be the first oystermen when Biloxi was only a small village. A few opened the oyster houses in New Orleans and other places.[16]

The mass cultivation and marketing of oysters was a new branch of the American economy. The "father" of this industry was one who came from the vicinity of Dubrovnik. Along with several countrymen he established his successful enterprise at Bayou Creek near New Orleans in 1855.[17] As camps in the Delta thickened through the influx of newcomers, there arose a miniature "Dalmatia on the Mississippi." By 1860 at least six hundred Dalmatians—along with a few Montenegrins—lived, worked hard, and succeeded in New Orleans. They were listed as sailmakers, cigar store owners, owners of bars, restaurants, coffee houses, fruit merchants, and oyster wholesalers; one of the women was registered as a midwife.[18]

To cover expenses for funerals and burials these immigrants, like many other ethnic groups, were compelled to found their own society. On May 1, 1874 some fifty Dalmatian Croats founded in New Orleans the United Slavonian Benevolent Association (Sojedinjeno Slovinsko Društvo od Dobročinstva). The society is still in existence. Over the past one hundred years it has paid hundreds of thousands of dollars in aid and funeral expenses. This was the first Croatian fraternal organization in the eastern half of the United States, the second oldest among all South Slav immigrants. In 1974, when the society celebrated its centennial, it had some three hundred members. Professor M. Vujnović, one of its former presidents, published on this occasion a book about its members and the life of the Croatians in Louisiana.[19]

A Louis G. Kovacevich arrived in Florida Territory in 1837 and traded as merchant with the Indians and whites. In 1848 he became the first pilot for the port of Tampa. A daughter married James Brandon, a Confederate veteran who built for his bride a mansion that still stands in Brandon, Florida.[20]

V   Croatian Confederate Soldiers

On the eve of the Civil War close to three thousand Croatians lived in the South. Besides New Orleans and Plaquemine Parish in Louisiana, they lived in Mobile, Alabama; and in Pascagoula and Harrison County, Mississippi. For them the South was their homeland.

Several hundreds served in the Confederate Army. An undetermined number were members of the Confederate Navy or were engaged as blockade runners, serving as sailors and captains. Usually they were known as "Slavonians." While some were natives of the South, most of them were born in Dalmatia.

Two Slavonian Rifle companies composed entirely of these South Slavs were attached to the European Brigade. The first company, as reported by the local Daily Crescent of May 4, 1861, numbered 118 men. Fourteen were officers, commissioned and noncommissioned, and 104 privates. Another unit was called the Austrian Guards. The best-known unit, a volunteer company of 110 men, was organized by Captain Anthony Cognevich. These companies together with several other European volunteer detachments formed the European Brigade. Some Croatians joined the Tenth Louisiana Infantry Regiment while individual men were in other units. They all saw action during the war. Some gave their lives to the Confederate cause. Even the oyster growers and fishermen supported the cause by supplying Forts St. Philip and Jackson with fish and oysters.[21]

One was taken prisoner at Gettysburg on July 2, 1863, was paroled, took the oath of allegiance to the United States, and enlisted in the Union Army. Another, named George Petrovich, was wounded in one of the battles, recovered, rejoined his unit, and on July 2, 1863 was killed at Gettysburg along with several of his countrymen.

Some Croatians served in Alabama and Mississippi units. Numerous captains and sailors rendered their services to the state of Texas. The Compiled Service Records of the Confederate Soldiers mentions hundreds of these "Johnny Reboviches" as they called themselves jokingly. At least twenty percent of them were listed as killed or "missing in action."[22]

After the defeat of the Confederacy in 1865, numerous Croation veterans joined thousands of Southerners moving to the new wild West. The long journey to the West was either by land across the whole width of the United States or by boat around the southern tip of South America.

CHAPTER 5

The Call of the West

AFTER defeating Mexico in war, the United States received by the Treaty of Guadalupe Hidalgo in February 1848 a territory that now includes the states of California, Nevada, Utah, most of New Mexico and Arizona, and part of Colorado and Wyoming. It was a huge, relatively unknown and sparsely populated country.[1]

By the time the first Yankees reached California many Croatians were old-timers there. Quite a few men from the shores of the Adriatic—their names ending with "ich"—who arrived then can now be found on lists of pioneers in local histories.[2]

The epochal event in California was the discovery of gold at John Sutter's mill on the American River in January 1848 in the northern part of the state. An eyewitness of the historic event was Matthew Ivancovich, who with his brother John was an immigrant from Dalmatia. Matthew had worked for Sutter since 1847; later on he mined gold in California and Oregon.[3]

Within a few months after the discovery of gold several thousand prospectors were already digging in the desolate mountain regions. The next year the big rush was on as "the forty-niners" from all parts of the globe hastened to join the search for the precious metal. By the end of 1849 there were one hundred thousand white settlers in California. In 1850 it became a state.

In this stampede of people seeking quick fortunes were numerous South Slavs. Some came from the South of the United States while hundreds came directly from the Adriatic coast and islands on privately owned vessels.

While Los Angeles remained a comparatively small town until 1900, the gold rush caused San Francisco to grow into an exciting and lively port city, a highly cosmopolitan crossroads

56

of two continents: America and Asia. After 1849 it became home to hundreds of additional Croatians.

The names of many pioneers have been registered in local histories. Americans called them "Slavonians," a name that was generally applied to all the Slavs and has survived to this day.[4] Between 1840 and 1861 hundreds of their countrymen came to San Francisco and its environs. They were lured by the prospects of getting rich quickly. Merchants and speculators realized it was easier and less risky to become wealthy in the city than in the mountains and deserts of California. In the furious expansion of the city and its frantic activity the Croatians played a prominent role.[5] By their nature enterprising and business-minded, some were doing a thriving business during the 1850s on the old Davis Street near the waterfront, later known as Embarcadero. They owned bars and saloons, grocery stores, restaurants, fruit and vegetable stands, and a variety of other businesses. Operating restaurants and taverns became a Croatian specialty in the West.[6]

I *John Owen Dominis*

The Dominis (Gospodnetić) family from the island of Rab, Dalmatia, gave to the world bishops, scholars, and sea captains. Captain John Dominis (born in 1803) started as a sailor in his teens, reached Boston in the late 1820s, and in 1831 married a young well-to-do woman of Puritan stock. Their son John was born in Schenectady, New York, in March 1832. Then they heeded the call of the West where the captain engaged in the trade with the Orient. They came to Hawaii in 1837, and in Honolulu Captain Dominis built a mansion called the Washington Place. It serves now as the Governor's residence. In 1846 the captain perished at sea on his way to China. His widow lived in the mansion till her death in 1889.

John, who was well educated, went to San Francisco in 1849 to join the gold rush. In 1850 he returned to Hawaii. By September 1862 he was married to Princess Lydia Kamekaha Kapaakea of the ruling royal family. He served as governor of the island of Oahu, and as adviser and secretary to four kings of Hawaii, including the last king. For four years he was also a general and commander-in-chief of the royal armed forces.

In 1874 he accompanied his brother-in-law, King Kalakau, on a trip to the United States. In Washington, D.C., they were received by President Ulysses S. Grant.

In January 1891 King Kalakau died and was succeeded by his sister—the wife of Dominis—who ruled as Queen Liliuokalani ("Queen Lil"). Dominis, now Prince Consort, died of pneumonia seven months after Lil's coronation. He was interred in the Royal Mausoleum in Honolulu. The couple had no children.

Dominis was a 33rd Degree Mason, a devoted public official. His widow's rule was brief. The islands were completely dominated by the United States, most of the land was owned by U.S. citizens, and in 1887 Pearl Harbor became a U.S. naval base. The American planters were importing a large amount of cheap Chinese and Japanese labor. The United States regarded Hawaii as a very important strategic outpost on the routes to the Far East. The queen rallied her natives with the slogan "Hawaii for the Hawaiians" and through a new constitution assumed autocratic powers. The Americans landed marines, organized a "revolution," and deposed the queen. First an American protectorate, Hawaii became a republic in July 1884. Exactly four years later the United States annexed it.[7]

Queen Lil died in 1917 at the age of seventy-nine. She always cherished the memory of her late husband, John Dominis, the son of a Croatian sailor and a Pilgrim mother. In Hawaii, too, he is still remembered and "only nice things are said about him in the Bishop Museum in Honolulu and in the Hawaiian Archives."[8]

Other Adriatic seamen besides Captain Dominis were engaged in trading with China. That boom had begun in the 1840s and 1850s when America made close contacts with the Celestial Empire. A captain who was a native of Dalmatia maintained for years traffic between China and California. It is alleged that during the gold rush he brought on his sailing vessel *Santa Teresa* the first laborers from China to California. His boat was later sunk off the coast near Santa Barbara, California.[9]

II *The First Fraternal Society*

These pioneers on our western shores were mostly simple, uneducated people; many were illiterate. Very few among them were educated and professional men. A member of San Francisco's Croatian colony was Dr. Vincent Gelcich, a physician, a native of Hvar in Dalmatia. During the Civil War he served as physician and surgeon with the rank of colonel in the Union Army. After the war he became a coroner in Los Angeles and married a daughter of the wealthy Pico family.

Before the war, while in San Francisco, Dr. Gelcich cared for his countrymen. On November 17, 1857 he helped to establish the Slavonic Illyrian Mutual Benevolent Society. It was the first Croatian and South Slavic fraternal society in the country and is still in existence. Its purpose was to aid stranded, penniless Croatian sailors, to provide hospital care, and to pay for and conduct the burials of its members and other countrymen. Within a decade after its formation it numbered some seven hundred members. Many of them were single men who were residents of San Francisco or other parts of the state. Rev. G. Zaninovich was their first priest.[10]

In April 1861 the members of the Society obtained a separate cemetery plot, the so-called "Slavonic Terra." This first known Croatian cemetery in America was a part of the Calvary Cemetery before the tragic earthquake and fire in 1906. Afterward all burials were removed from San Francisco proper to the present Holy Cross Cemetery in San Mateo County adjacent to the city.[11]

During the 1860s the San Francisco Croatian colony grew and prospered. The business directories register hundreds of Croatian names. A high percentage were U.S. citizens. Many of the Catholic Croatians married Irish, Spanish, or Mexican women because of their faith. However, other immigrants entered into marriage with women of other religions who were natives of various European countries. And those who preferred to marry their sweethearts from the homeland had to make the long journey to Dalmatia.

By the 1850s and 1860s many of these people were naturalized citizens and had grown prosperous. In the San Joaquin Valley, California, they owned restaurants and saloons and a variety of businesses. They were engaged in truck farming, gardening, in lumber, and also earned their living as laborers, cooks, carpenters, clerks, boarding house operators, bartenders, and coffee shop operators. Some women worked as milliners.[12]

III   *Antonio Milatovich vs. Mexico*

In the first part of the 1860s Mexico was torn by civil strife between the conservatives and the guerrilla forces of the Liberal leader, Benito Juárez. France under Louis Napoleon Bonaparte intervened. In June of 1863 the French troops took Mexico City. Maximilian Habsburg, the brother of Emperor Francis Joseph, came to rule as the Emperor of Mexico. Among his troops were numerous South Slavs including a number of Dalmatian sailors and ship captains. They especially frequented the port of Matamoras. However, by May 1867, the Juárez forces defeated Maximilian and his troops. After the execution of the unlucky Habsburg prince and the defeat of the French and the Austrians, some Croatian veterans crossed the Rio Grande and settled in the South. Some sailed for New Orleans. Others journeyed to the West.

A man who was deeply involved in Mexican affairs was Antonio Milatovich, a native of Dubrovnik, who had arrived in San Francisco in 1850 on his own brig *Portinia*. He managed to amass wealth through real estate speculations. By 1858 he had also acquired large tracts of land from individuals and from the Mexican Government in Lower California, the same region that had been explored and mapped by his countryman, Padre Consag. His holdings gradually amounted to about one million acres. He wanted to open this land for colonization after exploring its potential through several expeditions. Since the Mexican Government prevented him from taking possession of the land, Milatovich demanded payments for his property in the amount of $554,000. During the Mexican civil war Milatovich aided Governor Castro of Lower California with the sum of $5,000, and provisions and guns. In 1861 the Mexican army under Commandante Mendoza destroyed Milatovich's ranch at Sausal.

Demanding justice, Milatovich himself in 1864 took the journey to Mexico City. He sought out Juárez, but he was too busy fighting the French and Austrians and advised him to appeal to Maximilian, a member of the dynasty that ruled Milatovich's native land. A proud man, Milatovich, the supporter of the Mexican revolutionaries, refused to appeal to Maximilian. As a result, when he returned to San Francisco he was without money or land. In new ventures during the 1870s and 1880s he managed to recoup, died a rich man in 1901, and found his final peace under the cypresses of Calvary Cemetery among his family and countrymen.[13]

IV *The Pioneer Saga Continues*

With the completion of the first transcontinental railroad in 1869, the Atlantic and Pacific Oceans were linked. To many of the immigrants the West then became more easily accessible. A great majority of the Croatian immigrants were subjects of the Habsburg Empire, which in 1867 had became a dual monarchy, Austria-Hungary. Before the Austrians started to take regular statistics on emigrants (in 1869), the local authorities estimated that close to twenty thousand people from Dalmatia had gone to America.[14]

For many years San Francisco remained the principal settlement of the Adriatic immigrants. The Croatians loved the city. They attended Irish and German Catholic churches, one of which was St. Mary's. The beautiful Old St. Mary's, a brick gothic church, is in the midst of what is now China Town. The old San Francisco was a very lively place bursting with business activities. In 1869, of twenty-nine coffee houses eighteen were held by Dalmatians. They also owned eight of the sixteen best restaurants and were prominent in trade and commerce.

By 1869 they had formed the Pan-Slavonian Society (which included other Slavs) and even a Slavonian Reading Room or Čitaonica. It was a cultural oasis in a still somewhat backward and lawless city. The waterfront where many Croatians worked and lived was a dangerous area frequented by criminals from many lands. A few Dalmatians were known to have been assassinated. Jealousy and anti-foreign feelings engendered by the economic success of the foreign-born were widespread among native Americans. This was partly due to the participation of foreigners in crime and lawlessness. At the end of the 1860s one of the papers—which openly admitted anti-Slavic prejudice—printed the following under the title "Slavonians in San Francisco":

The Slavonian race is well represented in the large percentage of foreigners who inhabit this city. As a community, these people are clannish; they herd together, working solely for themselves, accumulating wealth and living it up; they have graduated social circles of their own and enjoy the pleasures of life in the fashion best adapted to the low level of their intellectual culture. They are an independent community. All its members are more or less civilized; that is to say they are not savages. The mercantile portion is principally engaged in the fruit trade; others devote their attention mainly to keeping bar-rooms, coffee-houses, etc. All are prosperous. The secret of their prosperity is in their clannish habits.[15]

However, the real cause of the success of the Croatians was their hard work, thrift, and ingenuity. The fame of their success spread to the shores and islands of the Adriatic. As years went by, hundreds of relatives and friends joined these "Slavonians." They purchased thousands of acres of land, created farms, orchards, ranches, and vineyards. And since their energy and vision knew no limit, their impact on the growth of California and the West became a lasting one.

V   The Saga of Nevada

During the late 1850s silver was discovered in Nevada Territory, a wild and isolated country of mountains and deserts bordering on California. Thousands of miners joined in the silver boom. The immigrants from the Adriatic were well represented in the crowd flocking to Carson City (today the state's capital), Virginia City, Aurora, Austin, Reno, and Tonopah. During the 1860s and 1870s these regions were the greatest silver-producing centers in the world.

The Croatians spread all over: Columbus, Lida, Pioche, and other places, where a town usually started under tents.

Two who struck it rich were Christ Novacovich and Nicholas

Trojanovich. They settled in Aurora, a prospering silver center right on the California state line. Wells-Fargo Overland Stage Coach Lines cut the first road through the mountains to Aurora, the seat of Esmeralda County. Novacovich was an agent for Wells-Fargo and owned the Merchants' Exchange Hotel while Trojanovich ran a "First Class Dining Saloon" as advertised in the *Aurora Times* of 1864. Novacovich later owned a bank in Aurora while Trojanovich moved to Treasure City, Nevada, to open a restaurant. Shootings and killings were a daily occurrence until the vigilantes took the initiative and hanged four members of the notorious Daley gang that terrorized the town. Mark Twain had spent some time here during 1861–1862. A well-known part of the town was the Boothill Cemetery where the number of graves was increasing steadily. Here was the resting place of gunmen, desperados, sheriffs, vigilantes, and miners. A few South Slavs were buried here too.[16]

Another Croatian, Marco Medin, came to Virginia City in 1861 and two years later established the Medin Gold and Silver Company in the Argentine Mining District with his brother. They also established other enterprises. Local newspapers highly praised his and his countrymen's role in developing Nevada. After it became a state in 1864, one of them, John Gregovich, was elected to the state legislature for two terms. However, violence and killings continued and several Croatians were among the victims, including Nikola Perasich who was killed by a hired gunman.[17]

Most of Nevada's pioneers came via California. San Francisco's voting records during the 1870s contained hundreds of Croatian names. The business directories listed them in many occupations and professions. On August 15, 1873 the Austrian Benevolent Society was formed in San Francisco. In 1874 the Slavonic Illyrian Benevolent Society built a home at Sutter Creek, the first Croation national home in America. Eventually, hundreds of such homes and halls were built all over the country. During the last two decades of the 1800s—as the number of their countrymen kept increasing—thousands of Croatians were well established in the West. By that time a new generation, the children and even grandchildren of these immigrants, had made its appearance.

VI   *Mazzanovich and Geronimo*

Anton Mazzanovich, a native of the island of Hvar, arrived with his two brothers and parents at Castle Garden in New York in October 1868. The family established itself in San Francisco. Father and sons worked as musicians. In January 1870, ten-year-old Anton enlisted in the U.S. Army as a musician. As the youngest soldier ever to enlist, he was honorably discharged in August 1873 at Fort Vancouver, Washington. The Mazzanovich brothers then played as musicians in the Bell Union Theatre and San Francisco Opera House.

In February 1881 Anton reenlisted, served in the 6th U.S. Cavalry, took part in the campaign against Apache Indians in late 1881, and met Geronimo, their famous rebel chief. After a skirmish on October 4, 1881, in which Mazzanovich took part, Geronimo escaped to Mexico. In July 1882 Anton was honorably discharged at Fort Grant, Arizona Territory. Then for a while he ran a saloon in the mining town of Shakespear, New Mexico. In 1885 he joined the New Mexican Rangers during the fighting with the Indians. Geronimo was never captured but finally surrendered in 1886.

During the Spanish-American War in 1898 and again during World War I Mazzanovich offered his services but was rejected by the Army. In 1931 he published his book of recollections, *Trailing Geronimo*. In it he describes his origins, his youth, and the campaign against Geronimo.

Mazzanovich was a colorful character, a typical man of the wild West. A versatile personality, he was musician, soldier, adventurer, frontiersman, saloon keeper, cowboy, ranger, and even a writer. The rest of his family left San Francisco in 1870 for Los Angeles to join hundreds of their countrymen, many of whom were also from the island of Hvar.[18]

During the late 1800s the restless immigrants advanced and spread to other western territories and states. Some were single men. Often several of them banded together, entered into joint businesses. Frequently two or three brothers or members of the same family, relatives and in-laws, braved the frontier together. Many lived in a sort of communal household or *zadruga*, a tradition which had existed for centuries in their homeland.

There were Croatians in Idaho Territory during the 1870s. Some sold liquor in Idaho City. Others owned restaurants in Nez Perce. One served as a captain of infantry in Wyoming; some served as common soldiers in various units engaged in Indian wars on the frontier. The Arizona Census of 1870 lists several Croatian and other South Slav farmers. A great many flocked to Butte, Montana, with its mines and promise of steady employment. Located in scenic hills, rich in ore, Butte became home to many Croatians and South Slavs. Miners, laborers, saloon and restaurant owners, merchants, craftsmen, and a large number of farmers established themselves in nearby Lincoln, Missoula, Helena, Dillon, Willis, and elsewhere.[19]

Long before Washington became a state in 1889, Croatians worked there as fishermen, sailors, laborers, merchants, and farmers. Many fishermen concentrated in the Puget Sound area. Some moved out to neighboring British Columbia in Canada. Others went all the way to Alaska, which they had occasionally visited for many years. Some of them were there as settlers long before America acquired it in 1867. The contact with the old Russian settlers was easy because of similarity of languages.[20] However, on the whole, Alaska with its cold and harsh climate did not appeal to the Croatians from the sunny shores of the Adriatic. It appealed more to people from Lika and other mountainous areas who were accustomed to cold winters.

CHAPTER 6

The Rising Tide

IN 1870 a unique visitor from Dalmatia came to the United States. It was Captain Nikola Primorac from Dubrovnik. In his sail boat, only twenty feet long, named *The City of Ragusa*, he was accompanied by Captain Buckley (an Irishman from County Cork) and a dog. They left Liverpool on June 3, 1870. The voyage was undertaken in response to a challenge and a bet of one thousand pounds. The tiny vessel, the smallest to attempt to cross the Atlantic at that time, reached New York harbor after a voyage of eighty-two days.

From September 1870 to May 1871, Captain Primorac sailed about New York and the principal cities along the coast. His crossing and visit attracted wide publicity in major American and English papers. On May 23, 1871, together with a young sailor, he left New York for Queenstown, Ireland, reaching it after thirty-six days. Ten days later he was given an enthusiastic welcome in Liverpool where he settled down.[1]

In the 1870s—at the height of the sailing ship era—significant changes took place in the shipbuilding enterprises of Dubrovnik and nearby Pelješac. Their wharves started to build sailing ships of two thousand tons capacity, large vessels which could ply all the high seas with considerable safety. It was on some of such boats that many Croatians from the Adriatic were sailing to the ports of the United States. The considerable increase in the size of sailing vessels was also supposed to challenge the competition of the emerging steamship fleets.[2]

As the number of people leaving Europe was steadily rising during the last three decades of the 1800s, more vessels—sail and steam—were needed. While in 1880 only 17,267 immigrants came from Austria-Hungary, in 1884 their number was over thirty-six thousand and in the year 1890 fifty-six thousand. In

1900 it jumped to more than 114,000. In 1907, the historic year when immigration to America reached its highest peak, the number of immigrants from Austria-Hungary was 338,452. Of these at least ten percent were of Croatian nationality.[3]

The period after 1880 witnessed the rise of the so-called "New Immigration." Most of these immigrants came from eastern and southern Europe. They were predominantly peasants from rural areas who belonged to three religions: Catholic, Eastern Orthodox, and Jewish. They came because the big expanding country with the richest economy in the world needed cheap labor.[4]

Between 1880 and 1890 some fourteen thousand emigrated from Dalmatia alone; their number increased to almost thirty-two thousand in the following decade. From the province of Istria at least twenty-five thousand Croatians left for America before 1900. Starting with the early 1890s the peasants from the Adriatic hinterland joined the exodus. One group was impelled by religious reasons to leave. After the Austrian occupation of Bosnia-Herzegovina in 1878, thousands of Croatian Moslems felt impelled to emigrate to Turkey or America because they feared the future in a Catholic-dominated empire. They were joined by their brethren from Montenegro who were threatened by persecution and massacres.[5]

This rising tide of immigrants presented an endless procession of desperate humanity and before the century ended "perhaps three million more were on the way from the Balkans and Asia: Greeks and Macedonians, Croatians and Albanians, Syrians and Armenians." And they all had one thing in common: they were uprooted.[6]

I *Pajaro Valley—New Dalmatia*

South of San Francisco lay the Pajaro Valley near Watsonville. When the young Dalmatian Mark Rabasa reached the valley, he saw acres of land planted with sugar beets, vegetables, and a few apple trees. He decided to grow apple trees as had been done for many generations in his homeland. He was the first man in Watsonville to go into the apple business. Apples were in high demand on the markets. Rabasa started to buy apples from his neighbors, joined with several countrymen, and soon created a new branch of California economy: raising apples and selling them profitably all over the country.[7]

The business required skill, energy, money, ingenuity, new methods of fighting apple disease, and building of proper packing houses. New methods in packing, drying, and marketing of apples were introduced.[8]

Jack London, the Socialist writer who knew this part of the country intimately, described these men and their success in one of his books. At this time (before 1914) there were twelve thousand acres of apple trees in the valley. London wrote:

Do you know what they call Pajaro Valley? New Dalmatia. We're being squeezed out. We Yankees thought we were smart. Well the Dalmatians came along and showed they were smarter. They were miserable immigrants. . . . First they worked at day's labor in the fruit harvest. . . . Pretty soon they were renting the orchards on long lease; now they own the whole valley, and the last American will be gone.

These men, the Dalmatians, had "a way with apples. It's almost a gift." They knew the trees. They could look at a tree in bloom and tell how many boxes of apples it would pack. They picked the fruits with love; their apples weren't bruised, fetched top prices at domestic and foreign markets. A hundred carloads of yellow Newton pippins were sent to England every year. Others exported apples even to South Africa.

The valley became a veritable show place during the spring when the trees were in bloom. To the Dalmatians, wrote London, the valley was their Klondike. It was said that no one but a Dalmatian would be allowed to pick a single apple. In 1914 the land in the valley was worth three thousand dollars an acre.[9]

Watsonville with its apple industry, numerous restaurants, and business places owned by Dalmatians, continued to prosper. In the early 1930s their land in Pajaro Valley was estimated at fifty million dollars.[10]

What these people did for the apple industry, Stephen N. Mitrovich did for fig growing, another important branch of the California fruit industry. Born in Dalmatia in 1859, he arrived in Fresno, California, in 1880. Fig trees were grown then only for shade and decoration. But in 1883 Mitrovich imported from Dalmatia one thousand fig cuttings and started to grow fig trees in the vineyards. The white Adriatic figs flourished in the California climate and within a decade Mitrovich's inventiveness, hard work, new system of growing, harvesting, curing, and packing resulted in a new booming industry. At the World's Columbian Exposition in Chicago Mitrovich was awarded the Premium Gold Medal for the best cured and packed figs.[11]

Mitrovich was also instrumental in organizing the All-Slavonic Society and the society called "The Wreath." During World War I he became very active in the South Slav unification movement.[12]

Throughout California new industries and enterprises were launched by many such individuals who had brought a special cunning which benefited the native fruit grower. They established beautiful vineyards in several parts of the state and expanded the raisin and wine industry. After 1882, the grape growers came to the huge San Joaquin Valley, became diversified farmers, raised cattle, hogs, sheep, goats, and poultry, besides tending their vineyards. They transformed large tracts of California into the most fertile fruit-growing orchards, vineyards, farms, and ranches. They also erected packing houses and canneries.[13]

II   *Newcomers, Fishermen, and First Journalists*

Because San Francisco already had a fair share of fishermen, the Adriatic fishermen looked for new opportunities in the south of California. At first a handful, then dozens, and even hundreds converged on San Pedro, the seaport of the growing city of Los Angeles. They acquired their own fishing boats and equipment. They banded together, working as teams of relatives, friends, villagers. They divided the profits and invested them. Eventually they owned several hundred fishing boats, many named after their native towns, islands, and saints. They founded and expanded the largest fishing center in the state. Then they established their own canneries employing hundreds of their own people. Their prosperity and success increased steadily. Their fleets plied the ocean all the way to the north: the shores of Washington State, Oregon, British Columbia, and Alaska. Along Puget Sound more and more of them fished and settled down. They formed new settlements and enterprises. They found permanent homes in Astoria, Oregon; Aberdeen, Billingham, and Tacoma, Washington. Their industries specialized in salmon, tuna, sardines, and mackerel.

Some took to shipbuilding in coastal cities. Hundreds worked in the growing redwood lumber industry. In Los Angeles and other cities before and after the turn of the century Croatians worked on the canals and sewers, built roads and bridges, erected public and private buildings. Hundreds of people from Herzegovina and Dalmatia became well known in the construction business.[14]

On July 3, 1895, the immigrants founded the Croatian-Slavonian Benevolent Society of Los Angeles. The Articles of Incorporation stated the purpose: aid to the sick, burial of the dead members, care of widows and orphans, as well as "the propagation of general intelligence, unity, friendship and brotherly love . . . and instruction as well as education of the good citizenship." Education and citizenship were ideals to these simple people many of whom had come to this country without any education.[15]

A high percentage of the Dalmatians persisted in their loyalty to the Habsburg monarchy. This was reflected in the names of some societies such as the Austrian-American Benevolent Society and others. (Some of these organizations use "Austrian" even today.) However, there were new organizations as, for instance, the Croatian Society "Zvonimir" (named after a Croatian king), formed in 1893 in San Francisco. Later on "Zvonimir" was instrumental in forming the Croatian Unity of the Pacific, a fraternal organization.[16]

Having come from a country which knew no free press, these people soon realized the potential and the power of the printed word. In America it was easy and simple to found and print a newspaper; most importantly, there was no censorship. The Croatians founded their first newspaper in the West in 1892—*Dalmatinska Zora* (Dalmatian Dawn) in San Francisco. But the paper could not survive. The paid circulation—between one and two thousand—was too small. Besides subscriptions, donations and paid advertisements were needed. It became evident that a foreign language paper could survive and prosper only if backed by some fraternal organization or business and bank establishments.

The struggle for survival by individual papers presented itself as an opportunity to the Austro-Hungarian embassy in Washington. In order to promote loyalty to the Habsburg monarchy among the immigrants, their representatives tried to gain control of some papers and subsidized the editors and papers. Through subtle means the Austro-Hungarian officials also promoted disunity among the South Slavs. But, while some editors were extremely pro-Austrian, a few of them remained staunch patriots, extolling Croatian independence.[17]

III   *Crested Butte and Some Mining Settlements*

The town of Crested Butte is located some 150 miles southwest of Denver, Colorado. It is a highly elevated beautiful country with long winters. The town was an offspring of the frontier. Some ninety years ago its mines by offering good wages and plenty of work attracted many immigrants. Mining was a dangerous occupation. In one of numerous disasters, that of Jokerville on January 24, 1884, sixty men were killed. Several Croatians were by then established there.

Like any other mining town Crested Butte had many strikes in its history. The first one broke out in 1890. The Italians, Croatians, and Slovenians were in the forefront of the labor movement. The strike failed. In 1903–1904 they struck again, responding to the call of John Mitchell, the popular leader of the United Mine Workers, who led 150,000 men in the coal fields of Pennsylvania. In this strike the state militia vented their wrath especially on the foreign-born strikers. The local Croatian Home served as the center of strikers' various activities. Besides the UMW, the "Wobblies" (IWW) participated in this strike. While many Croatian miners belonged to the radical Industrial Workers of the World, they were also members of their fraternal lodge which was called Immaculate Heart of Mary.[18]

When the young strong men from Croatia arrived in Gallup, New Mexico, during the 1890s, it was a small place with a railroad station and a few wooden buildings. The immigrants were lured to the coal mines because there was plenty of work and wages were better than in the East. A majority of the Croatians were from Gorski Kotar, northeast of Rieka. Gibson, some five miles away from Gallup, was the main Croatian settlement. As one of the eyewitnesses recalls, it was "like a real Croatian village and the people lived as they used to in the old country." The work was strenuous, the working hours long, but the pay was good for those days. Everyone "ate and drank to his heart's content and kept sending money to help their families in the homeland."[19]

Thousands of Navajo Indians lived in the area, and a few of them learned some Croatian. Several Croatian businessmen learned the Navajo tongue. With the gradual closing of the mines hundreds of Croatians flocked into Gallup, built their homes, acquired numerous businesses, and became well-known members of the expanding and prosperous city.[20]

The largest Croatian mining settlement was formed in Calumet, Michigan, which before 1914 became well known for its copper mines. The first Croatian immigrant arrived in 1881 and changed his name to Lucas. His first job was with the Slovenian-owned Ruppe Copper Company. Mrs. Lucas and her family were described by Louis Adamic, the American-Slovenian writer, in his dramatic story "Manda Evanich from Croatia."[21]

Living and working together, the Croatians and Slovenians founded in Calumet a common parish in 1889 and built the beautiful St. Joseph Church. With the influx of many Slovenians and Croatians it became necessary to separate the congregations. In 1900 the Croatians founded their own parish and in 1903 built their St. John the Baptist Church. For years it was the largest Croatian church in America.[22]

While in a dozen states the Croatian immigrants struggled as miners, another gold rush took place. It started in 1898 in faraway Alaska. One who joined the stampede and who had luck in mining became successful in real estate and business. Some fifty years later his son, Mike Stepovich, became the first governor of the new state of Alaska.[23]

IV   *The Industrial Settlements*

A considerable number of Croatians and other Slavs, coming in the late 1890s and early 1900s, were absorbed by the industrial cities of Pennsylvania, Ohio, and several nearby states. Here their largest settlements were established in Pittsburgh, Cleveland, and Chicago. In many ways these industrial settlements differed from the rural Midwest, the South, and the West. The prospects for economic advance were less favorable here than in the less industrialized areas. Thousands of the unskilled workers toiled in steel mills, heavy industry, construction, railroads, and mining.

Some of these immigrants preferred the factories of Ohio to the mines and mills of Pennsylvania. However, the largest concentration of Croatians did develop over the decades in and around Pittsburgh. With its steel and heavy industries it needed thousands of unskilled workers. As the state was close to New York harbor (where most immigrants landed) the trip to Pittsburgh or some other industrial settlement in Pennsylvania was relatively short and inexpensive. The influx of Slavs reached its height during the decade ending in 1908, when almost six hundred thousand Slavs came to Pennsylvania. Of these almost 150,000 were South Slavs. Among them were eighty-five thousand Croatians.[24] To no other state in the United States have Croatians and other South Slavs contributed more energy, creativity, and life-blood than to Pennsylvania.

As early as 1866, an Austrian, Max Schamberg, who was an Honorary Consul, established a business in Pittsburgh which was partly a bank and partly a travel agency. He named it the Croatian Bank. Because eventually most of the Croatian immigrants came from the town and district of Jaska, the East Ohio Street in Allegheny City (later Pittsburgh's North Side) became known as "Jaska Street."[25]

Steelton became another important settlement of the Croatians. The city's very name reveals the character of its main industry. The immigrants worked in the huge Carnegie Steel Mills as early as 1884. These and other mills later became the property of the United States Steel Company. The Croatians first shared their St. Mary's parish with the Slovenians. In May of 1909 the Slovenians formed their own parish.

In Johnstown, in the anthracite coal mining regions around Wilkes-Barre and Scranton, in Sharon, and in many other towns all over the state, the Croatian peasants, workers, and a small number of skilled and educated people found their homes. At the time when Pittsburgh, the "Smoky City," was an internationally known industrial colossus, the Croatians formed an important part of the huge foreign-born working force. By 1894 over nine thousand of them lived in Pittsburgh and vicinity. In 1909 their number in Pennsylvania was estimated at 130,000.[26]

What these people needed was a benevolent fraternal organization of the sort established by their countrymen in San Francisco and New Orleans. Zdravko Mužina, who had worked as a journalist in Chicago, and Petar Pavlinac were instrumental in establishing in January 1894 first a paper called *Danica—The Morning Star* and then a benevolent society called "Starčević." Ante Starčević was the popular nationalist politician in Croatia at the time. In September of 1894 the delegates of fourteen Croatian societies founded in Allegheny City the Croation Union of the United States. *Danica* was its organ. The dues were sixty cents a month. Death benefits were one hundred dollars for women and three hundred dollars for men. The initial membership was six hundred.[27]

The new fraternal organization gave rise to numerous new lodges in Pennsylvania and in several other states. Out of this modest organization grew the Croatian Fraternal Union, the largest of all South Slavic fraternal organizations.

The purpose of the Croatian Union was not only to assist its sick members, to pay for the burials of its members, and to "teach and spread enlightenment and culture . . . among the Croatian people," but also to promote brotherly love and good citizenship. The lodges were usually named after various saints of the Catholic Church or were given patriotic names.[28]

While most of the fraternal leaders were honest men who wanted to help their people, others caused friction and quarrels. The founding of Croatian churches was also sometimes marked by feuds and friction. Most of the priests who came from the old country were idealists and true friends of the people. However, there were individual priests who were unable to adapt to the peculiar conditions in America. Neither could the parishioners. In proportion to their numbers the Croatians formed few parishes. The principal reason for this failure was the lack of priests in the homeland.

A large number of Croatians realized that they were not welcome in Irish and German parishes. Or they would not join them because of the language problems. Some joined other Slav parishes (Slovak or Polish). Many simply ceased to attend any church.

The first Croatian priest to come to Pittsburgh, in August 1894, was Dobroslav Božić from Bosnia. The first Croatian church in Pennsylvania and in the United States, St. Nicholas on East Ohio Street, was dedicated on January 27, 1895. Another parish with a new church was founded in the beginning of 1900—also named St. Nicholas—in nearby Bennet (now Millvale).

Father Božić was a devoted and tireless worker. In 1898 he moved to his people in Steelton in St. Mary's parish; with his own savings of $750 he bought a wooden chapel for the first church. He died of overwork, strain, and sickness at the age of 39 on January 17, 1900; he did not live long enough to see the beautiful church and school that he helped to found.[29]

CHAPTER 7

Disasters and Problems

FROM Anaconda, Montana, in the extreme North, where the Croatians formed in 1888 a Sts. Peter and Paul Society down to Empire, Louisiana, in the South, the immigrant settlements grew stronger. In the Mississippi Delta the climate and the way of life were strikingly different from that of northern industrial settlements. The growing and selling of oysters became the lucrative Delta enterprise by 1900. While many engaged in the oyster business, other Croatians opened restaurants in New Orleans, competing in skill with native Creole cooks. Some branched into other businesses. By the late 1800s there were many women among them. Some of the men sailed regularly to Dalmatia, usually returning to the homeland in May and to Louisiana in September. This type of commuting was practiced until 1914. Around 1900 the steamship ticket from Trieste to New York cost about $30 in steerage.[1]

I A Terrible Disaster

On Sunday, October 1, 1893 a hurricane hit New Orleans and the Delta region. The whole area was devastated. All oystermen's camps were destroyed. Some two thousand people lost their lives in the hurricane. Among them were over two hundred Croatians, mostly the oystermen and their families. Entire Croatian families were wiped out in Empire, Bajou Creek, and Singer. Desperate and dazed people made their way to New Orleans by the hundreds, some of them after many hours in water whipped by wild winds. Many heartbreaking stories about the tragedy were related for years. As soon as the tragedy happened some of the wealthier countrymen and their benevolent society hurried to the rescue. A survivor of this disaster reported

76

on the event in the issue of *Napredak* (Allegheny, Pennsylvania)
on November 21, 1901, when the survivors were already recovering from the misfortune. This was the greatest single
tragedy that ever befell the Croatian immigrants in this country.[2]

It was but one of many disasters that struck these newcomers.
While most of those who survived recovered, starting again
from scratch, many of them were ruined for the rest of their
lives. Virtually thousands of people who had fled Europe for
a better and safe life in America ended as victims of natural
and industrial disasters. The survivors, though mourning their
dead, in most instances were not easily discouraged. In the
Delta they rebuilt their cabins, made them stronger to with-
stand the elements, rebuilt their boats, and worked harder than
ever before. And they still loved the sea.

A large number of Croatian captains and sailors served on
American boats with home ports on the Atlantic coast. Many
of them had simply left Austrian ships in America or a foreign
port and joined the American ships. Stjepan Radić, a rising
homeland politician and a critic of the Habsburg policies in
the early 1900s, observed that Croatian sailors were more appreciated in the United States than in their own country.[3]

New York City with its huge port attracted many of these
sailors. By 1880 the Dalmatians had organized an Austrian
Benevolent Society, later renamed the First Croatian Benefit
Society. Over the decades the immigrants found employment in
New York City as dock workers, longshoremen, members of
tugboat crews, also in restaurants and factories. Hundreds settled
in Hoboken, New Jersey, just opposite the Statue of Liberty.
There on March 30, 1890, they established the Slavonian Benevolent Society, and within months A. Škrivanić published the
first issue of a weekly paper, *Napredak* (The Progress), the first
Croatian paper in the eastern part of the country.[4]

With newspapers already in existence in the West and in
Chicago, the Croatian press now seemed to be firmly established. In Chicago Nikola Polić, a former deputy in the Croatian
Diet, published from October 1892 until 1896 a paper called
Chicago. Polić had left his home country because of Hungarian
persecution. In his weekly paper Polić devoted many pages
to extolling the American way of life and its ideals, urging

his countrymen to learn the English language and to become active in American life.[5]

A short-lived paper in Chicago was *Hrvatska Zora* (Croatian Dawn) in 1892, published by Janko Kovačević, another political exile from Croatia. He was a former army officer who came first to South Dakota and in 1890 enlisted in the last Sioux War. During the 1890s and in the early 1900s the Croatians grew so strong in Chicago that they created several societies and a national home. Eventually some fifty thousand were to live in the city and its environs.[6]

The large immigrant colony in Chicago maintained ties with their compatriots in Calumet, Michigan; Milwaukee and West Allis, Wisconsin; and St. Louis, Missouri. *The Copper Country Evening News* of Calumet reported on March 27, 1900, the presence of at least fifteen hundred Croatians in the city. In the early 1900s the colony was described as very progressive, consisting of thrifty and hard-working people, with many societies and a thriving parish of some five hundred families.[7]

In St. Louis, Missouri, one of the oldest Croatian settlements grew into a well-established community. The so-called "Bribirsko Selo" (The Bribir Village) composed of immigrants from Bribir and Novi Vinodolski in the Croatian Littoral was located around Gravois Avenue. Many also settled across the Mississippi River in East St. Louis and in other parts of southern Illinois. Hundreds also flocked to the mines of central Illinois.[8]

II *The High Tide*

The emigration from Europe between the late 1890s and 1914 was a real *exodus*, a mass flight of millions of people. The Croatians and other South Slavs joined them for a variety of reasons. Some areas of Croatia became depopulated. Entire regions were affected by the so-called "American fever." The native writers, lamenting the exodus of thousands, complained "Our strength and youth lie beyond the sea."

Thousands of peasant-emigrants left without being counted. Even when the Habsburg authorities introduced passports, during the high tide of emigration, the newspapers reported that more people left without them than with them.

When the U.S. Immigration authorities started to list the immigrants by their nationality at the turn of the century they grouped the Croatians and South Slavs in the following confusing manner:

1. "Croatians and Slovenians"; 2. "Dalmatians, Bosnians and Herzegovinians"; 3. "Bulgarians, Montenegrins and Serbs."

In the first category two distinct nationalities were lumped together. In the second they applied provincial names to all the Croatians and other South Slavs coming from two separately administered provinces. In the third, three distinct nationalities, coming from three independent states, were counted together.

After 1920, the Immigration and Naturalization Service began to list *all* the immigrants from both Yugoslavia and Bulgaria by the country of birth without specifying their ethnic origin.[9]

III   *From Bosnia and Herzegovina*

One of many Western travelers who visited this province during the high tide of immigration described it as:

A land of green pastures and rushing waters, of wooded hills and forest-clad mountains, a primitive pastoral land where shepherds still play their flutes and shepherdesses wander with their distaff in hand spinning as they watch their flocks, a land . . . still wrapped in ancient peace.[10]

While it may have looked peaceful, it had gone through a violent past. In 1914 the peace of the world was shattered in the capital of Bosnia-Herzegovina by the assassination of Archduke Francis Ferdinand, and World War I broke out.

Here the East and the West met. Through its southern parts, the land of Herzegovina, the large triangular province reached the Adriatic at two points. The population was mixed: slightly over 40 percent were the Orthodox; 20 percent belonged to the Catholic and 40 percent to the Moslem religion.

From these lands comparatively few people went to America before 1890. Because Bosnia and Herzegovina formed the hinterland of Dalmatia, the emigration from that Adriatic province affected that from the two areas. As they are geographically tied completely to Dalmatia and Croatia proper, all emigrants were leaving through these two adjacent lands. In 1905 the authorities in Sarajevo, the capital of the land, issued over 1,400 passports. In 1907 the number increased to over 6,000. In 1909 almost 3,000 people left, followed by 17,000 in 1910. In 1911 some 11,000 emigrated. Only a part of these went to the United States. U.S. immigration statistics between 1900 and 1914 included almost 50,000 "Dalmatians, Bosnians, and Herzegovinians."[11]

Some counties in Herzegovina lost thirteen percent of their population through emigration. Many of these emigrants chose California as their destination. The climate and land were similar to those of Herzegovina. Here they joined their neighbors and relatives, some of whom were from Dalmatia. When a few Franciscan priests before and after World War I left for America, some of their former parishioners followed them.

IV   *The Causes of Emigration*

Along the Adriatic and in its hinterland the most frequent reasons for emigration were: lack of land, high taxation, conscription, favorable reports by returned immigrants, and political oppression by foreign rulers. Other causes were the superior living conditions in America, much higher wages, the opportunity to rise, freedom of movement, personal liberty, and absence of high taxes.[12]

At the height of the European exodus a special delegation, as part of the U.S. Immigration Commission (which was established in 1907), went to parts of Austria-Hungary to study on location the moving forces behind immigration. Their verdict was that "the fundamental cause" for emigration of all South Slavs was economic besides a combination of others.[13] Emily G. Balch visited the same regions in 1905 and wrote subsequently:

I was told that emigrants from the rich eastern counties of Croatia-Slavonia, who seem to have no economic reasons for leaving home, when asked why they go, say: *"Mi idemo tražiti ima li još pravice na svietu."* ("We are going to find out whether there is still justice in the world.")[14]

In Croatia itself the additional reasons were: decline of the sailing vessel, the devastating effects of phyloxera disease ravaging the vineyards, the disappearance of the Military Frontier, the decline of the *zadrugas* (communal households), the increasing Hungarian oppression, especially during 1883–1903. In all parts of the Balkans each political crisis, war, or uprising set off another wave of emigration.

Stjepan Radić, co-founder with his brother Ante of the Croatian Peasant Party, accused the Habsburg authorities of mismanaging the rich Croatian forests and neglecting the merchant marine which caused the flight of some fifty thousand people. The departing emigrants had told Radić their destination was "a land . . . where one can live as one pleases, where there is less evil and injustice."[15]

Reluctant to fight the red tape with the authorities during the early 1900s, thousands of young male Croatians and their Serbian neighbors left the country illegally. The trips of individual groups were cleverly organized by steamship agents and some returned emigrants. They traveled partly on foot, crossed the border illegally, and made their way by train to France or some other country along the Atlantic. All along the route the agents and confidants placed them in an "underground emigrant-railroad" until the group reached the America-bound ship. In New York, too, the immigrants were received by another agent who sent them by train to a midwestern city, to the saloon or boarding house of a countryman. The saloon owner, who frequently was a steamship agent and a go-between for employers, found them lodging and employment. In no time the "greenhorn" immigrant joined the huge army of unskilled labor.[16]

V *Not All Made the Crossing*

The hazards and the perils have diminished in modern times, but the transatlantic voyage always presented a certain danger. The inland Croatians—unlike their brethren from the Adriatic—dreaded the crossing.

In the night of April 14–15, 1912, the White Star liner *Titanic* was hit by an iceberg off Newfoundland with many immigrants among the third-class passengers. Of 1,514 people that perished in the icy ocean were some thirty Croatians, over thirty Bulgarians, some twenty Serbs, and a few Slovenians, women and children among them. More immigrants and more people from the Balkans died in this single sea disaster than in any other such tragedy.[17]

The liner *Carpathia* (belonging to the rival Cunard Line) was on its route from New York to the Croatian port Rieka with many returning emigrants. Being closest to the place of tragedy *Carpathia* was able to save 715 survivors from the *Titanic*. The ship's physician and half of its crew who did a heroic job in saving the people and giving them comfort were of Croatian nationality. Ivan Jalševac, one of the *Titanic's* survivors, upon reaching New York aboard the rescue ship, gave a dramatic account of his experience in the issue of *Hrvatski Svijet* (New York) of April 22.[18]

Only a year after this tragedy, in October 1913, the last day before arriving in New York, twenty-six Croatians died during the fire aboard the ship *Volturna*, as reported by the New York daily *Narodni List*, on November 1, 1913. These two disasters belong to the long list of such tragedies involving the lives of thousands of immigrants.

Of the eight million immigrants who came during the first decade of this century approximately eighty percent arrived in steerage. The steerage was the immigrant's "purgatory" before entering the "paradise" of his dreams. Although numerous immigrants came as second-class passengers (and thus escaped the agony of Ellis Island because they were processed in the port), a typical immigrant was a steerage passenger. The anxieties, hardships, and sufferings of the travelers created over the years a "fellowship of the steerage."[19]

CHAPTER 8

The Exodus and World War I

WHEN in 1907 a total of 338,452 immigrants came from Austria-Hungary, "the Croatians and Slovenians" were listed first as "the most important races." The papers and agencies in Zagreb claimed that during the three years 1905 to 1907 alone some 120,000 people from all Croatian provinces left for America. One estimate for 1907 was as high as eighty-three thousand. An American reporter, watching the groups of peasants passing through the port of Rieka, noted that "tremendous hordes of immigrants" were sailing to the United States.[1]

Emily G. Balch estimated that at least 250,000 came from Croatia-Slavonia; close to 100,000 from Dalmatia; 25,000 from Istria; 20,000 from Bosnia; 15,000 from Herzegovina; and over 10,000 Croatians from the western and southern parts of Hungary. Most of them went to Pennsylvania, Illinois, New York, and Ohio.[2]

The provincial government in Zagreb found itself forced to issue several regulations to curb the emigration. The members of the national opposition in the Zagreb Diet (Sabor) bitterly criticized the Habsburg policies as responsible for the mass flight of the people, and praised democracy in America to which so many were obviously attracted.

To channel and control the emigration, the Austro-Hungarian government made, in 1903, an agreement with the Cunard Line for transport of emigrants from the ports of Trieste and Rieka to New York. The agency "Radnik" (The Worker) in Zagreb was the sole representative of Cunard for Croatia. The authorities controlled its activities.[3]

By 1910 and 1911 the depopulation of Dalmatia was so extensive that the current saying was: "the sole export was in human flesh—emigrants." On the island of Brač the fields were "already lying fallow" and "a large part of the population" had disappeared, as the deputy in Vienna's Reichsrat, Dr. Josip Smodlaka, passionately exclaimed in December of 1910. At another island, Vis, of ten thousand inhabitants a quarter were in America. On the whole "the exodus to America creates a scarcity of labor which is in turn met by an influx from the places that are still worse economically," observed Miss Balch, who was visiting Croatia.

In 1907 alone the emigrants from Croatia took with them to America over three million Kronen, according to the critics of emigration. The implication was that not all emigrants were necessarily poor. In 1911 the Diet in Zagreb passed the so-called Ordinance No. 166, entitled "Law on Emigration," trying to limit the emigration of certain categories of people. But, the flow was not stopped.[4]

I Life and Work in America

The 1910s and 1920s were years of growth, of very active life, and of some prosperity for all these immigrants in America. While in earlier years there were few women in their settlements, their number was now much higher. Thousands of families now lived and struggled together. Most of the women did not work outside their homes. The men were generally regarded as good providers and to let the women work would reflect on the husband's ability to provide for his family.

"Muscle, heart and endurance"—as some writers noted—was the work formula for all these people. They all tried to achieve the goal of financial security. They showed a great ability to live frugally. They lived mostly in clusters or formed smaller or larger settlements which we now call "ethnic neighborhoods." Over eighty percent of all Croatians and their Balkan neighbors were unskilled workers. Over a half of them worked in steel and iron industries, smelting plants, mines, lumber, construction, railroads, and stockyards. Before 1910 the unskilled worker made approximately 16 cents an hour. A machinist earned 30 to 40 cents an hour. Even with such low wages they were able to save money. Some bought modest homes. Such thrift and success amazed bank managers and other United States citizens.[5]

In scattered small towns of Pennsylvania, West Virginia, and other states where the Croatians worked in mines and heavy industry, many lived in small houses which usually had vegetable gardens. As their women were skilled cooks, and the butchers gave free liver and kidneys, all the hard workers ate well. With plenty of white bread, mostly baked at home, plenty of potatoes, vegetables, and sauerkraut, a Croatian ate well even in times of strike and unemployment. The women, burdened with incessant chores, worked usually between sixteen and eighteen hours a day.

In Pittsburgh where thousands of them lived many dwellings were "disease incubators." Some magazines like *Charities and the Commons* published numerous reports with very realistic photographs of "Painter's Rows," "Skunk Hollows," and other run-down settlements in which Slavic immigrants made their homes. The Immigration Commission Reports, especially the volumes of *Immigrants in Industries*, described in detail the deplorable housing conditions. Even in other parts of America, Indiana for instance, the situation was just as bad. Contemporary magazines show pictures of shacks, filthy courtyards, narrow alleys with barefoot, poorly dressed children, and dogs running around.[6]

Boarding houses varied. Some were bad and there was too much drinking, quarreling, and fighting in such places. But in thousands of instances the boarding house was for many immigrants a welcome and necessary institution. It was their transplanted home in which they all shared difficult and good times. It was especially good if a good boarding "missus" was in charge of it. Such a typical "missus" was Manda Evanich in Calumet, Michigan, some eighty years ago, whom Adamic immortalized. When her twelfth and thirteenth sons—twins—were born in 1902, President Theodore Roosevelt sent her a congratulatory letter, which was published in many newspapers.[7]

Those living on the land (the farmers, ranchers, fruit and vegetable growers in the West and South) were much better off than their compatriots crowded in depressing slums and company houses. Ante Tresić Pavičić who saw many of his countrymen in filthy apartments of St. Louis and other cities, observed later in his book that former proud peasants of Lika lived "like animals." The peasant-workers were ready to suffer such privations because some of them stayed only a few years and their main concern was to save money.

Many people kept their boarders even when they were jobless for months and unable to pay room and board. Most of the boarders paid their debts as soon as they could, but some left without ever paying, as the many complaints in numerous issues of Croatian papers evidenced.[8]

At the time the Immigration Commission was investigating conditions among the Slovenians and Croatians, a good third had wives in America. A high proportion of their children was at work. Some 34 percent of the men were employed twelve months of the year; 50 percent worked nine months or more; some 75 percent worked six months or more each year, earning an average of eleven dollars a week. The same Commission also found that the South Slavs committed fewer crimes than some other nationalities. They were usually sentenced for "gainful offense," personal violence, and as offenders "against public policy."[9] It is interesting that several publications concerned with immigrants quoted social workers to the effect that police brutality at its worst existed in all Slav industrial settlements.

In McKeesport, a suburb of Pittsburgh (population 32,000), some eighty saloons catered to the immigrants. Summer was a time for picnics. It was like being home for a day. Folk songs and tamburitza music were always on the program. Frequently the speechmakers reminded the immigrants of the old country, urging them to contribute funds for the various causes.[10]

Little did these homesick immigrants realize the significance of their contribution to Pittsburgh, of which a professor of Political Economy at the University of Wisconsin remarked: "Gigantic in its creation of wealth, titanic in its contest for the division of wealth, Pittsburgh looms up as the mighty storm mountain of Capital and Labor. Here our modern world achieves its grandest triumph and faces its gravest problem." He named the city "Pittsburgh the Powerful, the Iron City, the Workshop of the World."[11]

When Slavs came to the mills they replaced the Irish and Germans who moved up in the social scale. In Pittsburgh the Slavs constituted over one half of the workers in the steel mills.

Further up the Monongahela Valley were the milltowns: Homestead of Pinkerton fame; Braddock with its record-breaking mills and furnaces; Duquesne, where the weight of molten metal was a hundred tons; and McKeesport, home of the biggest tube works on earth. In the mills an open-hearth helper tapped fifty tons of molten steel from his furnace. Here were the vesselmen and the steel-pourers, rollers and hookers. Here five- and ten-ton steel ingots plunged madly back and forth between the rolls. The men worked in hoop mills and guide mills, where the heat was intense. Here were the ladles of molten steel, piles of red hot bars, straightening presses at the rail mills. A visitor in a mill saw only faces reddened by the glare of fire and hot steel, muscles standing out in knots and bands on bare arms.

Joseph Stella, an Italian-born painter, well known for his paintings of the Brooklyn Bridge, immortalized these steel workers in a series of drawings and paintings. This grim artistic chronicle and documentary of the immigrant at work was published in the issues of the *Charities and the Commons* weekly during early 1909.[12]

The work in the mines was particularly dangerous. In 1907 alone more than three thousand miners were killed on the job. The death rate was roughly constant in relation to the tonnage mined, rising slightly in relation to the number employed. It was two and a half times as high as the British rate! A high proportion of the killed were Croatians and Slavic people. The United Mine Workers fought for years to improve the lot of the workers, but it was a long struggle with many setbacks.

In steel mills and other heavy industries the rate of fatal accidents was also high. Big business, authorities, and writers have blamed the immigrants as chronically unsafe workers, "characteristically reckless" in mines and mills. This, however, is only partly true.

A variety of reasons for the accidents were cited by observers: carelessness, lack of attentiveness, intoxication, rashness, taking chances to save time, and also the lack of safety provisions by employers. Especially difficult was the lot of the families who lost their breadwinners in such accidents. Out of 304 cases of men killed in a year (1908) in Allegheny County, Pennsylvania, 88 of the families received not one dollar of compensation from the employers. Ninety-three families received not more than $100. Sixty-two families received over $100, but not more than $300. Sixty-one families received more than this, most of them under $1,000. In other words, 181 families, or roughly 60 percent, were left by the employers to bear the entire income loss, and only 61 families, or 20 percent, received in compensation more than $500—a sum which would approximate one year's income of the lowest paid of the workers killed.

Three hundred and four cases were under study, but the total number of those killed in industrial accidents in Pittsburgh and vicinity in 1908 was actually 526. Almost a half were married men and the others were supporters of their relatives. Three who perished were women. The 265 single men ranged in age *from thirteen to sixty-five!*[13]

The fate of those totally disabled for life by industrial accidents was tragic. Crystal Eastman, reporter for the *Charities and the Commons*, described the case of six men: one of them lost an arm and a leg; one was paralyzed; four were to walk with crutches for the rest of their lives. Of these six, three received no compensation at all; one obtained $30, one received $125, and one got $365. There were men also who had suffered the loss of an eye—who only in some cases received a measly compensation: out of eleven cases under study (all lost one eye), three received no compensation and the rest obtained between $45 and $200 for the loss.

Among the longshoremen in New York were many who were injured and disabled. The work was back-breaking since cargoes of one to one and a half tons were handled by two men. To obtain even such a job, the foreman had to be bribed. The Herzegovinians were pulling trucks—heavily loaded with cargo—for ten hours a night at the freight piers. The tall men from Dalmatia and Bosnia-Herzegovina, even though of exceptional height and endowed with rugged strength, after a few years of strenuous labor and unsanitary housing showed signs of exhaustion. Some five hundred South Slavs worked in their own gangs, but after they became too independent, the gangs were broken up and regrouped with other nationalities in order to "crush the spirit of rebellion." It seems that the employers did not trust Croatian foremen, and so they replaced them with Irish.[14]

Many individual South Slavs pushed themselves too hard in their drive to make money quickly before returning to the old country. In Pennsylvania, as observed by a contemporary writer, "they were willing at the outset to work at any wages and under any conditions."[15]

Going through the hazards of industrial work, injured and killed by the hundreds, cheated out of many millions in compensation, these Slavs quickly joined the ranks of organized labor. When "an arbitrary foreman or intolerable conditions affected them, they reacted as a community, en masse." While to the native white American "the strike was mainly an economic protest, to the Slav it indeed was more like 'war.' "[16]

As in all wars this, too, had its casualties. During the big strike in Mckees Rocks, Pennsylvania, in the summer of 1909 Stjepan Horvat was killed by a strikebreaker. A historic strike was one in the Copper Country of Michigan which started on July 23, 1913, and involved some fifteen thousand miners; it was marked by violence. During the violence the Croatian miners accidentally killed a deputy sheriff. Anthony Lucas, a son of the well-known Lucas family, as the district attorney did his best to save ten accused Croatians from the maximum penalty. Later on as a member of Michigan's legislature he pushed through the first miners' compensation law by the state of Michigan.[17]

At the time of the unsuccessful strike the Western Federation of Miners prepared a Christmas party for local children in the old Italian Hall. A false fire alarm caused chaos and a stampede against a jammed door. Seventy-four people—among them fifty-six children—were suffocated to death. Half the world telegraphed its condolences. The Sunday of the funeral was the saddest day in this mining town.

The strike lasted nine months and failed. It was not until July 13, 1943—thirty years later—that the Western Federation of Miners was recognized by the employers, but by then the mines were almost all closed and a great number of people had left the Copper Country.[18]

II *At the Crossroads*

It used to be said by old-timers that when there were strikes and violence, the suffering women dreamed of the quiet villages of their native lands.

The indiscriminate killing of strikers and their women and children at Ludlow, Colorado, and many other places, reflected the mood of the employers and of large segments of the American people. The guardsmen, sheriffs, deputy sheriffs, Pinkerton guards, and policemen were average Americans. In the Capitol of Washington, the legislators' criticism of and strong opposition to mass immigration mounted steadily. In 1907, the peak year of the immigration (which was also a year of economic depression), the U.S. Congress established the so-called Dillingham Commission, officially known as the U.S. Immigration Commission. Its purpose was to investigate the whole immigration problem and make recommendations for the future.

In 1917, the same year when America entered World War I, the U.S. Congress over the veto of President Wilson passed the first discriminatory restriction of immigration, the Literacy Test. The years between 1907 and the early 1920s should be regarded as a crossroads in the history of U.S. immigration.[19]

For many Croatians the period marked the realization of old dreams: they became farmers. Numerous former miners left the Michigan Copper country with their savings and acquired land in Minnesota, Wisconsin, Kansas, and as far south as Georgia, Alabama, and Florida. Some moved to Canada's wheat-growing provinces. The most prosperous Croatian farmers were in California. Miss Balch reported that here one of these farmers had property estimated at two million dollars. It was said that one could ride a horse for almost an hour past his corn on one side and wheat on the other.[20]

For a clear picture of America on the eve of World War I, it is necessary to look at its demographic composition. In 1900 the U.S. population reached almost seventy-six million. Of these, 10,214,000 were foreign-born whites. In 1910 there were 13,345,000 of these in a population of almost ninety-two million. In the first postwar census these foreign-born reached 13,712,000 out of a total of 105,710,000 people.[21] All the anti-immigrant elements considered the number of immigrants too high. They were determined to stop the free flow of immigration.

Dr. Ante Tresić Pavičić, mentioned earlier as a visitor in the Croatian colonies, published upon his return to Zagreb in 1907 a book entitled *Preko Atlantika do Pacifika: Život Hrvata u Sjevernoj Americi* (Across the Atlantic to the Pacific: The Life of Croatians in North America). It contains a great deal of information on the Croatians, it presents a well-written analysis of the American scene, and its purpose was to discourage the mass emigration to America. Interestingly, it had the opposite effect. After reading it many young people decided to go to America.

The prominent globetrotters and explorers, brothers Mirko and Stevo Seljan, came for a visit in 1912. They gave lectures to American and Croatian audiences and also formed with some Americans the American-Peruvian Corporation for exploration and exploitation of some parts of Peru. In 1912 a Croatian publisher in St. Louis printed the Seljan brothers' book *Through Desert and Jungle* in Croatian. A year later Mirko was killed by hostile Indians in the Brazilian jungles. Stevo died in Brazil in 1936.[22]

III *The Rise of National Movements*

In March 1909, President Taft received in the White House a delegation of Slavic representatives who were born in Austria-Hungary. He promised that in the forthcoming census the Slavic immigrants would not be counted as Austrians or Hungarians. However, the 1910 Census did not reflect the true status of these ethnic groups. This visit in Washington also indicated the anti-Habsburg feelings of many Slavs in America.

In 1904 the Convention of the National Croatian Society (now 25,000 strong) had appropriated $6,000 for the support of the anti-Habsburg parties in the homeland. On account of a split within the National Croatian Society in March of 1905, a new organization, the Croatian League of Illinois, was founded. In April 1910 the Croatian Unity of the Pacific was formed in San Francisco through the efforts of the Croatian Society "Zvonimir."[23]

When economic depression hit the United States in 1907,

Frank Zotti, the prominent Croatian businessman in New York and the president of the National Croatian Society, went bankrupt. Thousands of depositors lost some $800,000 in his bank. In December 1908 Zotti was deposed as president of the NCS. His widely circulated daily *Narodni List* was for years engaged in heated controversies with the new leadership of the NCS. It also denounced the anti-Habsburg activities of all South Slavs.

A new gynmastic society, Sokol (Falcon), was organized among the Croatians in Chicago in August 1908. The Sokol was also a patriotic organization which spread throughout America and was connected with the same movement in Croatia. It resembled the German *Turnvereine*; the Czechs popularized it among several Slavic groups in America and in the old countries.[24]

During the Eleventh Convention of the National Croatian Society in Kansas City (September 9–24, 1912) a political movement was formed, the Croatian National Alliance. It supported the activities of the South Slav unification movement in the old country, it voted financial aid for the political prisoners in Zagreb (including Stjepan Radić), and its resolution condemned the Austro-Hungarian rule in all South Slav lands of the monarchy. The founding of the Alliance marks the start of an organized anti-Habsburg political movement in the United States. Its organ was *Hrvatska Zastava*. Within a few months 110 lodges of the movement were organized all over the country.[25]

In their reaction to the Balkan Wars (1912–1913) the South Slav papers in America were divided. Some were openly on the side of Serbia and other Slavic states. A few Slovenian and Croatian papers—for instance Zotti's *Narodni List*—criticized Serbia as expansionist.

In the fall of 1912, Ivan Dojčić, a member of the Croatian National Alliance from Pittsburgh, having crossed the ocean in October, came to see the politician, S. Radić. He told him bluntly that he was sent by a group of revolutionists from Pittsburgh to assassinate the imperial viceroy, a commissary who ruled in Zagreb after the office of the *Ban* (representative of the king) had been temporarily abolished. Radić was shocked and told Dojčić that such terroristic acts would discredit the Croatian cause. Radić pleaded in vain with the young Dojčić.

On August 18, 1913 after the solemn services on the occasion of Francis Joseph's birthday in the cathedral in Zagreb, Dojčić fired shots at Baron Ivan von Skerlecz, the royal commissary, who escaped injury. The would-be assassin was arrested. For many weeks the press in America and Europe discussed the event and the political activities of the South Slavs in the United States. At his trial in Zagreb during September 24 and 25, 1913, Dojčić stated that he had come to kill the commissary and he was not sorry for what he did. Some South Slav papers in America hailed him as a hero.

Stjepan Radić, afraid that more revolutionaries might come from America, issued an *Open Political Message*, a pamphlet in Croatian addressed to his compatriots in America appealing to them to refrain from political violence and bloodshed. He considered Dojčić's deed political insanity. With the assent of authorities Radić mailed thousands of the pamphlets to individuals and organizations in America. Dojčić was sentenced to ten years in prison. His act as well as the many activities of thousands of his compatriots were indicative of their mood. Their newspapers now openly called for a revolutionary struggle against the Habsburg monarchy.[26]

IV *Wilson and Self-Determination*

In 1914 among the 1,218,000 immigrants who rushed through the open gates of America, over thirty thousand were Croatians. It was the last year of world peace and the last time in which the yearly number of immigrants exceeded a million. The guns of August in Europe announced the end of an era for both Europe and America.

The assassination in Sarajevo, Bosnia, of Archduke Francis Ferdinand and his wife (who was of lower Czech nobility) by a Serb nationalist caused Austria-Hungary to attack Serbia at the end of July. A worldwide conflict ensued. A majority of the Croatians and Slovenians abhorred the assassination and loyally served in the Habsburg armies on several fronts. The events in Europe inevitably influenced many immigrant colonies in America.

The Croatians, too, were divided and this division was most evident in their strong press. Zotti's *Narodni List*, a daily of twelve thousand circulation, favored a free Croatia and Slovenia under the Habsburgs. Another daily *Hrvatski Svijet-Croatian World* (New York), owned by the Slovenian businessman Franc Sakser, with a circulation of ten thousand opposed the Habsburgs and advocated formation of a South Slav state on the ruins of the Habsburg empire. And there were other papers either pro- or anti-Habsburg.

In March 1915 many Croatian delegates joined, in Chicago's LaSalle Hotel, other South Slavs in forming a South Slav National Council. The Croatian, Rev. Niko Grśković of Cleveland, became its president. A telegram was sent to President Wilson hailing him as friend of peoples oppressed by Habsburgs. A resolution announced that the Council represented all American South Slavs. Its goal was to work toward destruction of Austria-Hungary and establishment of a South Slav state.[27]

Subsequently, a South Slav or Yugoslav Committee was established in London. Among its members was the sculptor Ivan Meštrović who by then had gained international fame. Its main financial support came from wealthy immigrants in South and North America.

In mid-July 1915, the Croatians participated in another South Slav Congress gathered in Pittsburgh with some two thousand delegates. A few months later, Milan Marjanović, a journalist and writer, arrived from London in order to organize a propaganda drive in America for the South Slav cause. Frightened by the news of the secret Treaty of London, by which the Allies had promised (in April 1915) to Italy sections of Croatian and Slovenian lands, many Croatians and Slovenians remained staunch Habsburg loyalists. Even those who favored a union with Serbia advocated a republic for the future South Slav state. The United States, still neutral officially, advocated a reorganization rather than destruction of the Habsburg empire.[28]

After Wilson was reelected in November of 1916, the South Slav leaders spread the rumor that he had gained the crucial state of California through the South Slav vote; consequently, the South Slavs in the United States had elected Wilson over Hughes by a narrow margin. Over the past decades numerous writers have discussed this claim. The fact was never denied by Wilson.

In order to promote the work for the cause, the South Slavic National Council established its office at 932 Southern Building in Washington, D.C. It seems, however, that the Council's activities and influence were small, at least until the final months of the war "when American public opinion was aroused about the cause of subject nationalities in general."[29]

At another Congress held at Pittsburgh on November 29 and 30, 1916, the 615 delegates claimed to speak "in the name of more than 500,000 South Slavs." Represented here were the four major Croatian organizations with a combined membership of sixty thousand in about seven hundred lodges. The chairman of the Congress was the priest, Rev. Niko Gršković. The delegates recognized the South Slav Committee in London as the sole representative of all South Slavs from Austria-Hungary and greeted President Wilson in a telegram as "the defender of the rights of small nations."[30]

In anticipation of these deliberations a group of Croatian and Slovenian priests gathered on November 10 in Pittsburgh. There they composed a memorandum in which they hailed Wilson as defender of small nations, and three of their representatives went to Washington to hand the signed document to the President. The same group also issued "Our Declaration," which was printed and distributed among leading American journalists and politicians. The signers pleaded for "a union of all Croatian and Slovenian lands in an independent and free state." On December 6, 1916 the New York *Narodni List* issued a proclamation to the Croatians and a pamphlet in Croatian containing the same "Our Declaration" for wide distribution. It was signed by thirteen Croatian and Slovenian priests.[31]

The United States' declaration of war on Germany temporarily strengthened the South Slav activities in America. The whole movement was dominated by the American Croatians. It found a true supporter in the new Serbian minister in Washington, Ljuba Mihajlović. In July of 1917, Dr. Ante Trumbić of the Committee in London and Premier Nikola Pašić of the Serbian government in exile at Corfu signed an agreement about establishment of a future Yugoslav monarchy under the Serbian Karageorgevich dynasty. As many Croatians were opponents of the monarchy, the whole South Slav movement in America soon found itself in a serious crisis. To help save the movement Niko Gršković quit his job as priest in Cleveland, moved to Washington, and worked full time for the cause, while a Croatian politican, Dr. Hinko Hinković, a member of the London South Slav Committee, came to America for a lecturing tour. The disunity within the ranks of the South Slav movement was partly overcome when in December 1917 the United States declared war on Austria-Hungary. Now even the pro-Habsburg papers switched their allegiance and appealed to their readers for unity and support of the American war effort.[32]

Delighted by the U.S. declaration of war against the Habsburg government, Dr. Ante Trumbić sent a telegram to President Wilson in the name of his London Committee assuring the president that "our people, under the Austro-Hungarian yoke, shall receive in our territory the American troops as our defenders and liberators."

On January 8, 1918, the members of Gršković's Council sat in the galleries of the Congress when President Wilson delivered his speech setting forth his Fourteen Points. The fact that he demanded merely autonomy for the Slav peoples under the Habsburgs disappointed the South Slavs who were present. Consequently, in America and in Western Europe, the anti-Habsburg political activists demanded a more radical stand from the United States.[33]

However, the Fourteen Points were enthusiastically received by the Slavs in the Habsburg monarchy. Wilson's ideas especially influenced several political parties in the south of Austria-Hungary. In Washington Secretary of State Lansing reacted to Wilson's speech by recommending destruction of Austria-Hungary and creation of a free South Slav state.

Invited by President Wilson, Croatian members of the South Slav National Council and hundreds of countrymen, many dressed in colorful national costumes, participated in the festivities of July 4, 1918 in Washington. By now Wilson was in favor of destroying the Habsburg empire and giving complete independence to its Slavic peoples.[34]

In October 1918 the disintegration of Austria-Hungary began. A National Council was established in Zagreb on October 8. On October 19 the U.S. Secretary of State stated that the intention of the United States was to leave to the peoples of Austria-Hungary the decision of their own destiny. In its historic session of October 29, 1918 the Croatian Diet in Zagreb cut off all ties with the Habsburg state and a free South Slav state was proclaimed in all southern territories of the monarchy; its government was the National Council in Zagreb.

Invoking the Treaty of London (of 1915), the Italians started immediately to occupy the Adriatic shores. On October 30 an urgent telegram arrived in Washington from Dr. Ante Trumbić and on November 4 from the National Council in Zagreb. They implored the U.S. government to prevent the Italian occupation and to send U.S. troops. However, these pleas were in vain. The continuing occupation of the Italian and the invasion of Serbian troops in the old country caused disappointment among the members of the South Slav National Council headed by N. Grśković in Washington. The council met during four days: November 13–16. It issued a protest calling for "a republic after the model of the United States" in the homeland. On November 19 a group of Croatian and Slovenian leaders gathered in Pittsburgh and sent an urgent message to President Wilson begging for protection of their native lands from Italian and Serbian occupation.[35]

While the chaotic situation in their old country caused anguish to the political activists in America, the masses of their compatriots were happy that the war was over. The times had been good and these immigrants had earned good wages. Thousands of young people had served in the U.S. Armed Forces, many on the Western front in Europe. Hundreds of Croatians were killed in combat. A large number were decorated. Sergeant Louis Cukela, USMC, a native of Dalmatia, received two Congressional Medals of Honor for extreme bravery in France; he was the only man then who received two of the highest decorations in a single war. They were also awarded to Mate Kocak and Alex Mandusich while Jacob Mestrovic received the Congressional Medal posthumously for "conspicuous gallantry and intrepidity above and beyond the call of duty."[36]

CHAPTER 9

From One War Through Another: 1918–1945

IN World War I a significant number of South Slavs gave their lives in service of the United States. This undoubtedly helped to cement the ties between them and their adopted land.

The news from the homeland was sad: thousands of men had been killed on the battlefronts, leaving many widows and orphans throughout the old country. Their families sent frantic appeals for help to the immigrants here in the United States. In Croatia and other South Slavic lands the only hope lay in America.

I Disappointment with Yugoslavia

The Italian occupation of some Adriatic regions, the Serbian military occupation, and the subsequent reign of terror brought about a significant opposition to the new state. The Kingdom of Serbs, Croatians, and Slovenes was officially proclaimed on December 1, 1918. It included all Slovenian and Croatian territories which had been former Habsburg possessions as well as Montenegro and Macedonia. The multinational state of Yugoslavia was officially recognized by the United States on February 6, 1919. A group of immigrant leaders, bitterly disappointed over the turn of events in the homeland, convened on April 1, 1919 in Cleveland. Claiming to speak in the name of "500,000 Croatians and Slovenians," they addressed a Resolution to the Paris Peace Conference and to President Wilson. The Croatians and Slovenians protested the founding of the South Slav state as a violation of the principle of self-determination.

In Paris Wilson tried to save from Italian occupation Istria and some other regions for the South Slavs. An American observer in Zagreb, Lieutenant LeRoy King, stated in March 1919, in a report to the American delegation in Paris that "the Americans are very popular" in Croatia, and that all the people "look upon America as their last hope."[1]

In November of 1920, Istria, Rieka, Zadar, and some adjacent regions and islands with some 600,000 Croatians and Slovenians were handed over to Italy. This crass violation of the principle of self-determination caused a lasting disappointment among the Croatians and Slovenians in America. The South Slav movement in America was now dead. For the loss of their territories they blamed President Wilson who could not stop the Italian expansion. But in spite of this failure Wilson remained very popular among the South Slavs in the old country. To them he was a prophet whose ideas had instilled hope, a man who had destroyed the Habsburg rule.

Disappointed with the situation which meant virtual enslavement of their homelands by the newly established authoritarian regimes, millions of immigrants decided to make America their permanent home. While some South Slavs returned to the old country a great majority of them now made their final decision to stay in America.

II *The Agony of Becoming an American*

It was partly because of disenchantment with the postwar solutions that many Croatians and other South Slavs decided finally to "become Americans." The country which they had regarded as only a temporary residence now became their final home. In the process of adjustment their ethnic press played a large role. It was up to the editors, writers, and publishers to give the best advice possible to their countrymen, the new Americans by choice. The Socialist press in particular tried to point the way to adaptation to America. Milan Glumac, a typographer from Zagreb, here since 1907, edited the first issue of *Radnička Straža* (Workers' Sentinel) that appeared on December 24, 1907. He died from tuberculosis in 1914 at the age of thirty-one. In those years this disease was widespread and killed many young South Slavic immigrants. The newspaper he founded was the forerunner of a strong Croatian Socialist press in this country. Factionalism and controversies plagued the Croatian press. It was frequently an angry and ugly voice, indeed an immigrant version of "yellow journalism."[2]

One of the most successful and most durable Croatian newspapers has been the *Zajedničar* (The Fraternalist), the weekly organ of the Croatian Fraternal Union. Started in 1904, it is still being printed weekly in Pittsburgh on its own presses. It is not only the largest, but also a well-edited paper which has reported more on Croatian life in the United States than any other paper. Its role in bringing its more than sixty thousand readers closer to America cannot be sufficiently stressed.

One of the old school and one of the best journalists, editors, writers, and publishers in this group was Ivan Krešić. Originally educated for the priesthood, Krešić immigrated in 1906, joined first *Hrvatski Svijet* (New York), and afterward published several newspapers of his own. *Hrvatski List & Danica Hrvatska* appeared three times a week for twenty-three years. For forty years Krešić printed newspapers, almanacs, and books for large audiences, emphasizing American values and ideals. In 1945 he sold his paper to the Croatian Franciscans in Chicago. They have published the weekly *Danica—The Morning Star* ever since. It is now almost sixty years old and is excellently edited. Besides Krešić, Nikola Gršković (a former priest) deserves credit as a truly great educator of his people, a man who deeply understood America, a very able writer who until after World War II had great influence among his countrymen. He, too, helped thousands of them to adjust to the new country and to its ideas.

Professor Govorchin in his book on Americans from Yugoslavia mentioned forty-five South Slavic papers in 1939. Of them twenty-three were Croatian.

III   *Religious Activities*

For the older generations of the South Slav immigrants religion was a substantial part of their way of life. The church, usually with a parochial school, a teaching nuns' convent, a parish house (rectory) and church hall, remains in many settlements the hub of life. Considering the fact that a great majority of these immigrants were blue-collar workers, people with low incomes, it is amazing what they have been able to accomplish all over the country.

When Emily G. Balch was making a survey of all Slavic parishes in 1909 she counted ten Croatian churches. The Croatians established parishes in metropolitan Pittsburgh and Chicago (two of their strongest centers), in New York City, and in Cleveland; also in the states of Indiana, Michigan, Wisconsin, Kansas, Iowa, and Missouri. In California—where they are most prosperous—they founded only one parish, that of St. Anthony in Los Angeles (December 1910). The parish in San Francisco has always been Slovenian-Croatian. The first church was destroyed in April 1906, during the great earthquake. It was rebuilt in 1912.

St. Joseph parish in St. Louis, Missouri, was dedicated in September 1904, in a reconverted Jewish synagogue. In 1906 the grade school was opened, some fifteen societies formed, and in 1927 the church was moved to a new location at 12th and Russell Streets. Administered by secular priests and for a while by Jesuits, the parish was then taken over by the Franciscans. They now hold some fifteen Croatian parishes in the United States and Canada. In St. Louis the church, parish house, convent, school, and the adjacent "Sokol" building form a whole block of well-maintained, impressive buildings in the heart of the ethnic area.[3]

As teachers were badly needed, the teaching nuns had to be brought from the old country. In 1906 Rev. Martin D. Krmpotić invited from Banja Luka, Bosnia, sixteen sisters of the Order of Adorers of the Precious Blood. In 1909 he brought also a group of nuns from Maribor, Slovenia, members of the order of St. Francis of Christ the King. The Franciscan nuns established first their provincial home in South Chicago and then moved to Lemont, Illinois. In 1940 they established there Mount Assisi Academy for girls, built a new convent, and maintained St. Joseph's Home for the aged.

The Daughters of Divine Charity came from Sarajevo, Bosnia, in 1926. Their mother house is in Akron, Ohio. All these groups of nuns—joined by more recent arrivals—have grown and expanded and on the whole have been very successful in many activities: teaching at parochial schools, assisting at parishes, working in the hospitals, orphanages, and homes for the aged.[4]

The Croatian Franciscans (O.F.M.) from Herzegovina have their Holy Family Custody, a monastery, a Croatian Ethnic Institute, and a printing and publishing center at Drexel Boulevard in Chicago. They live in splendid buildings of the former Armour estate now in the midst of a Black ghetto. The Croatian Franciscan Tertiaries (Third Order Regular) are centered in McKeesport, a suburb of Pittsburgh. They administer three Croatian parishes in Greater Pittsburgh. The Dominican fathers administer one parish in Chicago and are forming a new one at Chicago's North Side. The parish in Gary, Indiana, St. Joseph the Worker, belongs to the Franciscan Conventuals.

The first known Croatian Lutheran minister in this country was Louis Sanjek. He was ordained in America in 1914 after studying first at the Catholic seminary in Zagreb. For years he worked among the Slovak and Slovenian immigrants. He described his American experience in an autobiography *In Silence*, a warm account of his own struggle and that of his people.

Some forty thousand Jews lived in Croatia before 1941. Many intermarried with the Croatians and quite a few were assimilated to the extent that they embraced the nationality of their adopted land. Some intellectuals, including several who were very active in nationalist movements in Zagreb and other cities, were of Jewish or half-Jewish descent. During the high tide of immigration a few came to America where they worked as merchants or bankers among the Croatians. Hundreds of Jews from Croatia made their way to the United States after World War II. (Thousands went to Israel where they hold important positions. For instance, two Israeli army leaders, including Bar Lev, were born in Sarajevo.) Many of the Croatian Jews, who now live in America and in other countries, made their escape during the horrible days of World War II with the help of the Archbishop of Zagreb, Alojzije Stepinac.

Various Protestant churches have been active among the Croatians (and other South Slavs) before and after 1945 in both Yugoslavia and in the United States. The Seventh Day Adventists, Baptists, and Mormons are very busy in Detroit,

Chicago, Cleveland, and Akron, among other cities. In recent years they have erected churches and halls, conducted religious radio programs, printed papers, periodicals, and books for the newcomers. They have also performed social work among them and helped them to get established in this country. *The Watchtower* of the Jehovah's Witnesses has a monthly edition in Croatian. Protestant Bibles in both Latin and Cyrillic alphabets are distributed either free or in very inexpensive editions. All these activities are bearing fruit. In the state of Utah some Croatian old-timers are members of the Mormon Church.

IV *The Moslems*

The contention of many western scholars that all Croatians are Roman Catholics was never accurate. For many centuries about twenty-five percent have been adherents of other religions. The largest non-Catholic religious group among them are members of Islam.

As a Moslem (or Muslim) scholar stated, before 1918 "from the poorer districts of Herzegovina and Montenegro many Muslims . . . emigrated to America." Quite a few came from Bosnia, Sanjak, and Croatia proper and "they identify themselves with the Catholic Croats, to whom . . . they are also akin in mentality." Moreover, "the Bosnian-Herzegovinian Muslims speak a fluent Croatian."[5]

The largest group of old Croatian Moslem immigrants settled in Chicago where they found some coreligionists from Macedonia and other parts of the Turkish Empire. A considerable number of them remained single. Because of the lack of mosques and religious instruction they found it difficult to practice their religion. At that time Islam was almost nonexistent in America. There were no *hojas* or *imams* to lead them in prayer and as a religious group, these Croatian Moslems were a lonely lot.

With the influx of Moslem immigrants from Croatian lands after 1945 came a revival of Moslem religious activities in several American cities. Over the years thousands of these Moslems, many of them educated and skilled people, have made their homes in the United States. The American-born, the old and new immigrants joined forces and in 1957 opened a mosque in Chicago and a religious and cultural center. Several of their religious leaders—some of them educated at the best Arab universities—have joined them in recent years. The Moslems have no ordained priests. Their *hojas* and *imams* lead the flock, kneeling and facing Mecca in prayer, and help them observe holy days, one of which is at the end of Ramadan, the forty days of fast and prayer. The two Bajrams, in the second part of each year, are observed by thousands. Other duties of the religious leaders are religious education and teaching from the Koran, the sacred book of Islam. One of the best-known of their religious leaders is Dr. Asaf Duraković, a scholar and author of two booklets on Croatian Moslems. Another is Dr. Kamil Avdić who lives in Chicago. There are many more women among them now than before 1945, and some Moslems have Catholic wives.

The Moslems participate in all old and new Croatian political and cultural organizations and collaborate in many political, cultural, and social activities. The predominantly Catholic societies and many individual Catholics, realizing the plight of their brethren in strange environments, generously contribute to the erection of new Moslem centers. This was best manifested four years ago when a new and large Moslem Centre was erected in Toronto, Canada. Many Croatian writers, scholars, and political leaders are Moslems. This does not necessarily mean that they and Catholics agree on all issues. Surrounded in the old country and in immigrant colonies by a Christian majority, as a religious group the Moslems have always been in a precarious position and therefore they are in some ways sensitive and distrustful. Despite the improvements and the new revival they are still exposed to prejudice and lack of understanding in a predominantly Christian country which knows little or nothing of Islam. Today every tenth Croatian newcomer is a Moslem.

Generally, the Moslem birth rate is much higher than that of the Christians. (In Yugoslavia the recent census shows a phenomenal rise of Moslems in Bosnia-Herzegovina.) These trends may change after a prolonged stay in America. Because of centuries of Near Eastern influences emanating from the Turkish era, and facing mutual problems, these Moslems are sympathetic to the Arab cause in America and in the Middle East.[6]

V *The New Americans*

When the flood of human migration became a mere trickle, an increasing number of scholars and writers started to analyze and scrutinize these people who were expected to join the Americans, quit their ancestral culture, and "melt" in the big Melting Pot.

The Croatians like any other "Balkanites" came here as peasants or children of peasants whose roots were in the soil for many generations.

According to a British writer, the people of Bosnia and Herzegovina are graceful and artistic. Their national dress is beautiful. Emily G. Balch was much impressed by the beauty of national costumes from the western parts of the Balkans. Lamenting the fact that they "leave their beautiful embroidered garments behind" to buy the "European clothes" which are cheap and ready-made, she wrote: "From the point of view of beauty they suffer immeasurably by this change to our sweatshops and factory-made clothes." She also recognized among the South Slavs a certain amount of instinctive fatalism, indifference to danger that swelled the terrible and excessive death rolls in the mines and in the steel industry. She was told that in mining company hospitals when injured Italians screamed from pain Slavs with similar injuries remained silent; if they complained, the doctors knew that they were badly, if not fatally, hurt.[7]

The Reports of the Immigration Commission made much of the illiteracy among Slavs in order to prove their inferiority but failed to explain its underlying causes. But Miss Balch remarks: "One must remember that illiteracy does not necessarily connote either stupidity or lack of desire to learn." She also praised these people's simplicity, a warm and quiet intensity of family life, their marked love of music and often of intellectual pursuits. "Splendid types . . . fine in their carriage,"[8] she remarked.

Others observed as a common trait of all Slavic peoples their traditional superstitions, remnants of old heathenism that curiously blended with their religion. They are charitable to the poor, although not always generous to the weak. An American writer frankly admitted: "It is hard not to be prejudiced against the Slav." The South Slavs differ from one another, and thus "the Dalmatian is the giant among them, and he of the Boche di Cattaro is a veritable Slavic Apollo, measuring, on an average, six feet three inches. He is dark skinned, and graceful in his movements." Similarly, John R. Commons wrote that "the Croatians from the southwest mountains are among the finest specimens of physical manhood coming to our shores. They are a vigorous people."[9]

Reuben Markham, who knew them well, considered the Croatians "a very estimable people," hard-working, self-respecting, lovers of liberty. They wear national costumes that are "among the most exquisite in Europe." They love music and song and they are "loyal and show great attachment to their leaders."[10]

Many thousands of these Croatian people spoke a special language: a mixture of Croatian and English words (or Croatian words with English endings). They were in the process of finally settling down as a whole ethnic group. And this process took many years. In 1919 an American periodical estimated their number at 450,000; the number of Slovenians was approximately 250,000 and of Serbians 80,000. The Bulgarians were not mentioned. The article stressed that the entire production of the staves and oyster fisheries in the South was controlled exclusively by the Croatians.[11]

VI The Immigration from Yugoslavia

In the years 1921 to 1929 (the year when the new restrictive immigration laws went into effect) over 83,000 from the Croatian provinces alone arrived in America. The U.S. Immigration and Naturalization Service reported that some 38,000 immigrants returned to Yugoslavia between 1919 and 1924. An American observed in Belgrade, the capital of the new South Slav state, "the large numbers of Croats and Slovenes who had gone to America many years ago . . . returned at the behest of the Serbs to fight in the Serbian army." Some who were American citizens spent years fighting Yugoslav red tape before they were allowed to return to the United States.[12]

In 1920 the Ministry of Social Policy in Belgrade founded a special Department for Emigration and Immigration. Emigration laws were passed by the Parliament in May and November 1921. An Emigration Service was established. The emigration was free, but could be restricted by various agencies. A special General Emigration Commissariat was established in Zagreb as the main center of the emigration. In March of 1923 it was abolished and the Ministry of Social Policy took over the entire responsibility.

. During the decade from 1931 to 1940 the immigration from Yugoslavia to the United States dropped to 5,835. Our authorities listed between the two wars only 56,787 newcomers from Yugoslavia. The writers in Yugoslavia consider this number too low. At least sixty percent of all immigrants from Yugoslavia after 1918 have been of Croatian nationality. A Serbian writer estimated the number of Montenegrins in America in 1925 at 8,000.[13] The U.S. Immigration quota for the immigrants from Yugoslavia was a mere 671 a year; it was later raised to 942. The Bulgarian quota amounted to only one hundred a year.

VII   *Taking Root in America*

To help people acquire their own homes, numerous building and loan associations were established. They financed the purchases of homes for their members. In this way thousands of immigrants fulfilled their old dream: to own their own house and the land around it.

Another old dream of many was to acquire land and to become farmers. For years various Croatian newspapers advertised lots available in a new Croatian colony called Velebit at the Eagle River, Wisconsin. This developed later into a strong and thriving colony, a prospering farming community, the largest of this kind among the Croatians. There was no better and more efficient way of settling down in the United States than by owning land and home.[14]

Choosing the new home did not necessarily mean forgetting the old country. When times were good and fraternal organizations were prosperous, they donated funds for relief and charitable causes in the homeland. For instance, on one occasion during the 1920s alone, the National Croatian Society contributed $25,000 to the economic organization Hrvatski Radiša in Zagreb; $6,000 for war victims in Croatia; and $11,000 for the starving people in Russia. Such generosity was repeated in the following conventions of this fraternal organization and many thousands of dollars have been given for various causes.[15]

Some of these causes were—in the view of critics and keen authorities—of dubious character. Some strikers or victims of labor violence who were being supported by fraternal donations, were members of leftist organizations. Croatian individuals and publications were branded as radical, Communist, and anarchist. A few men were deported during the Red Scare (1919–1920). Heated debates ensued in many Croatian newspapers, especially when leftists suddenly became very active in the main fraternal organizations.

All societies and organizations maintained keen interest in developments in the old country. Radić's Croatian Peasant Party and his struggle for a Croatian peasant neutral republic found many supporters among the immigrants. After he was mortally wounded in the summer of 1928 and King Alexander proclaimed his dictatorship in January 1929, the Croatian immigrant press and organizations announced an open struggle against the government in Belgrade.

Dissatisfied with leftist activities in fraternal organizations, a group of priests and laymen founded on October 12, 1921 in Gary, Indiana, a new fraternal organization, the Croatian Catholic Union. In 1925 it had some three thousand members in forty-five lodges. Its weekly organ was *Naša Nada—Our Hope* which for many years also printed an almanac. The Union later developed into an organization of some fifteen thousand members. For many years its president has been Joseph Saban. The long-time editor of *Naša Nada* is Stanley Borić. The C.C.U. besides being an outspoken Catholic organization, has always supported the idea of Croatian independence.

One man who took great interest in all fraternal movements and in helping his people to get acculturated (as he himself did) was Niko Gršković. Now a bitter critic of the Yugoslav state, which he helped to create in 1918, he closely followed developments among his countrymen in the United States. As

Adamic stated, Grškovic's *Svijet* (The World) in New York contained "some of the best editorials in America in any language." He called him "the dean of South Slavic editors in America" whose paper presented "a graceful balance between the Old and New World."[16]

A historic event in fraternalism was the founding of the largest of the South Slav fraternal organizations, the Croatian Fraternal Union, in November of 1925 by a merger of the National Croatian Society, the Croatian League of Illinois, the Croatian Unity of Pacific, the National Croatian Beneficial Society "St. Joseph," and the Young National Croatian Union. The combined membership was over 53,000; the assets amounted to $3.5 million; the insurance in force totaled almost fifty million dollars. Its first convention was held in Cleveland, Ohio, in May 1926.[17]

VIII   *Opposition to Dictatorship*

Chaotic conditions in the old country aroused a surge of protest among the Croatian immigrants, from the extreme left to the extreme right. An organization called Croatian Circle was founded in New York City and held its first convention in late October 1928 in Pittsburgh. Its organ was *Hrvatski List i Danica Hrvatska* (Croatian Journal and Morning Star). The leaders of the Circle were Ivan Krešić, Rev. Ivan Stipanović, and Joseph Kraja, a printer and publisher in Youngstown, Ohio. The organization advocated complete freedom for Croatia and mainly supported the policies of the Croatian Peasant Party.

The terror in Yugoslavia had among its many victims Dr. Milan Šufflay, a university professor of European reputation who was assassinated by police agents on a street in Zagreb. The *New York Times* and other leading newspapers carried on May 6, 1931, a protest signed by Dr. Albert Einstein, the great scientist, and by the German writer Thomas Mann who denounced the Belgrade authorities for the murder of Šufflay.

A Croatian National Council was founded to coordinate its activities against the dictatorship in Yugoslavia. In spite of the rising depression, substantial sums were collected to support propaganda and other forms of struggle against King Alexander.

The Croatian Fraternal Union, the largest organization of the South Slavs, gathered in Gary, Indiana, for an important convention during June 13–29, 1932. Its 260 delegates passed a strongly worded resolution condemning the dictatorship in the homeland and elected as the Union's new supreme president Ivan D. Butković. He grew up in Pueblo, Colorado. He emerged as one of the leading spokesmen of his people against the oppression in Croatia.[18]

In the dark days of the depression in the 1930s, in spite of poverty and joblessness, an amazing spirit of defiance and enthusiastic participation in all kinds of activities swept the Croatian, Slovenian, and Macedonian settlements. Thousands of jobless people and the fortunate few who had an income and some funds gave their small contributions for a cause they believed in. The press, too, in spite of the depression, was stronger and more active than ever. Except for a few that were subsidized by the Belgrade regime, a great majority of the newspapers and other periodicals denounced the royal dictatorship in Yugoslavia.[19]

To present the case of their people the Croatian National Council "in the name of more than 250,000 of American citizens of Croatian descent" issued in September 1933 a Memorandum addressed to the League of Nations, to the American leaders, to the press and the democratic world. On October 10, 1933, Rev. Ivan Stipanović presented it to President Roosevelt and to the State Department. He then traveled to Europe and on October 26, 1933 delivered the signed original Memorandum to the General Secretary of the League of Nations in Geneva, Switzerland.[20]

In 1934 a group of members left the political organization, the Croatian Circle, and formed its own organization called Croatian Home Defenders (Hrvatski Domobran). It supported the revolutionary movement in exile led by Dr. Ante Pavelić (1889–1959), a former lawyer in Zagreb and deputy in the Belgrade parliament. The weekly organ *The Independent State of Croatia* was printed in Pittsburgh.

There were many group visits to the homeland during the late 1930s. Many Croatians either saw the country for the first time after many years or—those born in America—for the first time. John D. Butkovich and a large group of Croatians were enthusiastically received by thousands of people in Zagreb in the summer of 1937. The people of Croatia showed their appreciation for all the support, material and moral, they had received from their brethren in America.

When Augustin Košutić, one of the leaders of the Croatian Peasant Party and son-in-law of Stjepan Radić, arrived in New York in August 1930, he was denied entry through the intervention of the Yugoslav embassy. He was sent back to Europe and then admitted in July 1931 after numerous protests by leading Croatians and Macedonians. The U.S. Commissioner of Immigration then was Edward Corsi, himself an Italian immigrant, who commented extensively on the Košutić case in his book on Ellis Island.[21]

IX   *Through the War Years: 1939–1945*

Just as the thunder of another war was approaching, a large number of Croatians (and some Slovenians) had become well-established farmers and ranchers. In California around Sunnyvale, Cupertino, Mountainview, and Watsonville they grew apples, grapes, other fruits and vegetables. New farming communities were established in San Bernardino and San Helena.

By 1939 the most successful rancher and grape grower was Peter J. Divizich, a Croatian immigrant from Konavlje near Dubrovnik. He came in 1920 and a few years later started his vineyards near Porterville in the central San Joaquin Valley which runs for four hundred miles from the north to the south between the two mountain ranges. Divizich knew everything about grapes and on the eve of World War II he owned over three thousand acres of vineyards near Ducor-Delano. Eventually he owned the largest vineyards in the United States. During World War II he supplied the U.S. Armed Forces with thousands of tons of raisins and other fruit products.[22]

Wealthy and prosperous farmers and ranchers also spread to other states. Some engaged in sheep raising; several owned flocks of more than ten thousand. Many moved to the South from the northern regions of the Midwest. Descendants of former lumbermen settled at the border of Louisiana and Arkansas. The town of Janesville was named after the Croatian pioneer Janeš. He was an important businessman in lumber and owned his little railroad. His former workers became farmers and orange growers. In order to do well one needed about five acres of orange trees. Such growers multiplied in Louisiana in Buras, Empire, and Triumph. Most of them were Dalmatians who took over thousands of acres of valuable land. Some around El Paso and Brownsville, Texas, became very prosperous. More than a hundred very successful farmers were established around Mobile, Alabama, in Baldwin County.[23]

The recovery of their compatriots in industrial settlements progressed at a slower pace. What delivered them from the misery of the Great Depression was the outbreak of World War II in Europe in September 1939, and America's entry into the great conflict in December 1941. Six and seven days of work a week and a lot of overtime brought the badly needed cash. A better life and even prosperity slowly returned to thousands of families. Men—those who were not drafted—and women alike were badly needed in the booming defense industry.

The politics of wartime brought many problems and controversies related to the situation in the homeland. It caused friction and struggle between the South Slavs and left scars on a whole generation which are still visible to this day.

Many organized groups expressed intense concern about happenings in the homeland. In Yugoslavia, after an agreement between the President of the Croatian Peasant Party, Dr. V. Maček, and the government in Belgrade, limited autonomy was granted to parts of Croatia. However, when Germany and her allies invaded Yugoslavia in early April 1941 there was almost no resistance. The country was overrun within a few days, the army surrendered, the government and the young king Peter fled the country and found safety in the British Near East. Later the Yugoslav government in exile was established in London. On April 10, 1941, the Croatian nationalists proclaimed in Zagreb an independent Croatian state which also included Bosnia-Herzegovina. Its southern parts were soon occupied by the Italians. Slovenia was divided between the Germans and Italians. Serbia became a German and Montenegro an Italian protectorate. The Bulgarians took Macedonia, the Albanians annexed the Kossovo region. What followed in the Balkans was a four-year period of warfare, civil war, destruction, and suffering in which some two million people perished. The Serbian nationalists (the Chetniks) under Draža Mihajlović and the Communist partisans under Josip Broz Tito, the Croatian troops, and those of several other countries—all were engaged in a fierce fight which showed no mercy to the adversary.[24]

In an orgy of savage brutalities reminiscent of those during the Turkish era, thousands of innocent civilians of all ages and many combatants were killed on all sides. The Italians deported many people from the Adriatic and Slovenian parts. The Germans deported thousands from Slovenia and Croatia. Thousands of villages and towns were destroyed by several armies and guerrilla forces. These tragic events and many of the actors in the terrible Balkan drama were extensively reported in the American press. They were also publicized in all South Slav immigrants' papers causing bitter accusations, quarrels, and attacks. After late 1941, the thin line between the homeland and the settlements in America, the mail service, was interrupted. With communications completely cut off, the immigrant families had no knowledge of what was happening to their families and relatives in the old country. This increased their anxiety and ill feelings.

Many Croatians in America favored the Croatian state as a fulfillment of the long struggle for national independence. Even most of those favoring independence disagreed with Ante Pavelić who was the head of the government in Zagreb. The Croatian Circle and the Croatian Peasant Party recognized Dr. V. Maček (who was imprisoned by Pavelić) as the only legitimate and democratic leader of the Croatian people. They opposed Tito's Communist movement for creation of a Communist Yugoslavia. All fraternal organizations pledged their unswerving loyalty and active support of the American war effort. Ivan (John) D. Butkovich, the president of the Croatian Fraternal Union, promised in a telegram to President Roosevelt to make the utmost contribution in order to bring about "a decisive victory for America and her allies."[25]

On the very first day of war the Croatians gave their first hero to the American cause. During the Japanese attack on

Pearl Harbor on December 7, 1941 chief Peter Tomich, water-tender on the *Utah*, anchored in the navy base, rushed down the hatch of the sinking ship. He got his men out, secured the boilers, and refused to leave his post as the ship rolled over in the sea. On March 4, 1942 Peter Tomich was posthumously awarded the Congressional Medal of Honor (along with fourteen other men from Pearl Harbor) for his heroism. However, no kin of his could be found and no one ever claimed his medal. In 1943 the U.S. Navy named a destroyer escort the USS *Tomich*.[26]

A high percentage of Croatians joined the armed forces. Thousands fought in the Pacific war theater and suffered high casualties. Almost twenty-five percent of the members of fraternal organizations went to war. Over three hundred members of the Croatian Fraternal Union lost their lives in the war. Of over ninety thousand American fighting men of South Slav origin, over fifty thousand were of Croatian descent. One war hero was Lieutenant J. Luksic, son of Croatian immigrants in Joliet, Illinois, commander of a P-51 Mustang who shot down twenty German airplanes in 1944. In 1945 the Congressional Medal of Honor was awarded to First Lieutenant John J. Tominac, son of Croatian immigrants in Johnstown, Pennsylvania, for exceptional heroism in France.[27]

John D. Butkovich was one of the main organizers of the huge All-Slavic Congress in Detroit in April 1942. The Croatians were instrumental in organizing many other congresses and conventions that were later denounced as a skillfully organized movement by the Soviet and Red agents to form a pro-Soviet fifth column in this country.

Provoked by constant attacks by the Serbian National Federation, its organ *Srbobran*, and other Serbian royalists, the Croatians convoked a large Congress in Chicago on February 23, 1943. Nine hundred and twenty-seven delegates represented 716 organizations. Main organizers of this Congress were J. D. Butkovich and Ivan Šubašić, former governor (ban) of Croatia. The assembly pledged loyalty of the Croatian people "to contribute to the victory of America and for salvation of our Croatian people." The present delegates came out in support of Tito's National Liberation Movement and ceased the support to the royal government in London. A Council of American

Croatians resulted from this event, and Zlatko Baloković, the well-known violin virtuoso, was elected its president. He donated fifty thousand dollars for the activities of the Council. In postwar years Baloković and many other collaborators were branded by U.S. authorities as pro-Soviet agents.[28]

The Croatian Fraternal Union and its president Butkovich remained in the forefront of these pro-Tito activities, a fact that perplexed many CFU members and other Croatians who were opposed to any Yugoslavia, royal or Communist. These activities were endorsed by the delegates of the Sixth Convention of the Croatian Fraternal Union meeting for twelve days in early September 1943 in the Sherman Hotel, Chicago. John D. Butkovich was reelected for another four-year term as CFU's president.

After the American government started full support of Tito's Communist partisan movement (December 1943), the whole left front movement among the Croatians became busier than ever. The Croatian War Aid Committee, founded in January 1944, collected more than one million dollars for aid to Communists in Yugoslavia. One of the leaders of the Central Organization of the American Croatian Women was the distinguished Metropolitan Opera star, Zinka Kunc Milanov. Baloković's Yugoslav Relief committee collected about a million dollars.

The daily *Narodni Glasnik* (National Gazette) in Pittsburgh was edited by Tony Minerich, a member of the National Committee of the Communist Party of U.S.A. He and several other Croatians were among the most active leaders of the whole pro-Soviet movement in America. Officially his paper was the organ of the Croatian Benevolent Fraternity, a section of the International Workers' Order, a Communist front organization.[29]

By the end of 1944 the Red Army was in Belgrade and northeastern Yugoslavia and in May of 1945 Tito's Communist forces held all of Yugoslavia under firm control. In the same month over two hundred thousand Croatians and thousands of Slovenian, Montenegrin, and Serbian anti-Communist forces surrendered to the British in Austria and were delivered over to the forces of Tito. In the following weeks these partisan forces massacred thousands of Croatian and Slovenian soldiers and civilians. Among the victims were many relatives of American immigrants. The few thousand Croatians who escaped British extradition found asylum as Displaced Persons in camps of Austria, Germany, and Italy. As soon as their plight became known, religious and patriotic organizations and many relatives and friends in America started to send them aid: money and parcels of food and clothing. Immediately steps were taken to provide the necessary legislation so that these refugees from war-torn Europe could come to America.[30]

X   The Aftermath

While the shocking news about the tragedy of many compatriots and the sad state of the old country was arousing the masses of immigrants in the United States, the leftist radical elements boldly continued their activities, including drives to send great amounts of aid to Yugoslavia to be distributed by the new authorities. A printed report in Pittsburgh stated: "The Slavs have found themselves. Tito is not alone. For the first time in history the Slavs are united and behind them is mother Russia."[31] However, this Pan-Slavic and pro-Soviet cry could not hide the brutal realities from millions of disappointed and deceived immigrants.

After November 29, 1945, when Yugoslavia was officially proclaimed a Communist republic, immigrants continued to send aid in millions of dollars. A few hundred immigrants duped by propaganda even returned to the homeland. Some of them, after losing everything, managed to escape after a year or two, returned to America or Canada, and related their bitter experiences. One of the leading men of the pro-Tito movement in America, Bogdan Radica (Raditsa) succeeded in leaving Belgrade for Italy after six months of agonizing experience. After joining his family in New York City in 1946 he published his revelations of the true nature of the new regime in Yugoslavia in *Reader's Digest* and all the leading American papers and periodicals. His writings received national attention. Raditsa later joined the movement against Tito.[32]

Many people, who had never accepted the Communist line, decided to speak up and do something for their dispersed compatriots and for the cause of their country. A group representing various Croatian patriotic organizations founded in Cleveland on March 17, 1946 the United Croatians of America. They convoked a national congress in Chicago on September 2, 1946. The main speaker was Dr. Vladko Maček, the democratic leader of the Croatian people who had managed to escape from Zagreb in May 1945, and had found asylum in Paris. A message was sent to President Harry S. Truman. Among the leaders present at the Congress was John D. Butkovich, the president of the Croatian Fraternal Union who had left the pro-Yugoslav movement. The organ of the United Croatians and other anti-Communist forces became the Chicago weekly *Danica–The Morning Star*, published by a group of Franciscans.[33]

The loud voices in the Croatian and Slovenian press were raised against what Baloković, Adamic, and others had helped to achieve. In many cases immigrants who had contributed thousands of dollars for the cause of "national liberation" found that they had been cheated and, worst of all, many of their sons or brothers were victims of the very movement they had supported from America.

In spite of these new trends, at the Seventh Convention of the Croatian Fraternal Union, held at Pittsburgh for eleven days after September 15, 1947, the newly elected president became Vjekoslav I. Mandić, who was supported by the so-called Progressive Bloc. This new leadership was in favor of a new Communist Yugoslavia, a stand which provoked a strong reaction on the part of anti-Communist and anti-Yugoslav members. The Union's membership was now over one hundred thousand. Mandić was to remain in office until 1967, when John Badovinac, a former member of the National Bloc in the CFU, was elected president. The close and friendly relations between the Yugoslav authorities and the leadership of the CFU remained a constant source of friction for many members of the organization as well as numerous American Croatians.[34]

In 1947 Zlatko Baloković visited Yugoslavia, was warmly received by the new authorities, and was decorated by President Tito with the Order of Brotherhood and Unity for his help in the establishment of a Communist Yugoslavia. By now the American authorities were showing a strong interest in the activities of the Yugoslav Relief Committee which had collected more than three million dollars as aid to Yugoslavia under

Baloković's leadership. Forty-three percent of the collected funds had been spent for overhead costs. The investigators claimed that funds were actually spent for Yugoslav Communist propaganda in the United States.[35]

After the outbreak of the Stalin-Tito dispute in June 1948, the Relief Committee ceased its activities. The split in international Communism resulting from the Cominform's expulsion of Tito's Yugoslav Communist Party caused confusion in the ranks of the South Slav leftists and delivered a severe blow to all their activities. It is interesting that Henry A. Wallace in his bid for the presidency as the candidate of the Progressive Party received the support of these leftist organizations, especially from the American Slav Congress. Its convention on September 26, 1948 was addressed by Wallace. The Convention endorsed him while the organ of the Congress, the *Slavic American*, and other leftist Slavic papers urged all Slavs to vote for Wallace in November of 1948.[36]

In the midst of investigations and hearings in the nation's capital, *The Guide to Subversive Organizations and Publications* listed as subversive about a dozen South Slav organizations. Among them were: the American Association for Reconstruction of Yugoslavia; the American Committee for a Free Yugoslavia; two Committees for Yugoslav Relief; the American Croatian Congress; the Central Council of American Croatian Women; the Croatian Benevolent Society; and the Croatian Educational Club. The names of some were later removed from this list.[37]

CHAPTER 10

Croatian Contribution: Present and Future

IN October of 1960, the Bruce family (for many years well-known Catholic publishers) unveiled a monument "Immigrant Mother" at the Cathedral Square in Milwaukee. The statue was done by the immigrant sculptor, Ivan Meštrović of Croatia. This well-deserved tribute to all unknown immigrant mothers reveals an ever-increasing recognition of all "anonymous," unknown immigrants whose contributions to this country have been too long ignored.[1]

These women helped in the building of America's mines, railroads, construction, factories, and in thousands of hazardous jobs by sacrificing husbands and children, thousands of whom died in accidents, disasters, and fires. The woman, especially the wife and mother, deserves the highest tribute. She was the greatest heroine of all!

A large number of widows were to be found in many mining settlements. On one occasion alone, in the gold mine of Jackson, California (of pioneer days fame), in the summer of 1922, thirteen immigrants from Croatia perished. In February 1924 in the flooded Ida May mine near Irontown, Minnesota, seven Croatians, eight Slovenians, and one Montenegrin lost their lives. In this and in many other disasters, before and after the turn of the century, and through the later decades, virtually thousands of Croatians (who were in the majority among the South Slavs) died in the mines, together with Slovenians, Serbs, Montenegrins, and Bulgarians.[2]

Many of the hundreds of mine accidents happened because of the lack of safety measures and because of neglect on the part of the mining companies. During the last hundred years more than 120,000 miners died in mines all over the country.

A present-day writer calls this tragic fact "the scandal of death and injury."[3] It can be estimated that among these dead close to thirty thousand were South Slavs.

I   Eminent Contributors to Industry

Other South Slavs contributed to industry and technology by their inventions and discoveries. The greatest of these, Nikola Tesla, a Serb who was born and grew up in Croatia, is discussed elsewhere in this book. Many American writers list him as a Croatian contributor. Another man who made a significant impact on industrial America was Captain Anthony Lucas (Lučić) who was born in Split, Croatia, in 1855. After leaving the Austrian Navy, he came to his uncle in Michigan in 1879, married Caroline Fitzgerald in 1887, and settled in Washington, D.C. As a geologist and mining engineer, Lucas struck oil on January 10, 1901, at Spindletop, near Beaumont, Texas. It was a historic day for the American oil industry. He later sold his property to the Mellon group for $400,000. Later on an Anthony F. Lucas Medal was established as an award to an outstanding contribution to the development of oil. On October 9, 1941, a fifty-foot granite monument was erected at Spindletop honoring Lucas for his discovery and contribution to our industry.[4]

Croatian workers and engineers invented numerous time saving devices to help decrease the cost of production and increase safety at work. Many of these inventions contributed to the modernization of American industry.

II   The Artists

The greatest artist was the sculptor Ivan Meštrović. He was born on August 15, 1883. The home of the Meštrović family was in Otavice, in the Dalmatian hinterland, where as a shepherd boy Ivan began to carve little figurines. He was discovered by a visitor from Vienna, sent to Split, and in 1901 to Vienna for education. In 1907 he became a student in Paris of the famous Rodin who called Ivan "the greatest phenomenon among the sculptors."

His first exhibit in America was held in New York in 1924.

He met Tesla and later made a sculpture of him. In 1928 Meštrović created the two huge equestrian statues of Indians for Grant Park on the shores of Lake Michigan in Chicago.

After 1918 he became a critic of the authoritarian rule in Yugoslavia. The authorities in Zagreb permitted him to leave for Rome and Switzerland in 1941. In 1945 he refused to return to the homeland, came to America, and until 1955 taught sculpture at the University of Syracuse, New York. In the same year he moved to Notre Dame University, South Bend, Indiana, where he created one of the best art departments in America.

His Notre Dame years were very productive. He taught sculpture and produced works of art in sculpture and other media. Many of his sculptures are gigantic in size. His works—in stone, bronze, plaster, and wood—are on permanent exhibit in all major museums, and adorn many churches and public buildings. He also created reliefs, drawings, and architectural designs. He has been praised by critics as the "artist of the universal," "the last living master of human form," and even compared to Michelangelo. His style was unique. His saints looked like peasants from his mountainous homeland. Many considered him the greatest religious artist in America.

In 1954 Meštrović became an American citizen. Several universities honored him with degrees and he received prizes and awards. In 1959, on a visit to his homeland, he donated his two residences there and many works to the Republic of Croatia. After his death in South Bend on January 14, 1962, his body was returned to his native soil and buried in the Meštrović Mausoleum in Otavice. Thousands of peasants paid their respects to their returned genius in silence while the authorities ignored the funeral. He had aroused their ire by publishing before his death his memoirs in Croatian (in Buenos Aires) in which he described his encounters with people and events, and was critical of the new and old regimes in Yugoslavia.[5]

Paul Kelečić Kufrin, born in Okić in 1887, after studying sculpture and architecture in Vienna, arrived in Chicago in 1907. In 1910 he opened his own art school and struggled in a society which had little taste for art, as Miss Balch observed in *Our Slavic Fellow Citizens.* He lived in Chicago until his death in November

1973. He executed works of many varieties and forms. Among his prizes he received a gold medal at the Chicago World Fair in 1934 for his bust of Clarence Darrow.

Joseph Turkalj, born in 1924 in Rakovica, Croatia, emigrated to America in 1957 after completing his art studies in Rome. At Notre Dame he worked for Meštrović and then taught there for a while. Turkalj has produced numerous statues, many of gigantic size like "Moses" in front of Notre Dame's library. He teaches art at Gilmour Academy in Gates Mills, a suburb of Cleveland. "Our Lady of Bistrica" in the National Shrine of the Immaculate Conception, Washington, D.C., is one of his best creations.[6]

Ivan Benković arrived in 1914 and worked as a commercial artist, illustrator, and painter. Tesla helped him to obtain a job in Chicago. At the end of 1918 he died of Spanish influenza. Vilko Gecan, a well-known painter in the homeland, lived and created in the United States from 1924 until 1928. And there were other visiting painters whose many paintings described the American scene.

Maksimilian (Maxo) Vanka, born in 1890 in Zagreb, a graduate of the Brussels Art Academy and professor of painting at the Art Academy in Zagreb, emigrated with his American wife in 1936. Commissioned by Father Albert Zagar of the Croatian St. Nicholas Church in Millvale, near Pittsburgh. Vanka executed ten large murals for the church. Five years later in 1941 he added five more huge murals, converting a simple workers' church into a great place of art. Newspapers and magazines all over the country noted that "The St. Nicholas Church has made a precious gift from its Croatian culture to this land" and paid highest tribute to Vanka and his murals. Most of them depict the life of the Croatian immigrants, their religion, and suffering.

Besides murals, Vanka painted in oil, watercolors, pastels, and made drawings during his travels all over the United States and the world. An Impressionist, he was a very good portraitist and among his favorite motifs were flowers and scenes of human suffering. Many of his paintings also describe Croatian peasant life. Adamic devoted a book and a short story to Vanka. Maxo, as his friends called him, drowned in the Pacific in Puerta Vallarte, Mexico, on February 2, 1963.[7]

Gustav Likan, born in Lika, Croatia, in 1912, was a recognized painter before he left Croatia in 1945 to find asylum in Argentina with thousands of his countrymen. In 1958 he had his first exhibit in Chicago where he settled as an immigrant. An American citizen since 1963, Likan has had many exhibits and his works are in many art galleries and museums. They range from murals to drawings, 250 of which were acquired by the Vincent Price Collection. Likan now lives in Austin, Texas.[8]

III *Singers, Composers, and Musicians*

Josip Kašman, a native of Istria, sang at the second performance of the newly opened Metropolitan Opera in New York in 1883. He was considered one of the best singers of his time. At the "Met" he performed for the last time in 1896. Only three years later, the enthusiastic crowds applauded Milka Ternina. Born in 1863 near Zagreb, she made a successful career in Austria and Bavaria, and was regarded as the best Wagnerian soprano. She returned to Zagreb in 1906, where years later one of her most talented students was Zinka Kunc-Milanov. Born in 1906, Zinka was an accomplished and successful operatic singer before she came to the United States in 1935. Her debut at the "Met" took place on November 17, 1935. She retired on April 13, 1966, after a long and successful career interrupted by trips abroad and four years in Yugoslavia. As one of the critics put it: "Zinka Milanov who graced the operatic stage from 1927 to 1966, brought the art of vocal perfection to a summit never believed possible. As a woman, as an artist, she truly deserves the title 'prima donna assoluta.'" In recent years Zinka's several countrymen were among the stars of the "Met": Mia Ćorak Slavenska (as prima ballerina), Marko Rothmüller, Biserka Cvejić (a mezzo-soprano), and the baritone Vladimir Ruždjak.[9] This was indeed a considerable contribution to the operatic arts by a comparatively small group of people.

Louis Svecenski, a native of Osijek, Croatia, came to America in 1885, and at the age of twenty-three joined the Boston Symphony Orchestra as first violinist. He toured the world, visited his native land several times, met Ternina in New York, and served for years as director of the Institute of Musical Art in

New York. He was one of the founders of the Curtis Institute of Music in Philadelphia.

Zlatko Baloković, born in 1885, was an internationally known violin virtuoso. He arrived in the United States in 1924 and two years later he married Joyce Borden of the wealthy Borden family. During the 1920s and 1930s his concerts received wide attention. During 1931–1932 he and his wife traveled around the world on their own 140-foot yacht, *Northern Light*. Baloković died in Venice in late March 1965, on his way to Yugoslavia.

Arthur Rodzinski, a well-known conductor, was born in Split in 1894. He emigrated in 1926. During his brilliant career he conducted the Cleveland Orchestra after 1936. He died in Rome in 1958; in 1976 his widow published his biography.[10]

IV *In Movies and on Television*

Like many of their countrymen, most of the Croatian contributors to the movies and entertainment industries disguised their origin by adopting Anglo-Saxon names.

Peter Coe's real name was Knego. John Miljan, too, was born of Croatian immigrants in Lead, South Dakota. He came to Hollywood in 1922 and played in some four hundred films, both in silent movies and talking pictures; one of these roles was General Custer in "The Plainsman." A veteran of silent and tone period was John Northpole (Kovačević) whose career in Hollywood began in 1912. Both Miljan and Northpole died in the 1960s.

Slavko Vorkapić, born in Srijemska Mitrovica in 1884, arrived in the United States in 1920 and became a successful actor. Later he was in turn movie director, painter, and sculptor. He introduced new concepts and innovations in film, one of them being montage: superimposing one picture upon another and using special effects. During World War II he produced the series "This is America" for the U.S. Office of War Information.

Joseph Zokovich of RKO Studios, Gloria Grey (Dragomanović) and Walter Kray (Krajačić) are also of Croation origin. Guy Mitchell, a popular singer and movie actor during the 1950s and 1960s, was born in 1927 Al Crnich of Croatian parents in Detroit.[11]

V   *Educators, Scholars, and Writers*

Henry Suzzallo, the eminent American educator and one-time president of the Carnegie Foundation, was born in 1873 of Croatian immigrant parents in San Jose, California. He received his Ph.D. at Columbia University in 1905. From 1915 until 1926 he was president of the University of Washington. During World War I he was an adviser to President Wilson. In 1927 he received his appointment at the Carnegie Foundation. During his scholarly career he wrote many books on education. He regarded democracy as a way of life, a means of developing the individual. When he died in September of 1933, the press called him "one of the nation's most distinguished educators."[12]

Victor G. Vecki, Ante Biankini, and Edward Miloslavich were physicians, scholars, and writers. Miloslavich, who died in St. Louis, Missouri, was an eminent pathologist and criminologist. Dr. Stephen Polyak, born in Zegreb in 1889, came to the University of Chicago's Medical School where he taught neurology and anatomy until his death in March 1955. His most important work *The Vertebrate Visual System* (some 1600 pages) was published in 1957; his *The Retina* (1941) was a classic in this field.

Dr. Milislav Demerec, a geneticist, was born in 1895 in Kostajnica. He arrived in the United States in 1919, received the Ph.D. at Cornell University in 1923. At the Long Island Biological Association in Cold Springs Harbor he did research in antibiotics; he taught at Columbia University and was later senior geneticist at Brookhaven National Laboratory at Upton, Long Island. He was the author of many studies and received various awards for his discoveries before he died in April 1966.

Francis Preveden was an anthropologist, historian, and linguist. He died in Washington, D.C., in 1959. Clement S. Mihanovich, a native of St. Louis and professor of sociology at St. Louis University, is an eminent sociologist. Engaged in the same field for many years was Professor Dinko A. Tomasic of Indiana University, the author of many books on East Europe and Yugoslavia.[13] He died in 1975 at Bloomington, Indiana.

Bogdan Raditsa of Fairleigh Dickinson University and Charles Jelavich of Indiana University are historians and authors.

Raditsa has also worked as journalist and columnist and has published in several languages. Many others of their country-men have contributed to the United States as educators and scholars.

Most of these men were sons of humble—sometimes illiterate—parents, and were the first educated generation in their families. They have enriched many scholarly disciplines, arts, and sciences, and they have contributed to engineering, architecture, medicine, economics, linguistics, history, political science, sociology, geography, and other fields.

During the last six or seven decades the Croatians and other South Slavs in this country have developed a whole literature of their own. Many of the emigré writers, especially during the last thirty years, have produced a wealth of literary works of lasting value both in their native tongues and in English. The homeland critics pay now increasing attention to the literary works of immigrant writers. In the upsurge of ethnic studies Americans, too, are now discovering the literature of immigrant writers, an area that has to be explored and assessed further.

The first repository of these immigrants' literature was their press. Before and after 1918 most of their writings were of popular and educational character, either religious or progressive and liberal. The latter was partly class-conscious and socialist. They were stimulated by freedom of expression, freedom of the press, and lack of the censorship that has prevailed in all South Slav lands. However, many immigrants themselves some-times encountered harsh criticism; Louis Adamic, for example, was harshly criticized by many ethnic newspaper editors.

A sizeable part of the popular literature was in form of pamphlets, booklets, books, and many almanacs—*Koledari*. Many of these writings in prose and verse were done by simple workers. Only a few were able and competent writers and translators from other languages into the Croatian. The only Croatian writer who succeeded as a writer in English was Joseph G. Hitrec who came after 1945 by way of India and was introduced to New York publishers by Louis Adamic. Harper published three of his books. Hitrec became a university pro-fessor and died in Buffalo, New York, in 1972.[14]

The many writers who emigrated after the late 1940s are

now busy and productive. They write in their mother tongue and in foreign languages through emigré or American and other publishers. The largest Croatian publisher is "La Revista Croata" (*Hrvatska Revija*) whose leading man is Vinko Nikolić, a poet, writer, and editor of the quarterly under the same name. This review is now in its twenty-seventh year, has attracted contributions from a large number of writers and scholars, and has published over thirty books of literary and scholarly character. Nikolić now lives in Barcelona, Spain. The dean of the Croatian writers in exile is Ante Bonifačić who lives in Chicago and came to this continent after 1945 an already recognized writer.

VI   *Successful Businessmen*

On April 22, 1962 the *San Francisco Sunday Chronicle* published the story of Mitchell L. Mitchell, "San Francisco's shyest millionaire." Surprisingly this "mystery man"—as the paper calls him—is "the son of the poor immigrant parents who came to the United States from Dalmatia, on the Adriatic Sea." We do not learn what Mitchell's original name was; however, his is an interesting story of success among these Adriatic immigrants.

Peter J. Divizich, mentioned already, who came from Dubrovnik in 1920, and by hard work, ability, and luck built a little agricultural empire in San Joaquin Valley, became a very rich man. He owned over five thousand acres of vineyards in the Delano area. However, agricultural conglomerates, unfair dealings of banks, and the United Farm Workers' strike brought about the loss of almost everything that had taken him fifty years to build. In his book—which is in fact Peter's memoirs—Henry A. Foley considers him one of the greatest men in the history of American agriculture. He now lives a lonely man in Ducor, California.[15]

John Slavic, born in California in 1899, was the founder of Delmonte Fruit Company and died a rich man in May of 1959. Nikola Bezmalinović came in 1910 as a penniless fourteen-year-old lad from the island of Brač. He started as a fisherman in the Puget Sound area on the Pacific coast. Nick Bez—as he became known—became a millionaire, a generous contributor to the Democratic Party, a personal friend of President Harry S. Truman. Before his death in the 1960s he was known as the "king of Alaska."

Some immigrants acquired wealth in boat building, construction and development, fish canneries, and food processing. Some struck it rich in salmon and shrimp fishing. Most of them were on the West Coast while several rich industrialists found their luck in the Midwest. All of them were self-made men.[16]

VII *Politics, Sports, and Folklore*

Mike Stepovich, whose father joined the 1898 gold rush in Alaska, is a graduate of Gonzaga University and the University of Notre Dame. In 1957 he had been the first Catholic and American Croatian to become governor of the Alaska Territory. When it became our forty-ninth state in January 1959, he was Alaska's first governor.

Nick Begich was born in 1932 in Eveleth, Minnesota, of Croatian immigrant parents. After graduating from the University of Minnesota, he moved to Alaska, worked as a teacher, and spent eight years in the Alaska State Senate. In November 1970, he was elected the sole Congressman from Alaska and thus became the first American Croatian Congressman in Washington. During his reelection campaign, on October 17, 1972, Nick Begich perished in a plane accident along with the House Majority leader Hale Boggs on a flight from Anchorage to Juneau.[17] Not a trace was found of the plane.

Prominent in Minnesota politics are the three Perpich (Prpić) brothers. Their father, a miner, immigrated from Krivi Put, Croatia. Rudy Perpich, a dentist by profession, was elected in 1970 Lieutenant Governor of Minnesota. In January 1977 he became Governor. He is very outspoken on many issues. The three brothers are referred to by local media as the "Kennedys of the Iron Range." Their brother **Joseph** is a psychiatrist married to the daughter of Arthur Sulzberger, publisher of the *New York Times*.[18]

At the end of 1976 Mike Bilandic succeeded Mayor Daley of Chicago as acting mayor. On June 7, 1977 he was elected as mayor collecting seventy-seven percent of all votes. Many Croatians served in state legislatures, as mayors of cities, judges, district attorneys, and sheriffs. Dennis J. Kucinich, an independent Democrat and only thirty-one years old, was elected mayor of Cleveland, Ohio, on November 8, 1977; he is the youngest mayor of a major American city. In state legislatures, the Croatians frequently sponsored the cause of labor. A majority of these politicians are members of the Democratic Party. Some supported the Socialists or various third parties. During the 1950s the younger generation joined the Republican Party in increasing numbers.

In one area—sports—the young men of Croatian descent have made considerable impact. The *Zajedničar*, a weekly organ of the Croatian Fraternal Union, in its issue of October 16, 1968, featured this headline: "CFU's Mickey Lolich Stars in Series." Lolich, the pitcher of the Detroit Tigers, is but one of virtually hundreds of Croatian athletes who have excelled in various sports, or have made names as nationally known coaches of some of the best teams in the country. The sports sections of many newspapers all over the United States frequently mention names ending with "ich."

Teodor Beg, a native of Žumberak, came to America in 1904 and as a wrestler won eight gold medals in national competitions during his career. Others of his countrymen have also done very well as athletes. The Chicago *Croatian Almanac* for 1943 listed over two hundred American Croatians who were by that time nationally recognized as outstanding sportsmen and athletes. Most of them were college football stars. Some were named the most outstanding "athlete of the year" by American media. During the last twenty-five years several Croatians gained national prominence as football coaches; some excelled in basketball. Fritzie Zivich of Pittsburgh won in 1951 the world's welterweight championship in boxing.

With the influx of more recent immigrants soccer has become very popular. The Croatians established a large number of teams, joined the official American leagues, and formed one of their own. Every year during the Labor Day weekend the Croatians hold soccer tournaments with at least a dozen teams participating and attracting thousands of people.[19]

Such sport events seem to gather more people than any political or cultural activity. However, some folkloric events are almost as successful in terms of attendance. The annual performance of the Duquesne University Tamburitzans in several cities attract as many as three thousand enthusiastic people. Folklore in its various manifestations is still very much alive among all South Slavs. The Croatian contribution to ethnic and American folklore has been outstanding. Several American authors expressed great admiration for the rich ethnic culture of the Croatians and other South Slavs. Their music, especially that of the *tamburitza* (a stringed instrument resembling a mandolin), their intricate dances, beautiful national costumes, handicrafts, and even their native dishes have added a colorful part to American folklore. More scholars and writers and more young people are interested in folklore now than ever before. Some cities with a large number of Croatians hold yearly folk fairs and festivals. Various radio—and most recently even TV—stations broadcast tamburitza and other folk music and show the lively dances.

The Duquesne University Tamburitzans Institute of Folk Arts is in the process of erecting a large museum to exhibit the huge collection of national costumes, instruments, handicrafts, and music of all Balkan nations. The Croatian Fraternal Union sponsors a Junior Cultural Federation which includes some forty groups of youngsters engaged in tamburitza music, folk dances, and singing. Their yearly festivals attract up to eight hundred young performers. In July 1976 the Tenth Festival was held in the Croatian capital Zagreb as part of the U.S. Bicentennial celebrations by Croatians in both the homeland and the United States.

The saga of Joe Magarac, Steelman, has been added to American folklore. It is a "tall story" about Croatian steelworkers in Pennsylvania inspired by a legend in Croatia, and is symbolic of the entire Slavic contribution to the American steel industry in which thousands of lives were lost and innumerable people were crippled. *Magarac* means in Croatian the donkey or jackass. One character in the story is called Steve Mestrovic; another is named Steve Pusic. Joe was a goodhearted giant who performed many feats in the steel mills around Pittsburgh and—according to one version of the story—went to a cave in the Allegheny Mountains to rest. Occasionally, his spirit returns to the mills and some workers can see him. Like the stories of Paul Bunyan, the woodman, Joe Magarac stories epitomize the workers in one of the basic industries, steel production. The model for a huge memorial, a giant sculpture of Joe pouring a ladle of molten steel to be erected in Pittsburgh, was the work of Cleveland sculptor Joseph Turkalj.[20]

VIII   *The Present and the Future*

In the 1970s the stories of the lives and contributions of the Croatians continue. Compared with approximately 600,000 Slovenians and some 300,000 Serbians and Montenegrins, the one and a half million American Croatians, many of whom have arrived in the last twenty years, are still the strongest of all South Slavic ethnic groups. They are ten times larger than the American Bulgarians and Macedonians (about 100,000).

It has been a long and arduous road from the era of pioneers to the present generation of thousands of educated, skilled, and professional people. Their forefathers paved the way. And for the prosperity and good life of today a high price has been paid.

Some years ago if one traveled through Montana, Utah, or other Western states, in small mining towns—which used to be almost purely South Slavic settlements—one could see large numbers of women who were widows of immigrants. Their husbands had died in accidents or from silicosis. In logging camps of the West the mortality was also very high. As an eyewitness observed: "The first generation died off like flies; it was simply a process of mass immolation."[21]

"Life was too cruel here," Milla Tanasich, a Croatian widow, stated to Louis Adamic in San Pedro. What she told him before her death might have been repeated by many other Slavic women: "America is big and terrible. I had seven children; they are all dead except one. . . . I had four husbands; three of them died. . . . America must become great. . . . We all came over from the Old Country to help America become great and terrible."[22]

In this great and terrible America some had more and some

less luck. Many saw their American dream shattered. Many succumbed to overwhelming odds. Others were disappointed. At the same time thousands succeeded after years of struggle. On the whole, the great majority of the Croatians today are doing well partly as a result of the heavy price paid by their forebears. Quite a few are prosperous and wealthy.

A profusion of all kinds of political, social, cultural, religious, and economic organizations, clubs, and societies was formed by the new immigrants after 1945. They represent a variety of causes ranging from extreme right to a fairly far left.

As one of the leading experts on problems of emigration from Yugoslavia recently stated: "Croatia not only has the highest absolute number of emigrant workers but also the country's [Yugoslavia's] highest rate of emigration, i.e., 8.2%, which is also the highest in Europe."[23] Another expert contends that *five million people* who were born, or whose origins are in Yugoslavia, are now scattered all around the world with the largest concentration in North America. The Croatians comprise more than sixty percent of these. Today almost every third Croatian lives outside his homeland, almost every fourth one lives in North America (the United States and Canada). The first expert mentions as the cause of Croatian emigration the "political situation." A careful analysis of this and a large number of other sources point to the fact that modern migration to the United States and other parts of the world from the regions that form Yugoslavia has been caused directly or indirectly by political factors. Thus in the case of the Balkan countries, as for all of Europe, America has been an escape from discontent, a refuge for a multitude of people searching for freedom, bread, and a better future.

During the last twenty years Yugoslav authorities have permitted hundreds of thousands of able, skilled young people to emigrate either temporarily or permanently to industrial regions of Western Europe and overseas. No wonder that by 1970 Yugoslavia was among the top fifteen sources supplying immigrants to America. (In 1970 alone 8,575 arrived in the United States.)[24] This emigration—especially from western parts of Yugoslavia (Croatia and Slovenia) has assumed proportions of a real exodus. As a result of this massive migration, many

Adriatic islands, coastal regions, and inland rural areas of the republics of Croatia and Bosnia-Herzegovina have been depopulated. In many villages one can see only old people and children. This exodus has increased during the last ten years. During 1965–1975 these newcomers have flocked especially to Cleveland, New York City, and Chicago. Many islands and towns in Adriatic regions now have more of their people in America than at home.

The continual exodus presented one of the most serious problems of the Socialist Federal Republic of Yugoslavia. The "brain drain"—the emigration of thousands of physicians, engineers, scientists, and professionals—has been particularly painful. However, these newcomers claim that they would be either unemployed or would have led a miserable existence in comparison to what awaited them in the United States. In many instances the people leave the homeland because they want a higher living standard which they cannot have under Communism and its restrictions in all walks of life.

The large number of unemployed, the inflation, and the presence of millions of illegal immigrants in the United States and Canada arouses public sentiment against the present level of immigration. It remains to be seen to what extent these factors will affect the exodus from the South Slavic lands. Judging from various reports, during the last three years mass emigration from Yugoslavia has temporarily stopped.

During the period of liberalization in Yugoslavia before December 1971, the ties between the homeland and the immigrants were especially strong. Among many visitors from the old country were also some of the highest church dignitaries. They were warmly received by thousands in many parishes and were given thousands of dollars for the needs of the Church in Croatia. When in May of 1966 Franjo Cardinal Šeper visited the immigrant colonies for the first time, the Croatians were very pleased to see their own Cardinal. On October 18, 1970, in the presence of thousands of people, Franjo Kuharić, the Archbishop and Metropolitan of Zagreb, consecrated the chapel of Our Lady of Bistrica in Mary's Shrine in Washington, D.C. (The sculpture was a work by Joseph Turkalj.) More than $150,000 was collected from the people for the cost of the chapel.

After the students' riots in Zagreb in late 1971, the nationalist movement in Croatia and the process of liberalization were stopped by Tito. Many liberal members of the Communist Party, numerous intellectuals, and those who had close contacts with compatriots in America were arrested and sentenced to prison terms. The Yugoslav government stated on several occasions that many anti-government activities in their land were supported by individuals and organizations in America. This charge was denied by all in America. The Croatians also appealed to the U.S. government and to the public to intervene on behalf of all imprisoned writers and liberal elements in Yugoslavia. To coordinate their political activities the Croatians formed, in 1974, a Croatian National Congress. New York, Chicago, and Cleveland became the main centers of these activities which were also strongly supported by the large colony in Toronto.

Meanwhile, the silent work of the fraternal movement is going on. The largest of all South Slavic organizations, the Croatian Fraternal Union, is still very strong. As a large number of the old members are dying, thousands of new members are recruited. The CFU's Thirteenth and Fourteenth Conventions were held in 1971 (in San Francisco) and in 1975 (in Pittsburgh). The controversies within its ranks still go on. Its national president is John Badovinac who with the other members of the Supreme Board is constantly attacked by the Croatian press as too close to the regime in Yugoslavia. This charge is denied by Mr. Badovinac.

Instead of holding joint bicentennial celebrations in Washington, the Croatian Catholic Union and the Croatian Fraternal Union held separate celebrations in late August, 1976. Both attracted several thousand participants. The Croatians were also well represented in the religious part of U.S. Bicentennial commemorations during the International Eucharistic Congress in Philadelphia in early August 1976.

While thousands of Croatians are making contributions to the CFU's Scholarship Foundation, they are also generous in their support of churches. In July 1967 a modern (built in circular form) Croatian Sts. Peter and Paul Church was dedicated in Omaha, Nebraska. It cost over $525,000. This is but one of many new churches, schools, convents, and other religious edifices that have been erected during the last decades at the cost of millions of dollars.

Every year many groups of American Croatians visit the old country. In the fall of 1973 members of the Croatian Fraternal Union were present at the unveiling of Matija Gubec monument in Stubica on the four hundredth anniversary of the peasant revolt. Various junior tamburitza groups also travel to Croatia for visits and concerts. "Matica," a society for emigrants from Croatia, founded in 1952, sponsors such group visits and guides the visitors around the country. It also publishes a monthly and an almanac for the emigrants in foreign countries. For Independence Day 1976, several thousand CFU members, including numerous junior tamburitzans, gathered in Zagreb to celebrate the U.S. Bicentennial. The Yugoslav authorities used this and other opportunities to gain political profit. The critics claim that the Communists skillfully exploit such mass visits for their propaganda.

Propaganda for the cause of Croatian independence was the main reason for the skyjacking of a TWA plane by five Croatian nationalists led by a recent immigrant, Zvonko Bušić and his American-born wife, Julienne. The incident that took place during the weekend of September 10–12, 1976, started in New York and ended in Paris. The demands of the highjackers to drop their printed leaflets with an "Appeal to the American People" and a "Declaration" stating the Croatian demands for independence be dropped over New York, Chicago, Montreal, London, and Paris were fulfilled. The bomb planted by Bušić at Grand Central Station in New York killed a policeman. On September 11 and 12, five major American newspapers printed the proclamations issued by the highjackers who were brought back from Paris to New York to await trial. Worldwide publicity again focused on the old Croatian question and the clandestine war between Croatian exiles and Tito's representatives in foreign countries. It should be emphasized that all four male highjackers were born and grew up under Communism. They learned violent methods from a violent regime in their homeland and used these means to force the American media—which usually followed the official line of Belgrade—to publicize the demands of the Croatian nationalist movement.[25]

CHAPTER 11

Early Slovenian Immigrants

AFTER the Croatians the second largest South Slavic group in America are the Slovenians. They are not seafarers like the Adriatic Croatians. People from the mountains and valleys—patient and hard-working peasants and artisans—they were among the first pioneers in inland America. The achievements of their missionaries deserve special attention.

In spite of very vigorous Protestant activities in Slovenia, after some success, Protestantism lost out in Slovenia because of Habsburg intervention. Another reason was that a majority of the Slovenians considered it a German religion. The Slovenians remained a Catholic people. Their priests had a very close affinity with the masses of the people. It is interesting that some of the priests decided many years ago to migrate to the New World. One of them was Rev. Mark Anton Kapus (1657–1717), a native of Kamna Gorica. A Jesuit, he explored with Francisco Kino the regions of Sonora (now Mexico) and Arizona during 1687–1717.

Many Slovenians living in the large Habsburg Empire started to migrate centuries ago to various parts of the multinational country. They also went to the German states as miners, trades-men, and artisans, and joined other Habsburg subjects—especially their Croatian neighbors—who headed for the lands beyond the sea. As one of their writers put it: "The Slovenians are a people of emigrants." Among the earliest were the religious dissenters who found their way to Germany, Sweden, and Holland. This same writer claims that a few Slovenians and their descendants were among the Pilgrims who in 1620 came to America from Holland by way of England.[1]

Some Slovenians were in the colonies when the American Revolution broke out, and several of them were soldiers in

Washington's army. Their family names were: Cesar, Cherne, Gorshe, Turk, Vavtar, Vertnar, Vidmar, and Volk. A man named Turk settled down in New York City in 1784, after the end of the War of Independence. *Volk* in Slovenian means "wolf" and it is not the German word for "people" or "nation." Two brothers Volk, Abraham and Thomas, settled in New York City before the end of the 1700s. They married Dutch and English women, respectively. A grandson of Thomas was Leonard Wolk (born in Wellstown, New York, in 1828). He became a well-known sculptor and a friend of President Lincoln. Leonard's son Douglas was a successful portrait painter in the late 1800s and early 1900s.[2]

I Rev. Frederick Baraga

Frederick Baraga was born on June 29, 1797 in Mala Vas, Carniola, then an Austrian province. The Baragas were a wealthy family. Frederick was educated in Ljubljana and Vienna. He was ordained in 1823 and then served at various parishes in Carniola. He wrote several books for the people. By 1830 he decided to carry the Gospel to the Indians of North America. The Leopoldine Society in Vienna, which sent missionaries to America, financed Baraga's trip and future work. He sailed from LeHavre, France, on December 1, 1830, and arrived in Cincinnati on January 18, 1831. His host and benefactor was Bishop Edward Fenwick. Here he studied English and the Ottawa Indian language. On May 28 he arrived at his first mission, Arbre Croche, Michigan.[3]

He stayed here for almost two and a half years baptizing some 550 Indians. After his transfer to Grand River in the lower Michigan Peninsula he founded a new mission in September 1833 at the place now known as Grand Rapids. After February 1835, he began work among the Chippewas at La Pointe, Wisconsin. Here, exposed to the elements and to disease, he stayed for about eight years. All the time he fought drunkenness among the Indians and the whites who sold them the liquor. A thousand Indians and whites joined his flock and he spent a great deal of time educating their children. Frequently he clashed with the unscrupulous Indian agents.

In early 1837 Baraga traveled to Paris, Rome, Vienna, and spent a few days in his native Slovenia. He collected ample funds for his work in America. In Paris he printed some of the books he had written for his Indians in their native language. His sister, Antonia von Hoeffern, a widow, accompanied him on the way back to the United States. They landed on August 3, 1837. *She was the first known Slovenian woman immigrant in America.* After helping her brother for ten years, she returned to Europe.

Moving back to Michigan, Baraga founded in October 1843 L'Anse Indian mission on the shores of Lake Superior where he stayed for ten years.[4] Even though he was frail, he endured great hardships. His face was tanned from exposure to the color of a half-breed. For years he taught the Indians the basics of farming and carpentry. He never tired in his efforts to help them. He was their real apostle and earned a reputation as the most productive missionary writer of Indian books.

His works comprised catechisms, prayerbooks, instructions, meditations, Bible History, Epistles, and Gospels for the Ottawas and Chippewas. In 1850 he published his monumental *Theoretical and Practical Grammar of the Otchipwe Language,* which was the first grammar of the Chippewa language. Three years later he published the first dictionary of the same language. He also compiled a Chippewa-French dictionary. For his work he was called "The Father of Indian Literature."[5]

On July 29, 1853, the northern peninsula of Michigan was detached from the diocese of Detroit and erected into a Vicariate Apostolic. Baraga was appointed its first bishop; he was consecrated on November 1, 1853, in the Catholic Cathedral of Cincinnati. Shortly afterward he left for Europe to obtain more funds and bring some badly needed priests. He visited Rome, several other capitals, and was a guest at the wedding of Emperor Francis Joseph in Vienna.[6]

Bishop Baraga always remained a simple Indian missionary. His diocese was huge; it included the northern Michigan peninsula, parts of the Lower Peninsula, as well as parts of northern Wisconsin and the northern shores of Lake Superior. In spite of advancing age and failing health, he traveled constantly. In canoes he covered thousands of miles during the navigation season. In October 1857 the Vicariate was elevated to the status of a diocese. Eight years later the see was moved from Sault Ste. Marie to Marquette.

After the second Plenary Council in Baltimore, where he suffered a stroke, Baraga returned to Marquette and died on January 19, 1868, at the age of seventy-one. He was mourned by Indians and whites, by Catholics and non-Catholics. A county in Michigan as well as several towns and post offices were named after him. One of the principal streets in Marquette, where he is buried in St. Peter's Cathedral, bears his name.

When Louis Adamic, the American Slovenian writer, visited Baraga County about forty years ago, he found that the Indians still remembered their apostle and defender. He was not only the greatest of Slovenian missionaries in these parts, but also a forerunner in the struggle for the civil rights of the Indians.[7]

II   *Other Slovenian Missionaries*

Baraga was instrumental in bringing a group of fellow priests from Slovenia. His work, fame, and writings inspired a number of his compatriots to follow his example. Thus it happened that little Slovenia proportionately gave more missionary pioneers to America than any other Slavic country. One of them was Rev. Francis X. Pierz (Franc Ksaver Pirc). Born on November 20, 1785 in Godič near Kamnik, he became a priest in 1813; inspired by Baraga's example he came to New York on October 18, 1835. For seventeen years he toiled among the Indians and white settlers—many of whom came from Germany after reading his reports in Catholic papers—in the missions of La Croix, Fort William, Sault Ste. Marie, Grand Portage, Isle de Castor, and Arbre Croche. In June of 1852 he came to the Chippewas of Minnesota in the diocese of St. Cloud, a part of the Archdiocese of St. Paul, Minnesota.

He founded several settlements and missions; one town owes its name to him. For twenty-one years he labored as a pioneer and frontiersman. At the age of ninety with failing sight Father Pierz returned to his homeland where he died seven years later.[8]

Ignatius Mrak was born in Hotovlje, near Ljubljana, on October 16, 1818. Upon his arrival in Detroit, Bishop Lefevre sent him to Arbre Croche to assist Pierz. A pious and a very humble man, he was extremely devoted to the Indians. In 1860 he traveled to Europe and visited his native land.[9]

He was consecrated as successor to Bishop Baraga on February 9, 1869 by Archbishop Purcell in Cincinnati, the city which at that time was very important for missionary activities in several states. After ten years in office he became ill and was permitted to resign in 1879. His successor was the Slovenian Vertin. Having regained his health, Mrak went as an ordinary priest to his beloved Indians at Eagle Town, Leeland County, Michigan. In his eighty-first year he retired to Marquette, outlived Vertin, and died at the age of eighty-nine on January 2, 1901. He was buried beside Baraga and Vertin.[10]

And they still continued coming, from the mountains and valleys of Slovenia. Baraga ignited the light that attracted the others. They knew no limits to sacrifice and hardships. And as the historian Rezek said, their charity was as proverbial as their humility.

Some of them stayed in eastern cities. Some journeyed to the extreme West like Rev. Andrej Andolšek, who was a missionary in San Francisco between 1863–1869. Most of them made their way to the Great Lakes region. Several assisted Baraga or Pierz at one time or another. Among these was Otto Skola who arrived in December of 1854 and worked with both of them among the Chippewas. He was the first Slovenian Franciscan priest in America. After Pierz took over La Pointe mission, Skola went to the Menomini Indians around Wolf River. He was a painter, poet, writer—like many other black-robed men in the wilderness. In 1871 he returned to Europe where he died in April, 1879.[11]

Another one who joined Baraga in October 1859 was John Cebul (Ivan Čebulj), who was born in Velesovo in 1832. He worked among the Indians around Lake Superior and spent some time in Duluth, Minnesota. After visiting his homeland in 1871, he was active among the Menominis in Wisconsin. He stood up for their rights, clashed with unscrupulous Indian agents, defended Indians at the court in Chicago. In 1878 he visited France and India. Four years later he was back in

America, welcomed by Bishop Vertin, and continued to work at numerous missions until his death in August 1898.[12]

Rev. Joseph F. Buh, born in Lučne on March 17, 1833 joined Pierz in November 1864 at Crow Wing, Minnesota. In July 1865 he arrived at Belle Prairie. In the next ten years he established several new missions. His territory came under the new diocese of St. Cloud in 1875. Buh, too, was a devoted friend of the Indians. In 1888 he moved to Tower, Minnesota, where in years to come he cared also for the newly arriving Slovenians. In 1895 a town near Little Falls was named Buh. He was promoted to a Vicar General under the Diocese of Duluth.[13] He died in Duluth on February 2, 1922.

The career of the great Baraga also inspired John Vertin (born in Doblice, Carniola, in July 1844) to come to America at the age of nineteen. After finishing theological studies at St. Francis, Wisconsin, he was ordained in August 1866. After twelve years of labor and the resignation of Bishop Mrak, Vertin was appointed by Pope Leo XIII as third bishop of Marquette. At the age of thirty-five he was the youngest bishop in America. He was consecrated on September 14, 1879.

On October 2, 1879 his cathedral burned to the ground. Immediately he proceeded to replace it with a new, more beautiful one. His father and brothers, wealthy merchants in Calumet, Michigan, aided him substantially. Within ten years the new cathedral was finished. Vertin and others like him built cathedrals in the wilderness.

In 1887 when he traveled on official business to Rome, he also visited his native village in Carniola. His relatives and villagers received him with great joy. Their former neighbors, the Vertins, were wealthy merchants in faraway America, and their son was a bishop! From poor hamlets hundreds of hopeful people were drawn to Minnesota and Michigan after each visit of a missionary. Bishop Vertin died on February 26, 1899 and was laid to rest beside Baraga under the new cathedral. This and some fifty other churches and schools are vivid monuments to Vertin's work.[14]

Among those who became bishops in America was James Trobec who was born in Log on July 10, 1835. He also joined Pierz in 1864 during his home visit. Having completed his studies at St. Vincent Abbey in Pennsylvania, he became a priest in September 1865, in St. Paul, Minnesota, and assisted Buh in Belle Prairie for a year. He devoted twenty-one years to his work at Wabash on the Mississippi River. He took care of numerous missions, built churches and schools, founded new parishes, helped red and white men. On July 8, 1897 he was appointed bishop of St. Cloud. Consecrated in his new office by Archbishop J. Ireland on September 21, his diocese comprised some 32,000 square miles. Here Trobec continued and expanded the work that Pierz had begun. Among the thousands of new Catholic settlers were a great many Slovenians. Retiring in 1914, Trobec went to Brockway, Minnesota, where he died on December 14, 1921.[15]

Philip J. Erlach, born near Ljubljana in 1839, became a priest in June 1865, in Omaha, Nebraska, worked around the Platte River, and then moved to Cheyenne, Wyoming. Two years later he returned to various posts in Nebraska and in 1885 was transferred to the Marquette diocese. In 1888 he was in Calumet, a rising mining center. Overwork taxed his health, and he died in Chippewa Falls in May 1894.

Ignatius Tomazin also belonged to the followers of Pierz. A native of Ljubljana (born in February 1843), he was ordained as a priest in St. Paul, Minnesota, and then took over several of Pierz's missions. One of his parishes was in Kraintown, Minnesota, a place named after a Slovenian town. Another follower of Pierz was John Tomazevic, a native of Brežnica. He was ordained in St. Paul and died of tuberculosis in October 1867. Among those who buried him was his father, one of the early Slovenian immigrants in Minnesota.

Ivan Stariha, a native of Sodinjavas, Carniola, fought as an Austrian soldier in the battle of Custozza, Italy (June 1866); he was decorated for bravery. Then he decided to be a priest in America where he arrived in May 1867 after a journey of fifty-seven days. His countrymen Vertin and Cebul helped him. In September 1869, he was ordained by Bishop Mrak. After arduous activities in Minnesota he was named Vicar General in 1890. On October 28, 1902, he was consecrated as bishop of the newly established diocese in Lead, South Dakota. He was another who built cathedrals in the wilderness and was a true friend of the Indian. By 1907 he had erected twenty-three churches. Tired and ill, he was permitted to retire, and after forty years in America he returned to Ljubljana. He died there in November 1915.[16]

The large number of eminent Slovenian missionaries, their proportionately high number of high prelates in the Church, and many achievements of these able and devoted men have left a lasting imprint on large sections of this land. This indeed is an epic and is proof of their amazing pioneering spirit. As the clergy and the people were closely knit, the activities of the former had an effect on the activities of the latter. Thousands of people followed their priests. To survive in a "foreign sea"— the priests believed—the Slovenians had to preserve their faith.

Even in faraway California, a few Slovenians joined in the gold rush after 1849. Again it should be remembered that traditionally many Slovenians were skilled miners, lumbermen, men of many trades, patient, frugal and hard workers and, unlike many of their Balkan neighbors, generally had a basic education. As many Slovenians have the same family names as some other South Slavs, it is frequently difficult for a groping researcher to determine among the names of pioneers who was a Slovenian and who was not.

In California some Slovenians tried their luck as gold prospectors. Some succeeded and some failed. They moved also into other occupations as excellent farmers, fruit growers, and gardeners. Porterville in central San Joaquin Valley was their first farming community in the state. As growers of grapes and other fruits, quite a few became wealthy. Around Porterville and in other regions of California's San Joaquin Valley they purchased a lot of land for fruit, cotton, and vegetable farming.[17]

In San Francisco, the most numerous South Slavic settlement in California of the 1800s, more Slovenians appeared after 1867. Several of them were veterans of the army of Emperor Maximilian Habsburg in Mexico. By 1890 at least twenty Slovenian families lived in the city. On April 17, 1893 they formed the Slovenian Benefit Society of California. They attended Irish and German churches. Most Slovenians spoke, besides their mother tongue, fluent German, which they learned in the Habsburg schools and in the army and which was the official language of the Austrian authorities in Slovenian lands. This knowledge of German proved to be an asset to many Slovenians in American factories as many of them were either owned by German-speaking people or employed foremen using that language.[18]

As they were subjects of Austria, the Slovenians (like the Adriatic Croatians) were before 1914 usually called "Austrians" by the Americans. Some were such loyal Habsburg subjects that they called themselves Austrians. Or they sometimes used even the provincial name of "Carniolans" derived from the name of the province in which most of them had lived. So many Slavic national and provincial names in the United States perplex American scholars and authorities to this very day.

CHAPTER 12

The Slovenians Establish Themselves

B UTTE is located in the southwestern part of Montana in the Rocky Mountains. It sits atop "the richest hill on earth." Its copper deposits mined by the Anaconda Company were enormous and as a prospering mining town Butte's population was at its peak: some ninety thousand (compared to today's twenty-three thousand).[1]

As early as 1885, the Slovenians were attracted to Butte by promise of steady employment. They were one of many nationalities working in mines, smelters, and other places. Miners, laborers, merchants, and craftsmen, they also moved into towns of Anaconda, Lincoln, Missoula, Helena, Dillon, Willis, and elsewhere in western parts of the state. As the growing population of the booming city of Butte needed farm produce and meat, some Slovenians became successful farmers in its vicinity.[2]

I *The Slovenians Are Coming . . .*

Slovenians were attracted to Colorado by its climate and resemblance of the land to Slovenia. They came to Canon City around 1880, also moved into Denver and other towns. The economic boom and the land attracted many more. They settled in Aspen, Leadville, Pueblo, and elsewhere.

Most of them came from the poor districts of the southern parts of Slovenia (then ruled by Austria), the province of Carniola. A great many came from the district called Bela Krajina (White Frontier Land). One of them came to America for the first time in 1868. He arrived in Baltimore on July 20 after ten weeks on the sailing vessel *Hermann* from Bremen and settled in Iowa. Altogether he went to America four times and died in Bela Krajina in 1931 at the age of eighty-two.[3]

145

Some of the Slovenian immigrants who came early were pack-peddlers who had traveled and sold their wares all over Europe. In America they continued their pack-peddling among the pioneers and Indians of Michigan, Wisconsin, Illinois, Minnesota, and Iowa.

What the Far West was to the Croatians, the Midwest was to the Slovenians. Joseph Gorshe came to the little town of Chicago in 1847. His wife, a half-breed, was an excellent seamstress. The story has it that one day a man paid her for a shirt with a piece of land he owned. It later became a part of the Chicago Loop. At any rate, Gorshe did acquire a lot of property in Chicago and through real estate transactions became a millionaire. The place where the Union Station is now located was once his property. When Gorshe died in 1902, he left an estate of several million dollars. Many Slovenians became wealthy from speculations in real estate.

Several prosperous Slovenian pioneers in Chicago were former pack-peddlers. They bought various notions, household goods, trinkets, and religious articles and, walking enormous distances, sold them to eager customers. The Meyer-Turk Furniture Factory in Lemark, Illinois, was founded by a former pack-peddler.[4]

Joseph Vertin, the father of the later Bishop Vertin, and Peter Ruppe were pack-peddlers in Chicago when they met Father Baraga in 1856. He urged them to go to Michigan's newly opened copper area. Soon they were on their way to becoming the wealthiest merchants in Calumet. Vertin's department store comprised one square block, the largest store north of Chicago, as recorded by Emily G. Balch.

The Chicago and other Illinois Slovenian settlements kept growing. In Joliet, southwest of Chicago, a rising industrial center, the first Slovenians appeared in 1870. Some worked in stone quarries. After their numbers increased they built their own church in 1891. In 1895 they established an eight-grade Slovenian parochial school. On account of its many religious activities, the Joliet colony was nicknamed the "Slovenian Rome" in America. The driving spirit behind these activities was Rev. Francis X. Sustersic who came in May 1891. He published a book for the Slovenian immigrants with instructions on how to get along in America. Later he established parishes in Chicago, South Dakota, LaSalle, Waukegan, Springfield, and Indianapolis.[5]

In Lincoln, Illinois, and in neighboring Indiana, the first Slovenians were from Carniola; some also came from the vicinity of Trieste and the region of the Isonzo (Soča) River. To Riggs, Iowa, the first Slovenian immigrants came around 1860. At about the same time many flocked to the good land of Kansas: in Frontenac, Meodesha, Olpe, Pittsburgh, and Yale. Some moved to Missouri; many of these had arrived from German Westphalia where they had lived for a while. Nothing was as attractive to these land-hungry peasants as the good and cheap land.

After discovery of copper in 1856, the town of Calumet at the Upper Peninsula of Michigan started its prosperous existence. It developed into a bustling mining town around huge copper deposits that at the time were estimated as the largest in the world. A number of Slovenians were living there in 1859. Peter Ruppe, after becoming a successful merchant, also acquired a copper mine company.[6]

After forming a parish with the Croatians in 1889 and then establishing a separate one, the Slovenians lost their church in Calumet through fire in 1902. Then they built an even larger and more expensive church. In September 1882, they founded their St. Joseph Society. It soon had some five hundred members. Other Slovenian societies were then formed in various colonies with the purpose of paying sick and death benefits to their members. By the late 1890s over two thousand Slovenians lived and prospered in the Copper Country and their number kept increasing. They also settled in Iron Mountain, Manistique, and in other places in Michigan. A group of farmers founded a settlement, Kraintown, in Ocenia County.[7]

II *Hard-working Farmers*

Just as their missionaries were erecting churches and cathedrals in the wilderness, the plain Slovenian peasants and workers were establishing farms, settlements, and towns. No one was more determined than these people to turn this wild, green frontier into thriving habitations. Patient, hard-working, thrifty, and enterprising, used to back-breaking work with axe, saw, pick, hoe, and plow, the Slovenian brought with him love and hunger for the soil. With his own piece of land he looked forward to the future no matter what hardships were involved.

One settlement established by these sturdy men and women in the wilderness was Brockway, Minnesota. Here seven farmers, who had come from the region of Ljubljana in 1865 and 1866, through hard work cleared the land, established farms, and built substantial homes. Other countrymen joined them in building a little Slovenia of their own. On the first Sunday after Easter 1871, the little farming community attended the first mass in the log church of St. Stephen. It was dedicated by the Slovenian missionary Ignac Tomazin. This is the first known Slovenian and South Slavic church in America. By the end of the century over seventy families and many single men inhabited this thriving community. On October 24, 1904 the Slovenian bishop, Msgr. **James** Trobec, consecrated the new brick church. For many missionaries Brockway remained one of their stopping places in Minnesota.[8]

After the discovery of iron ore in Tower, Minnesota, during the early 1880s, the Slovenians started to arrive in large numbers. The Minnesota Iron Range was to lure thousands of immigrants. A number of mining communities grew on the Range. The wages were good for the time: two dollars a day. A little Slovenian St. Martin Church was built in Tower in 1885. Their missionary, Joseph F. Buh, came as a pastor in 1888. There he founded the first Slovenian printshop in America and for several years printed the then only Slovenian paper *Amerikanski Slovenec* (American Slovenian). The first books he printed were a Catechism and the U.S. Constitution in Slovenian. The Sts. Cyril and Methodius Benefit Society was organized in 1888.

In 1887 the Slovenians came to Ely, Minnesota, located on a scenic plateau. By 1890 it housed over fifteen hundred of them. They built St. Anthony Church in 1900. Many societies and clubs have prospered in the city which has had over the years ten Slovenian mayors. By 1900 some two hundred Slovenian families inhabited the city of Eveleth, Minnesota. Others came to Duluth, St. Paul, Minneapolis, Chisolm, and other places. All over the Iron Range "a visitor . . . who sees the well kept homes and gardens abounding with flowers, pole

beans, lettuce, horseradish, and rozmarin (rosemary) realizes at
a glance that this is truly an area inhabited by Slovenians."⁹

Some early Slovenian pioneers, invited by Rev. Buh, settled
in St. Cloud, Minnesota. The local bishop, **James** Trobec, took
keen interest in the welfare of his countrymen. Kraintown,
about twenty miles distant from Brockway, attracted some fifty
farmers with their families.¹⁰

The Slovenians also came to the East, especially Pennsylvania
which was destined to have special significance for all the
South Slavs. The first Slovenians came to Johnstown already in
the early 1850s and in time many more arrived. Around 1890
there was a large number of them in Pittsburgh. There St.
Mary's Church was erected in 1897. Some three thousand came
to Forest City, near Scranton, in the anthracite coal region, where
by 1895 they had their benefit society and church. They also
founded settlements in Aliquippa, Ambridge, Bessemer, Braddock, Beaver Falls, Bethlehem, Etna, Clairton, Luzerne, Reading,
Steelton, and many other localities.¹¹

A rising industrial center on the shores of Lake Erie and
Cuyahoga River was Cleveland, Ohio. The city held promise
for the future to many thousands of immigrants. Josef Turk,
one of the first settlers, established a store on St. Clair Avenue
and East 30th Street. Hundreds followed him and over the years
a huge Slovenian (and partly Croatian) neighborhood formed
around St. Clair Avenue. In 1894 the Slovenians organized St.
Vitus parish which became with its church the center of the
Slovenian colony. The first pastor was Vitus Hribar. Forty
years later a beautiful church with two steeples was erected,
the largest Slovenian church in America. Decades ago its elementary eight-grade school numbered some 1700 pupils. J. Turk
had eleven children. He is buried in St. Paul's Cemetery on
Chardon Road in Euclid, Ohio. There another thriving Slovenian settlement was formed.¹²

Around the turn of the century the Cleveland Slovenian colony
was one of the busiest and most prosperous Slovenian settlements in America. By 1920 the city was, after Ljubljana, the
most populous "Slovenian City." Its outstanding leader was the
businessman Anton Grdina who arrived in 1897. He became
nationally known as a businessman and civic leader.

The Slovenians also established themselves in Newburgh, Collinwood, mostly in eastern suburbs, and then spread out into Cuyahoga County. They usually lived near the factories and shops where they worked, founded many businesses, and became over the years one of the most outstanding ethnic groups in metropolitan Cleveland.

Until the 1900s a comparatively small number of Slovenians settled in the North Atlantic states outside Pennsylvania. A few came to New York City during the 1870s. In 1879 Rev. Francis Pavletic came to Brooklyn; he had emigrated in 1864 and was ordained priest in Allegheny, Pennsylvania, in 1869. In 1893 the New York Slovenians started to organize their societies and parishes. The fact that they were scatterel over a large area of the city and in nearby New Jersey hampered their organizing efforts.[13]

III   The Slovenian "Paradise Lost" in California

Rev. Peter J. Jeram, a native of Smoljeva, Slovenia, was a very learned man fluent in several languages. In 1893 he served as a missionary for the Czechs in Tabor, South Dakota. In 1893 Monsignor Buh in Tower, Minnesota, published Jeram's English grammar for the Slovenian immigrants. Jeram was a peculiar and restless man.

In the summer of 1893, Jeram informed Buh of his fantastic plan to establish a large Slovenian Catholic colony in Eden Valley, in the Mendocino region some one hundred miles north of San Francisco. It was a wild mountainous country more suitable for cattle raising than for farming. In July 1895, Jeram bought ten thousand acres of this land from the real estate agent W. F. Lang in San Francisco for $75,000. The down payment was $25,000. The owner was the local bank in Ukiah, California. Jeram moved into a ranch house on the property and then started to sell through the paper *Amerikanski Slovenec* one-dollar shares to all Slovenians who were willing to settle here in the "Slovenian Catholic Colony Eden Valley" ("Slovenska Katoliška Kolonija Rajska Dolina").

Judging from the letters and articles sent to Monsignor Buh, Jeram wanted to found and develop a kind of Slovenian Utopia, a settlement of some four hundred families. The only way to preserve the Catholic religion, Jeram thought, was under strict control of a priest. As Buh's paper reported on February 21, 1896, Jeram had already sold some twenty-four thousand shares to Slovenians from several states. People came from as far as the states of New York and Mississippi. They had sold everything and struck out to a distant place in the wilderness hoping to find a new existence in what seemed to be a promising cooperative enterprise.

The *Republican Press* of Ukiah, California, of February 28, 1896, announced that Jeram's advance guard of "Austrians," consisting of fifty-three people had just arrived, and another two hundred settlers were expected soon. The colonists were to work cooperatively for four or five years; then small tracts would be made and stock raising would be attempted while the land was being prepared for cultivation.

The paper also added this interesting note:

When future colonists arrive in San Francisco they will be taken before archbishop Riordan, and when he shall have given them blessings they will be immediately brought to their new home in Eden Valley. There they will find their own Catholic church and the children will be able to attend parochial schools.

By May 1896 there were already some two hundred people in the settlement. Such activities did not go unnoticed by several papers. *The San Francisco Chronicle* denounced the establishment of this new Catholic colony, and the American Protestant Association, well known for its anti-foreign feelings, as well as the local German *Abendpost* joined the anti-Slovenian campaign. The Slovenian press continued to propagate the goals of forming "a new Slovenia in the Eden Valley of fertile California," ignoring the fact that the valley was not fertile at all.

Somehow, from the start, everything went wrong in the settlement. After only two months of existence the colony was plagued with strife, dissatisfaction, lack of food, insufficient milk for the children, and clearly lack of the discipline that the authoritarian priest expected from his flock. The people lived in temporary huts and soon some families left in desperation and protest.

They denounced the "dictatorship" of Jeram. By the spring of 1897 the situation had become unbearable.

On May 3, 1897, Jeram while trying to cross the Eel River in the colony on horseback drowned in the swollen river. His body was found two months later. As the real estate firm informed Monsignor Buh on June 28, 1897, "the colony enterprise had proved a complete failure." After Jeram's death the few remaining colonists abandoned the valley. The public administrator took possession of the land since there was a mortgage of $50,000. In the estate of the dead leader the officials found a rich library and the manuscript of an English-Slovenian dictionary Jeram was compiling, finished to the letter "T."[14] Thus ended the ill-fated attempt to establish a little Catholic Slovenia in the mountains of northern California.

The authority of the priest in Slovenia and even in several American settlements was still strong. Many priests were popular with the people who sought their leadership, help, and advice. But Father Jeram was not that kind of a man. However, the example of Eden Valley was also symptomatic of new times and trends. With the progress of time, with the gradual advance of liberal and socialist ideas among the Slovenians, numerous immigrants opposed the leadership and patronage of the clergy. After 1900, more and more skilled workers, printers, locksmiths— some acquainted with the ideas of labor unions and the German and Austrian Social Democracy—appeared among the South Slav industrial workers in America. They were extremely anticlerical, cared little for religion, or were non-believers.

The Slovenian Franc Sakser arrived in New York in 1892 as an experienced typesetter. He started to publish *Glas Naroda* (Voice of the People). He was its editor, manager, and printer. First a weekly, it later turned into a daily. In it Sakser attacked Monsignor Buh, Rev. Jeram, and their activities. He also founded an agency for railroad and steamship lines, selling thousands of tickets to Slovenians and other immigrants. Later he established his own bank in New York City and thus was able to secure the publication of his newspaper. It proved to be one of the most successful South Slav papers from 1893 to 1963. Sakser even took over some Croatian papers. His employees regularly met the immigrants who were coming by the thousands during the rise and high tide of immigration.[15]

Sakser represented a new brand of immigrant leadership. They were the product of changing times, strict enterprising business-men, men with progressive ideas. They believed in a strong nationality press. They provided their countrymen with service, advice, and leadership. And because their papers advertised their agencies and banks, the immigrants flocked to them by the thousands.

IV *The Miners*

Besides being farmers, tillers of the soil, thousands of Slovenians were miners; in this occupation they had a long experience in the homeland. For more than a hundred years the Slovenian miners have been working all over America. The contribution of these people to the American mining industry is significant; the history of this special breed of people—the Slovenian miners—is very interesting.

In Crested Butte, Colorado, the Slovenians were early settlers. Jacob Kochevar and his son Jacob, Jr., were the builders of the historic City Hall in 1883. Several other buildings they erected still adorn the town.

The Slovenian miners participated here in the strike of 1890 and then joined the turbulent one during 1903–1904, organized by the United Mine Workers led by the popular John Mitchell and supported by "Mother" Jones, the fiery Irish fighter for the rights of workers. In Crested Butte the Slovenians had a Saint Barbara Society, named after the patronesss of miners in the old country.

The Slovenians worked also in Kansas coal mines as early as 1881. They established their settlements before 1900 in Litchfield, Frontenac, Weir City, Daisy Hill, Fleming, Mineral, Stone City, Radley, Franklin, and Dunkirk. Their largest colony in Kansas was at Yale. The Americans called all these immigrants Austrians.[16]

In Frontenac, Kansas, the immigrants from Carniola founded in 1892 their own benevolent society. Another one, the Austrian-Slovenian Sick Benefit Society, was incorporated in 1896 in

Chicopee, Kansas. By 1912 it numbered over two thousand members in twenty-three lodges, thirteen of which were in Kansas. Monthly dues were fifty cents for sick and the same amount for death benefits. The sick benefits were three dollars a week; the death insurance was $300.00. The first member to be buried was John Selak who committed suicide in March 1893.

In Frontenac, the Society had its large home which was known as Austrian Hall. On August 23, 1931 the Austrian-Slovenian Sick Benefit Society ceased its existence because of lack of members.[17]

The Slovenian miners in Kansas were—as in other states—in the forefront of the labor movement. Their American fellow workers accepted them as hard-working, loyal, and dependable comrades. They admired them for their endurance, patience, and resourcefulness. The Slovenian custom of singing amazed the Americans. And while the miners sang their nostalgic songs in the dark pits under the black soil of Kansas, more of their countrymen were coming to these regions. After 1892 many settled in Kansas City. Here many worked in the stockyards. Within a few years they established a Slovenian parish, one of the most thriving in the country.[18]

At the same time in the copper region in Calumet, Michigan, many Slovenians were well established. Peter Ruppe became a millionaire, head of "P. Ruppe and Sons." His wealth came partly from speculating in industrial corporations. He also had interests in Arizona mining. Willing to help his people, he taught Slovenians to buy shares and speculate on the stock market. Calumet's boom reached the high point on the eve of World War I. Ruppe who lived through the best days of his city also observed its demise. He died in January 1923. By now Calumet, too, was dead. The same year his three sons sold the business to the Penney Company.[19]

In Ohio a fairly large Slovenian mining community was Bridgeport, at the border of West Virginia. Slovenians also settled in nearby Boydsville, Lansing, and Wheelingrock. By 1892 the Slovenians were so numerous in Bridgeport that they soon founded several societies, the usual sign that the group was fairly large and well established.[20]

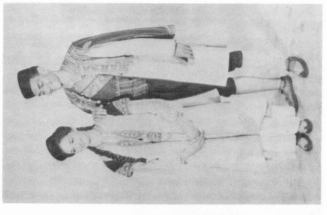

Members of the Duquesne University Tamburitzans in Serbian (left), Bulgarian (center), and Montenegrin (right) national costumes

John Radovich, a Croatian pioneer in New Orleans in the late 1800's

The Slovenian missionary, Rev. Frederick Baraga, first Bishop of Marquette, Michigan

Frank J. Lausche,
former U.S. Senator,
governor of Ohio
and mayor of Cleveland

Courtesy of Frank J. Lausche

Below, Nikola Tesla during the early years of his career

*Courtesy of the Croatian
Fraternal Union,
Pittsburgh, Pennsylvania*

Left, Gusle, an ancient, one-stringed national musical instrument of several South Slavic peoples

Courtesy of the Duquesne University Tamburitzans Institute of Folk Arts
(Walter W. Kolar)

Macedonian musical instruments, tupan (top, right), and zurla (bottom, right)

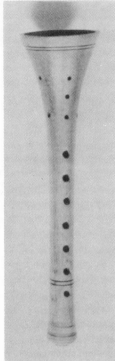

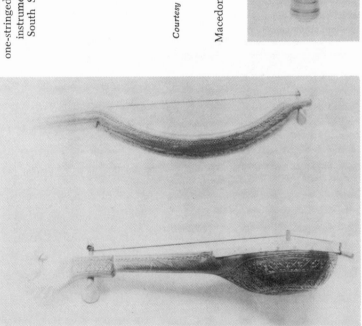

Courtesy of St. Vitus' Parish, Cleveland, Ohio

Above, St. Vitus Church, Cleveland, Ohio, the largest Slovenian Roman Catholic church in the United States
Below, Serbian St. Steven Orthodox Cathedral and parish hall in Alhambra near Los Angeles

Courtesy of Vladimir Novak

Above, Macedonian National Home in Steelton, Pennsylvania (1939)
Below, Croatian St. Anthony's Church in Los Angeles, California

Some of the last creations of Ivan Meštrović before his death in South Bend, Indiana

Joe Magarac the Steelman, a sculpture by Joseph Turkalj, a Croatian artist in Cleveland, Ohio

CHAPTER 13

Life in the New Country

THE first arrivals of the Slovenians in Johnstown, Pennsylvania, during the 1850s were constantly augmented by a huge army of newcomers, unskilled workers, most of whom were needed in the booming industries. In this city and elsewhere the newcomers joined the already well-established Slovenian communities. One was Forest City, where by 1904 they had their St. Joseph parish, fraternal societies, and business establishments. The Johnstown community prospered, but St. Teresa's Church was not erected until 1929.

By the early 1900s some six thousand Slovenians lived in Pittsburgh. They worked mostly in the steel mills and in foundries. St. Mary's Church, built in 1897, had a $3,000 organ which was donated by the industrialist Andrew Carnegie. In 1916, St. Mary's eight-grade parochial school was erected. A National Home had existed since 1911. Many Slovenian priests went through Pennsylvania on their way to assignments in other parts of the country.[1]

Steelton was home to hundreds of Slovenians. After sharing St. Mary's Church with the Croatians, the Slovenians formed in May 1909 their separate parish. Their new St. Peter Church was consecrated on December 11, 1910.[2]

When Emily G. Balch wrote her book on the Slavic immigrants (published in 1910), the editor of *Glas Naroda* furnished an estimate on the number of Slovenians. Around 1908 there were over 100,000 Slovenians in the United States, most of them residing in the North Atlantic and North Central region. Pennsylvania and West Virginia were home to some 25,000, located in twenty-three major settlements. Over 15,000 lived in Ohio, largely in Cleveland. Over 10,000 were in Illinois; some 7,000 in Michigan; over 12,000 in Minnesota; about 10,000 in

155

Colorado; 5,000 in Montana; 5,000 in California; 3,000 in Kansas; 15,000 in Washington; over 1,000 were scattered throughout Utah, Wyoming, and Idaho. Smaller groups existed in every state and territory.[3]

According to the official estimates, during the decade ending June 30, 1908, "Croatians and Slovenians"—as they were grouped by the Immigration authorities—preferred Pennsylvania to all other states. More than 121,000 chose to settle there. New York attracted 22,000; Illinois over 33,000. Some 3,000 settled in New Jersey; 29,000 in Ohio; 1,000 in Connecticut; 8,000 in Michigan; 6,500 in Wisconsin; 8,500 in Missouri; 8,500 in Minnesota; 1,000 in Maryland; 4,000 in West Virginia; 2,700 in Indiana; 1,000 in Texas; 3,000 in California; 6,000 in Colorado; 2,700 in Washington; 2,000 in Kansas; 2,200 in Montana; 1,000 in Iowa; 1,100 in Louisiana; 500 in Virginia; 700 in Wyoming; 1,100 in Utah; 500 in Oregon; 200 in Alabama; 800 in Tennessee.[4]

From 1899 to 1910, 355,543 "Croatians and Slovenians" were counted by immigration authorities. Of these almost 51,000 were women. Until 1923 an additional 225,000 were admitted.[5]

I *Life and Work in America*

In many parts of the country the Slovenians lived in well-organized, neat, and orderly boarding houses. In some instances, in Cleveland, for example, groups of girls lived together in such houses. The owners of these establishments during the high tide of immigration in Cleveland or Pittsburgh went to the railroad stations to pick up the newcomers and bring them to their first residence. They lived usually on credit until they received their first wages.

Even before 1920, a considerable number of Slovenians owned their modest homes. A Slovenian family patronized a Slovenian butcher, grocer, and other merchants. In many instances their own countrymen were the foremen in the factories where they worked. They existed for many years in a veritable "Little Slovenia" with almost no contact with the English-speaking American world.

In midwestern states—in Kansas, for example—a typical Slovenian dwelling was a four-room house with a vegetable and flower garden. Especially popular was the carnation which is the Slovenian national flower. Their homes were surrounded by a few fruit trees and grapevines.[6]

By 1910, when the U.S. Immigration Commission was investigating conditions among immigrants, about thirty percent of the Slovenians had brought their wives to America. Many men had acquired "picture brides" from the homeland. Many had never seen each other before; the prospective groom paid for the girl's boat ticket. After her arrival, if she was not willing to marry the man, either she or the man she married paid for her ticket.[7]

Exposed to the hazards of industrial work, injured and killed by the hundreds, in most cases deprived of any compensation, the Slovenian workers joined labor unions. This in turn involved them in strikes, labor violence, and loss of wages. In the Copper Country of Michigan the famous strike of some fifteen thousand miners began in July of 1913. It was organized by the Western Federation of Miners. The strike dragged on for nine months and failed. As already mentioned, it was not until July 1943—thirty years later—that the Western Federation of Miners was recognized by the employers. By then the mines were almost all closed and thousands of miners had already left Calumet and the Copper Country of Michigan.[8]

Many Slovenians either moved to other states to work in industry or bought land and became farmers in the Midwest or moved to the South or the West. In Kansas they joined their compatriots who had been farmers for a long time. The newcomers chose tracts of land consisting of between forty and sixty acres. This was the realization of their old dreams. They had tilled the soil in the old country for many generations.

II *World War I*

During this crucial period a large percentage of the Slovenians remained—like their Croatian neighbors—loyal to the Habsburgs. Some leaders like Franz Sakser became very active in the South Slav movement, which was against Austria-Hungary, and was intended to unite all the South Slavs. In New York City Sakser owned, besides other papers, the daily *Croatian*

World which was firmly opposed to the Habsburgs. Of the same orientation were the Slovenian *Glasnik* (The Messenger) with a circulation of twelve thousand and *Clevelandska Amerika* (Cleveland America) which was printed every second day of the week.

When the South Slavic National Council was founded in March of 1915 in Chicago, one of its members was Sakser. The Slovenian Socialists led by Etbin Kristan attacked the policies of the Council in their weekly *Proletarec* (The Proletarian). They were opposed to a future Yugoslav monarchy and favored a republic.[9] Sakser and other Slovenians participated in promoting the South Slav movement. Some Slovenian priests joined forces with the group of Rev. Martin D. Krmpotić, the Croatian pastor from Kansas City. They opposed the South Slav unification movement and envisaged an autonomous unit of Slovenia and Croatia in a Habsburg federation.

To attract the American Slovenians the South Slav Committee of London sent to America Bogumil Vošnjak, a Slovenian politician whose father had been a former representative in the parliament of Vienna. Vošnjak visited all major Slovenian settlements, explained the goals of the South Slav movement, published articles and appeals in Slovenian papers. He also printed several books in English (in London) all directed against Austria and the German menace to the future of all Slavs. (After World War II, Vošnjak died in exile in Washington, D.C.)

On July 29, 1917 a group of Slovenian Socialists gathered in Chicago and issued a statement against the agreement that had been signed between the Serbian government on the island of Corfu and the Yugoslav Committee of London on a future Yugoslav monarchy. The Socialists demanded a republic based on a democratic national referendum.[10]

A Slovenian Republican Alliance was also organized and it sent memoranda to Washington demanding establishment of a South Slav democratic republic instead of a monarchy. The Socialist Etbin Kristan appeared before the Senate Foreign Relations Committee in Washington and spoke out against arbitrary creation of a centralistic Yugoslav monarchy.[11]

As soon as a free South Slav state was established in late October 1918 with a National Council in Zagreb as its government, the Italian troops started to move into Slovenian territories in Istria, around Trieste and parts of Carniola. The American Slovenians denounced this action as a violation of the principle of self-determination. The same principle was also denied later on at the Paris Peace Conference, where President Wilson was unable to save Slovenian lands around Trieste from Italian occupation. Many Slovenians blamed these losses on the South Slav movement in America.

III *The Slovenian Press and Religious Activities*

The newspapers and other publications were of great importance in the life of the American Slovenians. The Slovenian press was well established before 1920. In 1924 the *Novo Doba* (New Era) became a weekly organ of the South Slavic Catholic Union. *Amerikanski Slovenec* (American Slovenian), founded in 1891, remained an influential paper even after 1920. So was the Socialist *Proletarec* (Proletarian). Several Slovenian papers were printed in Chicago which remained a strong center for Socialist activities. One of their publications was *The American Family Almanac* (Ameriški Družinski Koledar), an excellent yearly almanac, a real repository of Slovenian literature in this country. Some of the best and lengthy studies on the history of the American Slovenians were printed there. It was founded in 1914 and had a wide circulation among those who sympathized with Socialist ideas. One of its able editors was Frank Zaitz, a prolific Socialist writer. The *Almanac* was published by the Yugoslav Workmen's Publishing Co., and co-sponsored by the Fraternal Slovenian National Benefit Society. This was founded in 1904 and later reached a membership of sixty-five thousand. By 1945 it had paid $22 million in benefits; its assets were $11 million. In 1926 a subsidy of $15,000 made possible a history of their people *Ameriški Slovenci* (American Slovenians) written by Joseph Zavertnik. It sold six thousand copies and was a lengthy book of over six hundred pages.[12]

The Socialist publications denounced the power of the Church among the Slovenians, among whom the priests were very influential. Here in America the Socialists, freethinkers, even Communists and anarchists, frowned on religious activities.

Around 1910 the Slovenians in America included forty-two priests, two bishops, twenty parishes, and a number of young seminarians trained for priesthood. In 1912 the Slovenian Franciscans established a Commissariat of the Slovenian Holy Cross Province in Brooklyn, New York. For a while it had jurisdiction over the Slovak and Croatian Franciscans.[13]

Like their Socialist foes, the Slovenian priests realized the potential of the press, and printed many papers and periodicals, almanacs, and books. During the last ninety years large sums were devoted to publishing activities. In the midst of the Great Depression the anti-Church *American Family Almanac* for 1933 reminded their countrymen that some $3,500,000 had been spent for churches, schools, convents, and rectories. By 1930 some $250,000 were spent annually for the maintenance of parishes and schools. In 1930 the number of Slovenian priests was around one hundred.

Minnesota has the largest number of Slovenian parishes—ten of them. Five are located in Illinois, while metropolitan Cleveland has four. Others are located in other parts of the country. Their largest parochial schools were founded in Joliet, Illinois; Chicago; Pueblo and Denver, Colorado; St. Vitus in Cleveland. In 1925 there were fifteen Slovenian schools with some seven thousand pupils. In the early 1950s there were some eight thousand Slovenian grade-school pupils in over fifty parishes.[14]

The best years for Slovenian parochial schools were between the 1920s and 1940s. In the agonizing process of becoming American, the teaching of the native language was stopped years ago. Today English is used as the only language of instruction even though today many pupils in the first grade do not speak English. St. Vitus in Cleveland, the largest Slovenian parochial school, teaches Slovenian after regular school hours. The trends in Americanization among the young Slovenians have been supported by the Roman Catholic bishops. These assimilating policies are now being challenged by a large number of ethnic priests.

In resisting the Americanization process the Slovenians knew what was at stake: a rich tradition, culture, and heritage. Reuben Markham, the Balkan correspondent of *The Christian Science Monitor*, one of many who wrote about them, had the highest praise for these people who developed "a very high degree of literacy, maintained schools in every town and village . . . and made their little country a model for Central Europe." They also have, he said, "the noble tradition of building statues to poets." He put them "among the most advanced nations."[15] William L. Shirer, the American journalist and writer, in his *Berlin Diary* in March 1938 observed that Ljubljana, the Slovenian capital, "is a town to shame the whole world." Louis Adamic, the American writer and controversial World War II activist, born in the vicinity of Ljubljana, wrote about his countrymen most extensively in his many books and articles. He really introduced them to the American people.

R. A. Schermerhorn, a historian who for many years was a professor at Case-Western Reserve University in Cleveland, stated that the Slovenians and their Croatian neighbors have much in common. They have been "cooperative" to a marked degree both in Europe and the United States, "frequently burying their differences in a common cause." In America the close-knit character of the Slovenian communities "retains a social cohesion that serves to keep delinquency and crime to a minimum. Offenses against property are almost nonexistent." Big-time racketeers did not flourish among them. As a matter of record "it was the testimony of a Slovenian immigrant, Gus Kovach, backed by many other Slovenians, including Frank J. Lausche, later governor of Ohio, that broke one of the largest 'mobs' in that city."[16]

In his book on America and the Americans, J. Trunk wrote more than sixty years ago to his fellow Slovenians: "If you can, stay at home. And if you have to leave, don't drown in the foreign sea. If America really becomes your beloved bride and you are happy and proud with her, if you do become an American citizen, don't forget to remain a loyal son to your mother, the Slovenian Fatherland!"[17]

IV *They Were Very Busy*

On the main street of their largest settlement, St. Clair Avenue, Cleveland, Ohio, the Slovenians built in 1924 the Slovenian National Home at a cost of $300,000. It is their largest in this country, the center of innumerable activities, the site of many events in the life of Slovenians and other South Slavs. Around 1930 some 28,000 Slovenians formed a compact settlement within its vicinity. After 1945 thousands of its residents moved out to the suburbs.[18]

Seldom has any Slavic nationality group shown as much constructive creativeness as the Slovenians did. By 1930 they had some eighty national homes valued at more than one and a half million dollars with some 20,000 affiliated members. Forty of these homes were in Pennsylvania, ten in Ohio, while the rest were scattered in ten different states. They were centers for many activities and many had well-stacked libraries with books in Slovenian and English.[19]

In Cleveland alone the Slovenians have founded over forty singing societies, fourteen of which are still in existence. In 1932 there were in the country fifty-five Slovenian singing societies and thirty-six drama groups. Five of them owned their own buildings, over twenty of them held their own libraries, six had private schools for adults, while some thirty offered regular lecture programs. Prosvetna Matica (Educational League) of the Yugoslav Socialist League in Chicago coordinated its cultural activities with many Slovenian settlements.[20]

In 1932 the Yugoslav Socialist League held its ninth convention during May 28–30 in Milwaukee with seventy-five delegates present. The Slovenian Freethinking Beneficial League had its eighth convention in Pittsburgh. Seventy-one delegates were present. The Yugoslav Catholic Union (Slovenian) held its fourteenth convention during July 25–August 2 in Indianapolis with 136 delegates. The Yugoslav Benefit Union (Slovenian) gathered in Milwaukee at its eighth convention attended by seventy-two delegates. The American Yugoslav Union (Slovenian) convened on September 25 in Eveleth, Minnesota.[21]

The Slovenian press was the most active of all South Slav presses. It was well edited and attracted a large reading public. *Amerikanski Slovenec* of Chicago still appeared five times a week; it was owned by the workers' printing association "Edinost" (Unity). Dailies in Cleveland were *Ameriška Domovina* (American Homeland) and *Enakopravnost* (Equality). The old *Glas Naroda* (Voice of the People), owned by Frank Sakser, still appeared in New York as a daily. *Prosveta* (Enlightenment) was a daily in Chicago owned by the Slovenian National Benefit Union. Adamic considered it "one of the best balanced, most effective immigrant publications."[22]

The Socialists were very busy during the 1930s. Their paper *Proletarec* had its editorial offices in the Slovenian Workers' Center at 2301 S. Lawnsdale Avenue, Chicago. Their Educational League distributed over 100,000 copies of free books and pamphlets among the people. *Proletarec* also owned the largest South Slavic book store. All major Slovenian papers on the eve of World War II were printed in their own printing establishments.

During these years the young writer Louis Adamic, whose book *The Native's Return* made him well known, not only reported about the difficult political conditions in Yugoslavia but also about the plight of his compatriots during the depression. His book became the Book-of-the-Month selection for February 1934 and sold immediately fifty thousand copies. This and subsequent books and articles made Adamic one of the spokesmen for the South Slavs in America. When in 1935 he published his book *Grandsons*, a fiction describing a Slovenian gangster, a segment of the American-Slovenian press denounced him for such portrayal of their kin.

CHAPTER 14

Slovenians After 1939

AFTER the crucial summer of 1939 the attention of all American Slovenians turned to their homeland. The ensuing years of war brought many bitter and emotional controversies, the central figure in which was the writer Louis Adamic.

In April 1941 Slovenia was occupied by foreign invaders: the Germans in the northern parts (mostly southern Styria with the city of Maribor) and the Italians in the southern parts (Carniola and the capital Ljubljana). The Germans and Italians deported many Slovenians and sent thousands to concentration camps. During the guerrilla warfare with Tito's partisans, the Germans burned thousands of homes. They killed a large number of people of all ages, combatants and civilians alike.

In April 1941, in Cleveland, Ohio, a Slovenian Section of the Yugoslav Aid Committee was formed to help their homeland under foreign occupation in any way possible. On December 5 and 6, 1942 the Slovenian National Congress convened at the Slovenian National Home on St. Clair Avenue in Cleveland. Louis Adamic was elected as honorary president of the Slovenian American National League. The next year he published his book *My Native Land*. In it he denounced all the anti-Communist Slovenians and pleaded for the establishment of a Communist federal Yugoslav Republic. The book caused controversy among the Slovenians who responded in their press and at various meetings. *The Daily Worker* of New York, the official organ of the Communist Party of the U.S.A., praised the book very highly.[1]

Adamic also became the editor of *The Bulletin of the United Committee of South-Slavic Americans* whose first issue appeared in September 1943. This organization was later branded as a Communist front organization. The Slovenian National Congress was affiliated with the American Slav Congress. Some 550

164

delegates of the S.N.C. claimed to represent 250,000 American Slovenians. Adamic remained its main ideologist.[2] He became the leader of the pro-Tito movement and together with several South Slavs denounced the royal Yugoslav government in exile and their supporters in America.

After America entered the war in December 1941, thousands of American Slovenians joined the armed forces and fought with distinction. Among the first American war casualties was Louis Dobnikar from Cleveland, a water tender on the USS *Kearny*, a destroyer that was torpedoed in the North Atlantic. In the sea battle off Guadalcanal in November 1942, Lieutenant Commander Milton Pavlic, an Annapolis graduate of Slovenian origin, died a hero's death on the USS *South Dakota*. He had helped put three Japanese warships and thirty-two planes out of action. A new destroyer was named after him. And there were many others who fought and died valiantly.[3]

The Slovenian delegates participated at the first All-Slavic Congress in Detroit in late April 1942 and in all following activities of the American Slav Congress. Louis Adamic was one of its main leaders. Under his initiative the leftist representatives of all South Slavic groups gathered on August 7, 1943 in the Slovenian National Home in Cleveland and formed a United Committee of American South Slavs. Its main purpose was to support creation of a Communist Yugoslavia under Tito. Its president became Louis Adamic. Zlatko Baloković was its vice-president.[4]

Adamic's actions and writings continued to provoke a strong reaction, especially on the part of anti-Communist Slovenians. The Union of Slovenian Parishes responded to Adamic's *My Native Land* with a pamphlet *Shall Slovenia Be Sovietized? A Rebuttal to Louis Adamic*. In spite of his controversial behavior Adamic entertained good relations with many American politicians. He and his wife Stella were even invited by President and Mrs. Roosevelt for a dinner at the White House in January 1942. The British Prime Minister Churchill was also present and Adamic later described this event in a whole book.

Adamic's name and activities were well known among the Communist partisans and people in the old country. Ater 1942 the U.S. government supported Tito and his forces. They took control of the country in the spring of 1945. Tito and his government recognized the valuable support of Adamic and his friends. Thousands of Slovenian refugees who, in 1945, escaped to Austria and Italy and eventually were admitted to the United States cursed Adamic for his role in creating a Communist Yugoslavia. When the American Slovenians learned about massacres of many of their relatives and compatriots by the Communists, the blame was put on Adamic and his men.

I   *After 1945*

By 1948, the same year when Tito and Stalin broke their close relations, the American media were publishing all details of Adamic's and his collaborators' pro-Soviet and pro-Tito activities. In the beginning of 1949 Adamic flew to Yugoslavia, met its new leaders, and stayed there for seven months collecting materials for his new book *The Eagle and the Roots*. It was an emotional apology for the Communist regime in Yugoslavia. On September 5, 1951, the American news media reported that Louis Adamic had been found dead at his farm near Milford, New Jersey. He had been shot through the head. It was alleged that he committed suicide. Thus Adamic's last book *The Eagle and the Roots* was published posthumously in 1952.

What transpired here in the leftist movement and what the repercussions were in Yugoslavia was described after the war by one of Adamic's Croatian friends, Bogdan Raditsa, in all leading American publications. An American Slovenian, M. Cvetich, who during the war was planted by the F.B.I. in Communist-supported organizations, described the controversial activities in a series of articles in the *Saturday Evening Post* during July 1950.[5]

II   *The Slovenian Contribution*

Gerald G. Govorchin, who as a young man worked for years in various factories, remarks in his book:

Thousands of South Slavs have for many years devoted their talents and energies to the two great basic industries of America: mining and the manufacture of steel. But miners and laborers cannot, as a rule achieve fame or fortune; their names are seldom seen in head-lines of newspapers. Nevertheless, their work . . . has helped to transform the United States into the richest nation on earth.[6]

Thousands of Slovenians are among these anonymous con-tributors. However, many others, including the missionaries, received deserved recognition.

In the development of a modern America, Max Stupar, a native of Metlika, Slovenia, gave his contribution. In 1909 he built one of America's first airplane factories. Many of his country-men—frequently not recognized as Slovenian—continued to give their talent and energy in all branches of American industry as engineers, innovators, and inventors.[7]

In the arts, Slovenian-born Franc Gorshe—a student of Meštrović—excelled in sculptures. He arrived in 1945 and for years had a studio in Cleveland. He produced many sculptures with religious themes. Then he moved to New York and finally to Carinthia, Austria. He exhibited his works in the United States, Canada, and Europe.[8]

The paintings of Harvey G. Perushek who emigrated in the beginning of the 1900s, were exhibited all over the United States. Before he died in 1935, he was the president of the United Art Gallery in Chicago. His countryman, Božidar Jakac, visited in the United States and was especially impressed with Pittsburgh.[9]

Anton Schubel, the Slovenian contributor to music and musical pedagogy, was born in Rodice near Ljubljana in 1899. From the Slovenian National Opera he came to America in January 1928, gave a series of concerts, returned to Slovenia, and then came back to America in 1930. From 1931 until 1945 he sang in the chorus of the Metropolitan Opera in New York. Then he became a talent scout for Carnegie Hall. He was the first to sing Slovenian songs on television. In 1949 he became the director of the Slovenian Glasbena Matica in Cleveland, one of the best ethnic singing and operatic societies in the United States. Many of his songs were recorded. He died in Cleveland on June 9, 1965.[10]

In the movies Laura La Plante (real name: Turk) was of Slovenian origin. Zala Zarana was born in Kranj and so was Zalka Srsen, to mention a few.

All these contributors, including many educators and people in other activities, are included in a lengthy study that Professor E. G. Gobetz is publishing in a book on the Slovenian contribution to America and to the world.

The Slovenians are also talented writers. One of the earlier writers was Rev. Jurij M. Trunk who in 1912 published in Klagenfurt, Austria, his bulky *Amerika in Amerikanci* (America and the Americans) after his visit in 1909. After World War I he settled in America and wrote columns for Slovenian papers, articles, studies, books in Slovenian, and translated from the Slovenian into English. For many years he lived in San Francisco where on September 1, 1970 he celebrated his hundredth birthday. He died on March 11, 1973, the oldest Catholic priest in America.[11]

Louis Adamic, the best known Slovenian writer in the United States, has already been discussed in this book. Some of his fifteen books, innumerable articles, and other writings in English dealt extensively with the Slovenians and other South Slavs. He definitely is the most eminent Slovenian contributor to American literature. In the present revival of ethnicity some of his books— long out of print—have been reprinted.

Frank Mlakar immortalized the Slovenian St. Clair neighborhood of Cleveland in his powerful novel, printed in 1950 by Harper, *He, the Father*. He was born in 1913 in Cleveland of Slovenian parents.

One of the many Slovenian writers who found asylum in free countries of the world was Karl Mauser of Cleveland. Mauser came to the United States after the war, worked for many years in the Cleveland Twist Drill Company (where many postwar refugees obtained jobs), and continued writing. He wrote only in Slovenian. His best known work is a trilogy *Ludje pod bičem* (People Under the Whip) depicting the fate of the Slovenians. Mauser's books were translated into other languages. He died suddenly in January 1977.[12]

In America, Canada, Argentina, and other countries the Slovenian publishing activities continue and their writers are still very productive. The Slovenians in exile have a literature of their own. This is acknowledged even by literary critics in the Slovenian Republic of Yugoslavia.

Of all South Slavs, the Slovenians have been most successful
in American politics. Their most eminent politician was Frank J.
Lausche, who was born on November 14, 1895 of immigrant
parents in the heart of the Slovenian settlement in the St. Clair
area of Cleveland. Lausche grew up in modest conditions among
the immigrants and always retained his pride in the Slovenian
heritage. He graduated from the John Marshall School of Law
(Cleveland) and after working as an attorney-at-law became a
municipal judge in 1932. During 1936–1940 he forced the
racketeers out of Cleveland. In 1940 he was elected mayor of the
city on the Democratic ticket, and reelected in 1943 with an
overwhelming majority. In 1944 he won the governorship of
Ohio. He served five terms as governor. In November of 1955
Lausche was mentioned as a "Favorite Son" candidate for the
Democratic presidential nomination in 1956, but his candidacy
did not materialize. In 1956 he was chosen by the people as
their Senator in Washington and served for twelve years in
the Capitol where he attracted national attention. He served
on the Foreign Relations and Foreign Commerce Committees.
All the time he "exhibited the same qualities of sincerity, frank-
ness, aggressiveness, and ingenuity."[13]

As governor and U.S. Senator, Lausche spoke out firmly against
Communism in Yugoslavia and East Europe. He was often seen
at various ethnic rallies and maintained close ties especially
with the Slovenian community in Cleveland where he was loved
by the people. Having reached the highest public office ever
attained by a South Slav, Frank J. Lausche became a living
legend among the American Slovenians. He still comes to
visit Cleveland.

John A. Blatnik became a well-known U.S. Congressman of
Slovenian descent. Born in August 1911 in Chisolm, Minnesota,
of immigrant parents, after graduating from Winona State
Teachers College he was elected state senator. During 1942–1945
he served in the armed forces. In 1944 he became a liaison
officer between the partisans in Slovenia and Croatia and the
allies in southern Italy. In 1946 the people elected him in Minnesota's Eighth District as a Democratic Congressman. During
his twenty-eight years in Washington he was a member of
important Congressional committees, did a lot for the Iron

Range region, advocated housing for low-income families, and championed civil rights for all Americans.[14]

Joseph Skubitz, of Slovenian descent, was the representative of the Fifth Congressional District in Kansas. Ludwig J. Andolsek, another Slovenian and native of Denver, was appointed in April 1963 by President Lyndon B. Johnson—and approved by the Congress—as the U.S. Civil Service Commissioner. As such he was in charge of over two and a half million civilian employees of the federal government.

According to Professor E. G. Gobetz, "Slovenian Americans are proud that they have given five admirals to the U.S. Navy, including Clevelander Rear Admiral William Petrovic." Ferdinand J. Chesarek, son of Slovenian immigrants, born in Calumet, Michigan, in 1914, and a graduate of West Point, is a Lieutenant General, U.S. Army. He served as an assistant of the Army Chief of Staff in the Pentagon and as supreme military representative of the United States to the United Nations. There are four more U.S. Army generals of Slovenian descent.[15]

Many Americans of Slovenian descent have also served in state legislatures, as mayors of cities, judges, district attorneys, city councilmen, and sheriffs. Traditionally, most of them tend to support the Democratic Party. They were staunch supporters of Roosevelt's New Deal. Wherever they live in large numbers, they are very interested in local politics.

In the past many Slovenians supported Socialist and other third party political candidates and, as already explained, were involved together with Louis Adamic in leftist activities and in 1948 in the campaign to elect Henry A. Wallace as the candidate of the Progressive Party to the presidency of the United States.

As for the Slovenian women, they made a substantial contribution: in politics, the labor movement, in singing and music, and especially in education. Many teach in high schools, colleges and universities. Voda Ponikvar is co-publisher of the *Tribune Press*, Chisolm, Minnesota. The women are also eminent as leaders in several fraternal organizations.

At many universities, large and small, eminent and less known, many Slovenian men teach in various fields and disciplines. Many are authors of scholarly books. A fair number are in sciences and engineering, some working in nationally known laboratories and institutes. Alexander Papesh, the architect, is the leading designer of stadiums in America. Aldo Kosuta designed the new Christian Science Center in Boston.[16]

As mentioned before, in sports and coaching the Slovenians have also made a considerable contribution.

The accordion is the most popular musical instrument among the Slovenians. The Glasbena Matica under the directorship of A. Schubel performed several of the classic operas in the Slovenian language. Unfortunately, the flourishing period of Slovenian singing and operatic activities is now over because of insufficient new members. However, this decline is less noticeable in polka music and dances. In these the Slovenians excelled, especially during the 1940s and 1960s. Cleveland has been called by many the "Polka Capital of the World." One man who helped to establish this reputation was Frank Yankovic, the "Polka King" of America. Born in 1915 in Davis, West Virginia, he grew up in Cleveland. With his polka orchestra he traveled all over the country, appeared on TV shows, and made many reecordings. His accordion interpretations of numerous Slovenian songs are being played all over America. Several of his former associates then formed their own polka bands. Yankovic's records "Just Because" and "Blue Skirt Waltz" have sold well over a million copies.[17]

If one counts several generations of Slovenians there are 500,000 to 600,000 of them. Many live, of course, under adopted Anglo-Saxon names. All of these people, regardless of names, whether they admit their ancestry or not, are now part of the mainstream of American life.

Adamic in many of his writings stressed the high price they have paid for a better future in this country. As he put it in his autobiography *Laughing in the Jungle*—a characteristic title—he and every one of his countrymen had to struggle in this jungle in order to survive and succeed. Many were swallowed up by the jungle. One of them was Adamic himself who died with a bullet in his head.

Thousands of educated and skilled Slovenians have emigrated to this country after World War II. Of all immigrants from Yugoslavia (in recent years an annual average of six thousand), approximately twenty-five percent are of Slovenian nationality. Thousands of these new arrivals grew up under Communism. Paradoxically, the young generation that was raised under it in Yugoslavia is very nationalistic. Here in America they have a variety of political organizations. Having achieved tremendous economic progress and having the highest living standard in all Yugoslavia, many Slovenians believe that their country, highly industrialized and rich in resources, should have an independent existence. From Cleveland and from other cities thousands of Slovenians travel by jet plane to Ljubljana to visit the Slovenian republic which attracts hundreds of thousands of tourists from all over the world. The leader of the Slovenian independence movement in the United States and Canada is Professor Cyril Zebot of Georgetown University in Washington, D.C. An economist, he published two books on the present and future of Slovenia. His articles appear in the issues of *Slovenska Država* (Slovenian State), a monthly printed in Toronto.

Over twenty-five percent of all Slovenians live presently in the United States and other countries of the world. They are the only South Slavs in the United States who still have daily papers. The combined circulation of their papers—several of which are printed in Cleveland—is estimated at 78,000. The daily *Ameriška Domovina—American Home* (established in 1898) still appears in Cleveland. The editors are Vinko Lipovec and Mary Debevec. It is sponsored by the American Home Publishing Company of 6117 St. Clair Avenue. The religious monthly *Ave Maria*, founded in 1909, is published by Slovenian Franciscan Fathers in Lemont, Illinois. The daily *Prosveta—Enlightenment*, founded seventy years ago, is still printed in Chicago, sponsored by the Slovene National Benefit Society with a circulation of nine thousand.[18]

In proportion to their number the Slovenians have of all South Slavs the strongest press, the largest number of members of fraternal organizations, and the highest number of parishes. While only ten percent of all American Croatians belong to their fraternal organizations, more than fifty percent of all Slovenians are members of their own ten fraternal organizations, some 250,000 in all. This is a remarkable achievement. As already explained, the achievements in American politics and the participation in the earlier Church activities (with half a dozen bishops) are also astounding.

Thousands of Slovenians were in attendance when on August 15, 1971, their chapel of Our Lady of Brezje was dedicated in the National Shrine of Immaculate Conception in Washington, D.C. The chapel was consecrated by Maksimilijan Držečnik, Bishop of Maribor, and Bishop Janez Jenko of Koper, both from Slovenia. Hundreds of pilgrims from the old country joined their countrymen in America in one of the most memorable events in the history of the American Slovenians. A beautiful souvenir book *Slovenian Chapel Dedication* printed for the occasion included among other congratulations one by the statesman Frank J. Lausche.

A recently founded Society for Slovenian Studies under the leadership of Professor Rado Lenček promotes the interest in Slovenian history and culture, organizes panels at Slavic scholarly conventions, and publishes a bulletin. The Slovenian Research Center of America is directed by Professor Giles E. Gobetz of Kent State University, Kent, Ohio.

James S. Rausch, who was born of a Slovenian mother in Albany, Minnesota, in 1928, is the most recent Catholic bishop of Slovenian descent. He was consecrated as bishop in 1973 in Collegeville, Minnesota, and is now secretary general of the Conference of the Catholic Bishops of the United States. He is proud of his Slovenian descent just as the Slovenians are proud to have acquired another bishop in America.[19]

CHAPTER 15

The Serbs and Montenegrins

BEFORE 1920 few Serbs emigrated from the little Balkan country of Serbia which in 1918 became a part of the Kingdom of Serbs, Croats, and Slovenes. A great majority of the people of ethnic Serbian origin came from the Habsburg-ruled lands, especially from Croatia proper, Dalmatia, Bosnia-Herzegovina, and southern Hungary. During the decades ending with the early 1920s the U.S. Immigration authorities counted Serbian immigrants from the Kingdom of Serbia together with Bulgarians and Montenegrins. Among the immigrants from the South Slav state (Yugoslavia) the Serbs have comprised approximately fifteen percent.

Montenegrins, closely connected with the Serbians in modern history and sharing the same Orthodox faith, joined their Croatian neighbors in southern Dalmatia on their migrations to America. Quite a few of the Montenegrins—after leaving their rocky principality under the rule of the Petrovich dynasty—settled in the region of the Bay of Kotor (Bocca in Italian) before embarking on the long trip to America. Along with the early Croatian settlers in California after 1849 and 1850 there were many Montenegrins, or, as they called themselves, *Crnogorci*. Both Croatians and Montenegrins from the "Bocca" were popularly known as *Bokelji*. In America the Orthodox Montenegrins and the Catholic Croatian Dalmatians worked together, lived in the same settlements, and were commonly known by the natives as "Slavonians."

After 1850 some Montenegrins lived in Louisiana and settled in increasing numbers in other parts of the South. Their number increased after 1860, especially in New Orleans. As many of their last names were very similar to—or exactly like—those of the Adriatic Croatians, it is difficult to distinguish between a

174

Montenegrin and a Croatian. However, every immigrant from Dalmatia, if he was of Orthodox faith, was either a Montenegrin or a Serb.[1]

The Montenegrins had for centuries an independent country. Many of them in America insisted on their own separate identity. In present-day Yugoslavia they are recognized as a distinct nationality and Montenegro is one of the six republics. Therefore, wherever necessary, we mention them as a distinct national group.

I *George Fisher, the Pioneer*

The first prominent Serbian pioneer, George Šagić-Fisher, was first known as Djordje Šagić. In America he adopted the name George Fisher. He was born in April 1795 in Stuhlweissenburg (Stolni Biograd), in the Serbian diaspora in western Hungary. As a young man he fought against the Turks with the Serbian insurgents under the leadership of George Petrović (Karageorge) whose descendants later ruled Serbia as princes and kings. After the defeat of the revolt, young George Šagić emigrated to Philadelphia, reached that city in September 1815, moved to Mississippi, and in 1818 became an American citizen. He then lived for a while in Mexico City, was expelled by the Mexican authorities for his liberal ideas, and moved to Texas. He fought with enthusiasm for Texan independence against the Mexicans. In 1832 he was in the port city of Matamoras where he tried, in 1834, to print a liberal newspaper in Spanish, *Mercurio del Puerto del Matamoras*, but was again banished by the authorities. As an ardent Mason he established lodges in Mexico, Texas, and even in Panama where he journeyed in 1851.

After Texas finally became independent in 1837, Fisher helped to organize the Supreme Court of the Republic. When Texas became an American state he served it in various capacities.

During an expedition to Yucatan, Mexico, in 1841, he met John Lloyd Stephens of New York. In his *Incidents of Travel in Yucatan* (New York, 1843), Stephens devotes a number of pages to Fisher as a "citizen of the world." In December 1851 Fisher sailed from Panama to San Francisco. For six years he served as the Secretary of the California Land Commission, then was appointed as the Justice of Peace and judge at the

County Court. In 1870 he became Greek Consul in the same city as recognition for his earlier advocacy of the Greek cause. He died in mid-June, 1873.[2]

II The Golden West

The gold rush contributed to a fast expansion of San Francisco, where among other nationalities more and more Montenegrins and Serbs found their home. Some ventured into various businesses. As thousands of new settlers were attracted to the golden West, some Montenegrins joined the Dalmatians in San Joaquin Valley, the largest valley in America. Over the decades some Serbs and Montenegrins did fairly well as ranchers and farmers but very few came close to the fabulous success and wealth of the Dalmatians who were probably more enterprising and had more sense for business than all other South Slavs.[3]

In 1857 a Slavonian-Russian-Greek-Orthodox Church and Benevolent Society was formed in San Francisco. Its president was the Russian Consul. This reflected the traditional Tsarist interest in Orthodox peoples from the Balkans. The vice-presidents and trustees were all Montenegrins except for one Serb from Belgrade. The objects of the Society were "to have a church wherein will be held on Sundays and other holy days services to the ritual of the Orthodox Eastern Church, to care for its members and bury its dead."[4] It was incorporated on September 2, 1862. Out of this society emerged the Serbian Orthodox Church in America.

On June 21, 1863, a son was born to the Montenegrin immigrant Nikola Dabovich who, with his brother Ilija, had arrived in San Francisco in 1856. He was to become the first Orthodox missionary among the Montenegrins and Serbs as Rev. Sebastian Dabovich. Many members of the Dabovich clan lived in and around Jackson, Amador County, California, which was well known during the pioneer days. A majority of the Montenegrin miners lived in this county where they prospered as miners and businessmen. With their Dalmatian friends they formed several mining companies. One of them in 1876 was called the Serbian and Slavonian Gold and Silver Mining Company.[5]

In Jackson and Sutter Creek the Croatians first got their gold and then moved out to invest it in business. The Montenegrins and Serbs stayed and later on formed a majority in these two places. Their many descendants still live there.[6]

In 1880 the First Serbian Benevolent Society was formed in San Francisco, composed mostly of Montenegrins. When in 1888 Simica, the wife of the Serbian immigrant Petar Vignjević, came from Serbia, she probably was the first Serbian woman to come as an immigrant to California. Another immigrant from that Balkan country was Sava Hajdin; he was the first president of the Serbian Orthodox Federation "Sentinel." From this developed later the Serbian National Federation, a fraternal organization.[7]

Few Serbs or Montenegrins settled in Los Angeles and the southern parts of California before the 1880s. John (Ivan) Lazarevich was one of the earliest immigrants from Montenegro. After a career as a gold miner during the 1850s he settled in the sleepy town of Los Angeles, married an American citizen, and raised a large family. It was customary for many Montenegrins to marry in their late thirties and even forties because they spent the first years in America seeking their fortune and then after some success settled down and raised families. Lazarevich retired as a wealthy businessman. Another Montenegrin, Nikola Bieladenovich, in partnership with two Dalmatians, with a capital of $60,000, established in 1863 the Illyrian Gold and Silver Mining Company in San Domingo District of Calaveras County.[8]

III *Very Reverend Sebastian Dabovich*

This offspring of fortune-seeking people turned out to be a man who never cared about material wealth. As a child he attended the Russian Orthodox Church in his home town, San Francisco; decided at an early age to be a priest, and as a young man studied at the Russian Theological Seminary of St. Petersburg, then the capital of Russia. He was ordained as a priest by Archbishop Tihon in 1887.

Several years later Tihon arrived in America as the newly appointed Metropolitan of the Russian Orthodox Church for North America. He wanted to nominate Rev. Dabovich as bishop of all Orthodox Serbs and Montenegrins, but a majority of these people refused to have their Church under the jurisdiction of the Russian Orthodox Church, preferring instead that of the Orthodox Church in Serbia. Tihon then appointed Dabovich to the lower office of an Archimandrite in charge of his Orthodox people.

After the Russian Revolution in March 1917, Tihon, having returned from America, became the Patriarch of all Russia and died in a Bolshevik prison in 1924.

Dabovich was an ascetic and pious man who denied himself all the luxuries of life, lived in poverty and humility, and worked extremely hard as the first Serbian and Montenegrin Orthodox missionary and spiritual leader in America. Though in delicate health he traveled widely and carried his faith to the most obscure places. He preached love and tolerance, ministered equally to the needs of city dwellers and those in mines, lumber camps, and farms. He established the first Serbian Orthodox Church in this country, that of St. Sava in Jackson, Amador County, California, in 1894. Tireless and devoted he led campaigns to build additional churches including one in Los Angeles. After moving to Chicago he formed a new parish consisting of two hundred families, and built a little church, parish house, and school. In recent years it has been replaced by a beautiful church. He stayed in Chicago four years and made it headquarters for the Serbian Orthodox Church in America. By decrees of the Serbian and Russian Church, he became its administrator.

He established other churches, schools, cultural and national centers for his people. For a while he also taught at the Russian Orthodox Seminary at Tenafly, New Jersey, and ordained several Serbian priests. He baptized more Serbian children than any other Serbian priest in this hemisphere. He wrote a great number of articles for papers in America and abroad. He published scholarly studies which dealt with problems of Orthodox theology, history, and culture of Montenegrins and South Slavs.

In addition, he translated Orthodox liturgy into English, edited and published a periodical called *Orthodoxy*, promoted the establishment of Orthodox churches among the Rumanians, Bulgarians, and Syrians in America. With some Anglican leaders he explored ways of encouraging unity between the Anglicans and the Orthodox. When the Balkan Wars broke out in 1912, he rushed with hundreds of Montenegrin and Serbian volunteers to participate in the war against the Turks. He served as chaplain on the front during 1912 and 1913. Returning to the United States shortly after the outbreak of World War I in 1914, he stayed here only a short while. Again he went back to Serbia to do his share. After the defeat of Serbia by the Central Powers in late 1915, Dabovich participated in the retreat of the Serbian army and civilians through Macedonia and Albania. The Allies evacuated them to the Greek island of Corfu where the Serbian government in exile spent the rest of the war. From Corfu Dabovich again made his way to America to secure aid and relief for Serbia until the end of the war in late 1918. With the coming of the peace he returned to Yugoslavia to participate in the reconstruction of the country.

When the Serbian Orthodox Diocese in the United States was finally organized, Dabovich was not named its bishop as he had hoped. Disappointed by this decision of the church authorities in Belgrade, he refused to return to his work in America. He became ill and tried in vain to recover his health in the mild climate of Boka Kotorska. His wish was to see once more the Golden Gate and his beloved San Francisco. This, however, did not happen for he died on November 30, 1940 in the ancient Serbian monastery of Žiča. This was only a few months before the war came to these regions and caused horrible destruction and suffering. Of the seventy-seven years of his life Dabovich spent fifty-seven years in his native land, the United States. He was a great patriot, a religious man, a scholar, truly the greatest missionary the Orthodox South Slavs ever had in America.[9]

After 1885 many Montenegrins and Serbs moved to Montana. In Butte, the lively and prosperous mining settlement, the Montenegrins formed a sizeable colony, and banded together almost in a military fashion, a carry-over from the homeland. When gold was discovered in faraway Alaska many Montenegrins rushed there. As mountaineers used to harsh conditions they didn't mind the cold climate; as members of the Orthodox Church they had been in contact with the Russian settlers and frequented their churches. From their homeland, which was for a long time supported by Tsarist Russia, they brought over their sympathy for everything Russian.[10]

Stephen N. Mitrovich, a native of southern Dalmatia, participated as a young man in the Montenegrin-Turkish War of 1877. In 1880 he came to Fresno, California, where over the years he established a new industry: the growing and drying of figs. In 1912, in his fifties he went with a dozen Montenegrins to Montenegro to take part in the Balkan War against the Turk, the traditional enemy of that country. He participated in campaigns, was decorated for bravery by King Nikola, and then served for a while as an interpreter for the war ministry. Barely escaping death from pneumonia, he returned to Fresno after a year and a half. His adventures and success were reported extensively in the local press and history books.[11]

Among the Orthodox immigrants from Montenegro and other parts of the Balkans few were educated. Two of these who came before the rise of the "New Immigration" deserve special attention. Michael (Mihajlo) Pupin, a peasant son from Idvor, Banat (southern Hungary), arrived penniless at Castle Garden in 1874. Later he became a well-known scholar and scientist. The other man, a finished scholar who came in 1884, was Nikola Tesla, son of an Orthodox priest from Smiljan, Croatia. Both were Serbs from the Serbian diaspora, descendants of Serbian settlers on the Austrian Military Frontier. Both Pupin and Tesla helped by their inventions in the expansion of an industrial America to which thousands of their countrymen contributed their hard work, energy, and skill. The significance and contribution of Tesla and Pupin will be discussed later.

CHAPTER 16

After 1890

THE turn of the century marked an intensification of the exodus from the Balkans by many Serbs and Montenegrins who joined in the trek to America. During the decade ending June 30, 1908, according to the U.S. statistics, most of the people classified as "Bulgarians, Servians [sic] and Montenegrins"—a total of 18,548—came to Pennsylvania. How many of these were Montenegrins and Serbs is impossible to determine since they were counted together with the Bulgarians. Over fourteen thousand of them emigrated to Illinois and almost twelve thousand to Ohio. Smaller numbers—between a thousand and three thousand—went to other mid-Western states wherever cheap and unskilled labor was needed.[1] However, a few thousand were distributed among the states of the West and South. For years, Pennsylvania attracted more Serbs than any other state. By 1910 Pennsylvania was home to some ten thousand Serbs. A great majority were natives of Croatia proper, Dalmatia, and Bosnia-Herzegovina.

By the early 1900s, there were in Chicago over three hundred Serbian families and many single men. In 1903 they established the First Serbian Beneficial Federation. In 1905 the Montenegrins formed the society "Love of Montenegro" which soon had some seventy members. In Chicago all these men worked in iron foundries, in the Carnegie steel plant, in construction, and in factories. Most of them were unskilled workers. Many steel workers lived in a settlement near the Carnegie plant.

By 1909 several Serbian and Montenegrin fraternal and burial societies had been formed. In that year the First Serbian Beneficial Federation, the First Montenegrin Federation, and the Serb Montenegrin Federation (of Butte, Montana, founded in 1906) merged into the United Serb Federation Harmony. This

181

was accomplished at a meeting in Cleveland, Ohio. However, bitter feuds arose among the membership, partly caused by political friction in the old country. The Serbian Karageorgevich dynasty in Belgrade (after the overthrow of the Obrenovich dynasty in 1903) was engaged in a serious struggle with the Montenegrin Petrovich dynasty in Cetinje. The Serbian nationalists openly propagated the absorption of Montenegro by Serbia. The diplomatic representatives of both countries in America and the immigrants of both nationalities were affected by the tense political situation growing out of the old country struggles.

The societies that belonged to "Harmony" soon split into separate original groups. Then some new benevolent separate Serbian and Montenegrin societies were organized. The better-known among them were: Serb Federation Freedom and United Federation Serb Sentinel-Harmony. Thus, the federation formed in Cleveland ceased to exist. After years of friction several Serbian societies from Cleveland, Chicago, and Los Angeles founded in Cleveland in 1920 the Serbian Beneficial Federation Unity (Srpski Narodni Savez Jedinstvo). A final union of the main Serbian fraternal groups was achieved in 1929, when they formed in Pittsburgh the Serb National Federation (Srpski Narodni Savez). On June 26, 1931 it gathered in Pittsburgh for its first convention which lasted ten days. One hundred fifty-two delegates represented some twenty-one thousand members. The S.N.F. is the largest Serbian fraternal organization today.[2]

I   The Sons of Black Mountains

Even in the first decade of the 1900s the Montenegrins were almost unknown to the American public. Emily G. Balch, writing her book on Slavic immigrants, had a hard time in collecting information about them.

Most of the Montenegrins came during the rule of Prince Nikola Petrovich who in 1910 proclaimed himself king. When in 1907 some twenty-seven thousand immigrants were counted by United States authorities as "Bulgarians, Servians and Montenegrins," more than ten percent were Montenegrins. For a small country of some 250,000 inhabitants (in 1912) several thousand emigrants a year was a considerable drain on the population. Among the "Dalmatians, Bosnians and Herzegovinians" there were undoubtedly some Montenegrins.

Montenegrin authorities did not count their emigrants, as Miss Balch found out when she visited the little capital of Cetinje in 1905. A Dalmatian emigration agent (in Austrian-controlled territory) told her that some two thousand Montenegrin emigrants were leaving their rocky mountains yearly. A considerable number were going to Alaska. In Douglas, Alaska, a Montenegrin paper was printed and was being received in the homeland.[3]

It was also known that many of these sons of the "Black Mountains" headed for Pennsylvania, probably the best known of all American states among all South Slavs. A large number went to Illinois, Ohio, and New York. Some joined the old settlements in the West. Very few women were among them. In Montenegro, no less than in Bulgaria and Macedonia, they had to stay home, raise children, and with the remittances from America improve households and estates. They were the obedient, silent, and patient guardians of the ancestral hearth-fires, the symbol of a family's continuity.

Most of the Montenegrins were leaving without passports; only fifty-four were issued in 1904 for North and South America. One of the reasons for the reluctance of the authorities to issue passports was "the recent rejection at Ellis Island of some hundred or more Montenegrins. These men borrowed the money for their tickets, and their forced return was a serious matter for them and theirs," wrote Miss Balch.

Admitting that she had "not been able to learn much about Montenegrins in America," Miss Balch recalled having run across traces "of a party of 35 of them in a Colorado mining camp, where they had left an unenviable reputation for low grade living." She saw the rough shacks, the low huts of un-mortared stone, with roofs of grass, and filled with smoke and children. And she adds:

I thought of the still frequent newspaper accounts of clashes of their bands with the Turks on the frontier, and of how close they stand to the heroic age in which the woman also labors, since the man must fight and hunt. I recalled the Homeric figure of the blind gusla player singing epic songs in the square of Cetinje (I suppose the only instance in Europe of a living epic), and I did not wonder that the Montenegrins cannot meet standards of the tenth and twentieth centuries.[4]

In Montenegro every man was considered a soldier regardless of his age. Even those in America were considered soldiers on leave, expected to return at once and fight if a war with Turkey broke out. A Serbian author discussing the emigrants in America stated: "Only in the period between 1904 and 1907, were there found in America fifteen thousand Montenegrin soldiers or men fit for military service." On the eve of the Balkan Wars—at the peak of mass immigration—at least twenty thousand Monte-negrins were in the United States, thousands of whom returned in 1912 to fight the Turks.[5]

Milovan Djilas, whose books in English dramatically describe his native Montenegro which he calls "The Land Without Justice," mentions his uncle Lazar who spent three years in America. "He learned hardly a word of English, and earned no money. As he went, so he returned. But bad luck followed him there; his wife had thrown off her yoke and had become pregnant by another man." Upon his return, to save the honor of the clan he drove her away.[6]

Of the 11,543 "Bulgarian, Servian and Montenegrin" new-comers in 1906, fully ninety-six percent were listed as unskilled laborers. Some sources indicated that about eighty percent of Montenegrin immigrants were completely illiterate because there were very few elementary schools in the homeland. In America, the Montenegrins worked as hard as their Balkan neighbors and proved themselves vigorous and diligent workers. This was testified to by several historians of immigration[7]

Parts of Montenegro formerly belonged to Turkish-held Herze-govina, where the Serbian Orthodox people were related to those in the little principality of Montenegro. Before the turn of the century some Herzegovinian Serbs left for America via Dalmatia. A typical example is that of an immigrant from the region adjacent to Montenegro who preferred to leave his homeland in order to avoid serving in the Austrian army. Austria had acquired Herzegovina after 1878. With a group of young fellow Serbs such an immigrant traveled from Kotor in Dalmatia and sailed for New York in 1906. Eventually they came to Anaconda, Montana. One of them, Maksim Slijepčević, worked for forty-seven years in a smeltery with many other South Slavs. He founded and was for years active in the society "Herzegovinian Unity." He died in 1970 at the age of eighty-four and was buried in the cemetery owned by the society.[8]

Why did many of these mountaineers leave for America? First of all, for economic reasons: poverty due to lack of land. They lived under the most primitive conditions. Their standard of living was the lowest in all the Balkans. But there were also other causes. Many men were tired of constant wars and guerrilla fighting with their Moslem neighbors. And there was the long practice of blood feuds on account of which "the inherited fear and hatred of feuding clans was stronger than fear and hatred of the enemy, the Turks."[9] Sometimes these feuds were carried over and practiced even in America, especially in the West, where the lawlessness in some mining towns encouraged it.

A considerable number of Montenegrins emigrated because they were dissatisfied with the autocratic rule of the prince and chieftains. Distant America became so attractive to the mountaineers that even a folk song stated:

> America, you dewy flower,
> everybody desires you:
> a child of two years,
> or a man of hundred years.[10] (author's translation)

This is but one of many songs that villagers of Montenegro and other Balkan countries composed in honor of America. America figures even today in Balkan folklore.

The most dramatic and most painful part of the emigrants' long journey was the departure from the Bay of Kotor. Mount Lovćen looms above it and for miles the emigrants kept their eyes on the mountain peak as they proceeded on their way. And when it disappeared in the blue distance, it is said, the sad passengers watched the clouds over Lovćen's peak and only then said the final farewell to their land.

In his new homeland the Montenegrin gradually earned the esteem of many who praised his courage and endurance. As an American observed, "there is no more sturdy stock in Europe than the Slav of Montenegro, none more ready to turn from gun to the wood axe, from blood-revenge to citizenship." Louis Adamic described him as "a tough guy, agile and hardy, fearless, impatient of restraint; and moreover, a poet and philosopher despising life when it is separated from freedom."[11]

II *The Rising Frictions*

Michael Pupin, who sailed aboard the *Westphalia* from Hamburg in 1874 for New York, observed in his autobiography: "He who has never crossed the stormy Atlantic during the month of March in the crowded steerage of an immigrant ship does not know what hardships are."[12] In years to come many of his fellow Serbs and many Montenegrins dreaded that transatlantic crossing regardless of the time of year. Most mountaineers from the Balkans and the peasants from inland regions feared the sea. In mid-April, 1912, when the *Titanic* sank, some twenty Serbs and a few Montenegrins were among those who drowned in the Atlantic.

In 1907, according to the estimates of Rev. Sebastian Dabovich, there were about 200,000 Serbians, or "certainly 150,000" in America. Of these, 50,000 settled in New England; 5,000 in the Southern states; 20,000 in the North Middle states; 20,000 in the Northeastern states; 15,000 in the Southwestern states and territories; 5,000 in Alaska, Canada, and British Columbia.[13]

Wherever Slavs labored and struggled, Serbs and Montenegrins were present. The Serbs from the Austrian and Hungarian Croatian provinces usually lived alongside their Croatian neighbors but they had their own separate parishes, fraternal organizations, and social and political societies. They also participated in many labor struggles before and after World War I. In the winter and spring of 1913–1914 among the strikers in Colorado who were finally suppressed by the infamous Ludlow Massacre, there were Serbs and Montenegrins. Some of them were returned veterans of the Balkan Wars.[14]

In those wars the Serbs and Montenegrins fought together

as allies against the Turks. However, after the defeat of Turkey in which Serbia doubled her territory by acquiring Macedonia, the old friction between the ruling dynasties of Serbia and Montenegro increased sharply. These in turn caused continuing animosities between the Serbs and Montenegrins in America. The emotional quarrels among them broke out, especially in the West even before the Balkan Wars. At the Serbian Congress in San Francisco in May 1910, a Serbian speaker denounced the King of Montenegro, Nikola Petrovich. Stephen N. Mitrovich (the pioneer of the fig industry), a great admirer of the king, angrily responded to the speaker and even carried the dispute to court. The *Serbian Herald* was obliged to retract and to publish one of the strongest apologies. However, the frictions remained and kept increasing during World War I, when the same Mitrovich, now fifty-seven years old, offered his services to the Secretary of War, but was politely rejected. His two sons then went into the service: one in the engineering corps and one as an aviator.[15]

During the Balkan Wars 1912–1913—a prelude to the great war that broke out in Europe in 1914—all Serbian papers in America favored the cause of the Balkan allies against the Turks. The ensuing Balkan turmoil led to the terrible conflagration which became World War I. A young Serbian nationalist, Gavrilo Princip, triggered it in Sarajevo on June 28, 1914, by assassinating Archduke Francis Ferdinand, the heir apparent to the Habsburg throne. His deed was applauded by all Serbian publications, a fact that caused increasing friction among the South Slavs. Two of the papers that supported the cause of Serbia and denounced the Habsburgs and Bulgarians (the Habsburg allies in the war) were the *Srbobran* (The Serbian Defender) in New York and *Srpski Glasnik* (The Serbian Messenger) in Chicago. The most active in Serbian circles was Professor Michael Pupin of Columbia University. He also served as an honorary Serbian consul. An ardent Serbian nationalist, Pupin advocated with all his power the formation of a Greater Serbia in the Balkans instead of a South Slavic federation which some Slovenians, Croatians, and a few Serbs and Montenegrins supported in the South Slav movement in the United States.

Dr. Paul Radosavljevich, a Serbian scholar from New York

City, was one of the vice-presidents of the South Slav National Council that was formed in Chicago in March 1915. Nikola Tesla, the famous inventor and scientist—also living in New York City—sent his best wishes to the Council, but stayed away from South Slavic politics. The main obstacle to the movement, which envisaged a future democratic South Slav state on the ruins of the Habsburg empire, was Pupin's Great Serbian policies and his attacks against the South Slav movement in the Serbian press.

In late 1915 and early 1916 little Montenegro was overrun by the superior Austrian forces, King Nikola was forced to leave the country, the Montenegrin army was captured, and a Montenegrin government in exile established at Neuilly, near Paris, France. American Montenegrins in considerable numbers supported the king. Before their country was overrun, two of the king's representatives came to America to recruit several thousand Montenegrins for the war in the homeland.[16]

After the defeat of Serbia by the Central Powers and the establishment of the Serbian government in exile at the Greek island of Corfu, Colonel Milan Pribičević was sent to America to recruit volunteers for the Serbian army which was prepared by the Allies for the Salonica front in the Balkans. As the Serbs openly denounced the Montenegrin government and King Nikola and announced that Montenegro would be annexed by Serbia in the future, the animosities between the diplomatic representatives and the immigrants of both countries in America steadily increased.

At the South Slav Congress in Pittsburgh during November 29–30, 1916, one of the Serbian organizations represented was the Serbian Orthodox League "Srbobran" which had some seven thousand members. Among the telegrams that were sent was one to the Serbian government at Corfu under the premiership of Nikola Pašić who—like Pupin—favored a Great Serbia rather than a South Slav state (Yugoslavia). He also insisted that the future state must be a monarchy ruled by the Karageorgevich dynasty, an idea that was supported by a majority of the American Serbs and defied by a majority of the Montenegrins who realized that this scheme would deprive their country of independence.[17]

The new Serbian minister in Washington, Ljuba Mihajlović, took a keen interest in the South Slav movement and sympathized with the idea of a South Slav state of equal partners. This caused troubles for him with Professor Pupin and Premier Pašić who kept pushing the Great Serbian designs. In a note to Secretary of State Lansing in March 1917, Mihajlović pointed out that "the noble expressions of President Wilson" had caused outbursts against the Habsburgs in Zagreb, the Croatian capital. With the minister's help the Serbian military mission under Pribičević was able to send by June 1917 the first two thousand volunteers for the Serbian army at Corfu.[18]

The American Montenegrins who opposed annexation of Montenegro by Serbia complained in their publications that they were hampered in their activities by the intrigues of the "Great-Serbian agents." The paper *Crnogorski Glasnik* (Montenegrin Messenger) in Detroit under the heading "Yugoslavia or Greater Serbia" attacked "those who appointed themselves as creators of a future Yugoslavia and who are ignoring the rights of the people." The Montenegrins repudiated the idea that the "Kingdom of Serbia become an unlimited master of all South Slavs" among whom, the *Messenger* wrote, the Croatians, Slovenians, and Montenegrins have a great past and deserve "the right to independence and self-government." Both dynasties, they argued, the Serbian as well as the Montenegrin, should be removed and "leave it to the people to elect their leaders as it is done in the United States." Instead of a Great Serbian monarchy they advocated a "South Slavic Republic."[19]

This was basically the stand of all opponents of a Yugoslav monarchy. The Serbian agent Ivanović stressed in his reports to the Serbian government "the republican spirit" among the American Montenegrins. He and other Serbian agents falsely accused these Montenegrins of being pro-German agents and by his intrigues caused the arrest of some of them by American authorities.[20]

The visiting Serbian minister from Paris, Dr. M. Vesnić, the recently arrived members of the Serbian military mission, and the Serbian diplomatic representatives in Washington sat in the galleries of Congress when on January 8, 1918 President Wilson read his Fourteen Points. Point XI demanded restoration of occupied Serbia and Montenegro; Serbia should also be awarded free access to the Adriatic Sea. Point X required only autonomy for the Slav peoples of the Habsburg Empire, not complete independence, a fact that dismayed Vesnić and other South Slavs in America.[21]

On May 6, 1918, in Rome, King Nikola of Montenegro handed the U.S. Ambassador a document expressing the aspirations of his country. The old king expressed his hope in America, "the champion of liberty and Democracy." Fearing the Serbian designs aimed at destruction of an independent Montenegro, he wanted to send his minister to Washington. In America, a group under the name of the Montenegrin Committee for National Unification favored a union with Serbia and denounced the king's demands for restoration of Montenegro which even President Wilson favored by including it in his Point XI. This committee sent in August 1918 a Memorandum from New York signed by 126 American Montenegrins. It demanded a South Slav state and repudiated King Nikola's government in Neuilly, France.

On June 24, 1918, U.S. Secretary of State Lansing addressed a statement to the Serbian ambassador that "the position of the United States Government is that all branches of the Slav race should be completely free from German and Austrian rule." This negated the Fourteen Points regarding preservation of Austria-Hungary and opened the way for creation of a South Slav state.[22]

On July 4, 1918, the leaders of the South Slav movement along with the Serbian diplomats and delegates of many organizations were guests of President Wilson in Washington. Thousands of people, dressed in national costumes, marched in the parade; at the head of their long column was a group in Serbian military uniform. This event was widely publicized afterward by the American and South Slav press.

What was not publicized was the growing opposition to a union with Serbia. The ambassadors of the United States in both Paris and Rome sent repeated messages to the State Department that the Montenegrin government in exile rejected any annexation of Montenegro by Serbia.[23]

When, at the end of 1918, the war ended Italian and Serbian troops occupied the Adriatic regions and the former Habsburg lands. The Kingdom of the Serbs, Croats, and Slovenes, pro-claimed on December 1, 1918 in Belgrade, annexed Montenegro. This was a victory of the pro-monarchist Great Serbian group. The South Slav state was established because President Wilson had agreed to it. This presented a violation of his own principles of self-determination. This victory for Pupin and his group sowed the seeds of discord which led to a permanent animosity between the American Serbs and the rest of the South Slavs in America.

CHAPTER 17

After 1918

T HE Kingdom of Serbs, Croats and Slovenes under the Karageorgevich dynasty annexed Macedonia, Montenegro, and the former Habsburg provinces. Many loyal Montenegrins mourned the loss of their state. Because of the new political situation in the homeland the divisions between the American Serbs on one side and the Montenegrins, Macedonians, and Croatians on the other side remained permanent. In fact, in later years the feuds between them intensified.

I The Role of the Newspapers

These feuds were vividly reflected in the press over the decades. The Serbs published several papers, some Socialist. A Yugoslav League of Independent Socialists existed in San Francisco as early as 1909. It published *Volja* (The Will) in both Latin and Cyrillic script. Some Serbian papers were printed exclusively in Cyrillic.[1]

As late as 1939 there were still seven Serbian papers of which one of the oldest was the weekly *Radnička Borba* (Workers' Struggle) in Cleveland, an organ of the South Slavic branch of the Socialist Labor Party. The paper also maintained for many years a bookstore where pamphlets, books, and an almanac were sold. The Serbian Socialists translated many works of the leading Socialist theoreticians into Serbian and sold them in inexpensive editions.

There were many pioneer journalists among the Serbians. One who became a well-known Serbian publisher, journalist, and bookstore owner in Chicago was John R. Palandech. He had arrived in 1887 at the age of 13. The *San Francisco Chronicle* of July 16, 1925, remarked of him that he was "the Northcliffe of the foreign language newspapers." Another was a woman, Leposava Djordjević, who also was an active publisher in California.[2] The main characteristic of the Serbian press was its intense nationalistic line. After 1918 most of these papers supported the centralistic policies of the Belgrade government and suppression of the non-Serbian peoples in Yugoslavia.

II *The Serbian Orthodox Church*

Rev. Sebastian Dabović, already mentioned, laid a strong foundation for the Serbian Orthodox Church in America. The church organization was to include both Serbian and Montenegrin immigrants. From its very beginning in 1894, this church was confronted by the attempts of the Russian Orthodox Bishop for North America to control it. In proportion to their numbers the Serbs and Montenegrins succeeded in establishing a fairly large number of churches. As the Serbian Orthodox Church is a national church it became in America the most important institution for the preservation of their ethnic identity.

By 1916 there were twenty-eight Serbian parishes of whom five were without pastors. Most of the parishioners were natives of the Habsburg provinces and from Montenegro. The U.S. Bureau of Census in 1916 offered data for only twelve Serbian parishes with a membership of 14,301, ten churches, and eight Sunday schools with 653 pupils.[3]

Because the religion of the ruling people and of the dynasty of the new South Slav state was Orthodox, the Serbian Orthodox Church became a privileged church. It was headed by a patriarch whose see was in Belgrade and who closely collaborated with the government. In 1921 with the support from Belgrade the Serbian Orthodox Diocese of the United States and Canada was established under the jurisdiction of the Serbian Orthodox Church. The constitution of the diocese stated that the diocese considered itself "canonically as an organic part of the Serbian Orthodox Church in Yugoslavia and enjoys the benefits which derive therefrom." It also stated that the diocese should have full administrative freedom in accordance with the laws of the United States and Canada. Any possible changes in the future of the diocese shall depend on a final approval by the patriarch in Belgrade.[4]

During the 1920s and 1930s the diocese grew and according to one source it had some thirty-five churches with about one hundred thousand members. Some eight Serbian churches in America are dedicated to their national saint, St. Sava; one of them is the beautiful cathedral in Milwaukee. Another cathedral is St. Steven's in Alhambra, California. Their churches are located in all major Serbian settlements.

Millions of dollars have been spent for these churches and other buildings. The St. Sava Monastery and the see of the diocese are located in Libertyville, Illinois. The Serbian churches are among the most imposing church edifices in America. The most beautiful are the Church Ravanica in Detroit and St. Sava Cathedral in Milwaukee. The latter was built largely of imported Italian marble in classical Byzantine style which is characteristic of all Serbian and Bulgarian churches; it was opened in November 1957. The impressive St. Sava Church in Parma, Ohio—a suburb of Cleveland—was dedicated in early 1967. It cost more than $600,000.[5]

Michael Pupin, the American Serbian scholar, refers in his autobiography to "Slavs with Americanization grafted upon them." He himself remained a Serbian nationalist to the end of his life. While among several Slavic ethnic groups the Roman Catholic Church was very eager to "Americanize" the immigrants, this was not so in the Serbian Orthodox Church. On the contrary, it helped the Serbs to retain their national identity. The Church and the people are tightly knit together.

III Nationalism

On the whole, the Serbs are a proud people. Serbian national consciousness was highly developed when they came to America. They were "essentially people of the soil . . . grubbers with toil-eager hands." A peasant from Shumadia region south of Belgrade is "a grand, proud character . . . a free tiller of the soil for over a century." He is "at once democratic and aristocratic, always civilized, sometimes remote. He is unfailingly polite and hospitable, even when he does not entirely accept or trust you."[6]

Hospitality is part of their tradition. As Pupin stressed,

tradition was "spiritual food" to his fellow Serbs. It nourished and sustained them in their hardships and belief that "the noblest thing in this world is the struggle for right, justice and freedom."[7] Their traditions, the long struggle against the Turks, and the character of their Church made Serbs fiercely patriotic and nationalistic. Konrad Bercovici in his book on the Balkans calls Serbs "the most chauvinistic people in Europe."[8] This of course is debatable.

Inevitably the nationalism of the Serbian immigrants in America was bolstered by the government in Belgrade through its diplomatic representatives and through the Serbian Orthodox hierarchy. But at the same time it was also influenced by events in the old country. Nationalism was on the rise among other South Slavs. During the decades after 1920 the new arrivals were generally more nationalistic than earlier immigrants.

Like the rest of the South Slavs, the Serbs, too, got involved in the radical movements. This trend reached its culmination in the activities during World War II. A majority of the American Serbs, however, were during the royal dictatorship in Yugoslavia and during 1941–1945 loyal royalists. The Serbian press denounced the writings of Louis Adamic which were critical of King Alexander's rule. As Adamic himself commented, he received threatening calls on many occasions and after he got involved in anti-monarchist activities during the war he had reason to fear for his life. In the old country the ruling Serbian class regarded Slovenia, Croatia, and Montenegro as conquered provinces and Macedonia simply as Southern Serbia. They did not even acknowledge the existence of the Macedonians, while the Bulgarians from Bulgaria were looked upon as outright enemies of the Serbian people. This attitude was carried over to the immigrant colonies in the United States. The animosities continued even among the leftist organizations belonging to the several branches of the South Slavs.

IV *World War II*

On the eve of World War II a great many Serbs were prospering in industry, in various professions, and in farming. Along with the Slovenians and Croatians, the Serbs and Montenegrins were successful in California's San Joaquin Valley. Some were fairly wealthy truck farmers. Some worked for the wealthy Dalmatians. All over the country they were well established, and their children were attending colleges. In politics they supported Franklin D. Roosevelt's New Deal.

Several thousand returned to the old country between 1920 and 1939. Some went back without any money, and more single men returned than families. But a great majority stayed in America and in late 1939 looked with apprehension on the developments in the homeland. A great deal of suffering was caused when in April 1941 Belgrade was bombed by Germans and the whole country was overrun by them as well as by Bulgarians and Hungarians. The fate of their homeland and their people caused great anxieties to the American Serbs.

The establishment of a Croatian state, which included Bosnia-Herzegovina, dwelling place of many Serbs, infuriated their compatriots abroad. Hungarians occupied Bačka and Banat where some American Serbs, including Pupin, had been born. Serbia proper was occupied by the Germans. The Bulgarians occupied Macedonia and parts of eastern Serbia. Albania (under Italian protectorship) annexed Kossovo and the Metohija regions. On July 12, 1941—with Italian assistance—a group of Montenegrin nationalists in Cetinje proclaimed an independent Kingdom of Montenegro. It was short-lived because a few days later a Communist uprising against the Italians and the nationalists suppressed the Montenegrin independence. But this proclamation of independence revived again the old struggles between the Montenegrins and Serbs in the United States.[9]

In Serbia and Bosnia a Serbian army colonel who did not, like most of the highest officers and troops, surrender to the Germans, Draža Mihajlović, organized nationalist armed detachments called Chetniks. They started to massacre Croatian Catholics and Moslems. Then the Croatians retaliated and the old hatreds between the Croatians and the Serbs, between Serbs and Bulgarians, Serbs and Albanians, and Serbs and Hungarians erupted in mutual killings. Thousands of combatants and civilians on all sides fell victim to wholesale Balkan butchery. These events reported through the American media (and often distorted) caused an immense flare-up of hostilities among the

American Serbs on one side and Croatians and Macedonians on the other.

When, after the German attack on the Soviet Union (June 1941), the Communist partisans under Josip Broz Tito started their armed struggle against all foreign troops as well as against the anti-Communist forces in Croatia, Montenegro and Macedonia, the signal was given to all American South Slavic leftists, Communists, and Communist-front activists to get into action. In these endeavors the American Serbs contributed their share. Like the other South Slavs, thousands of American Serbs were alarmed and confused by the events in the old country.

After the United States entered the war in December 1941, it actively supported the royal Yugoslav government in exile in London under young King Peter who came to this country for a short visit and was welcomed by the leading Serbs. His ambassador in Washington, Konstantin Fotich, along with several Serbian organizations and papers like *Srbobran*, denounced all Croatians as destroyers of Yugoslavia and enemies of the Serbian people. Until late 1943, the U.S. government supported Draža Mihajlović (leader of the Chetniks) and his guerrilla action in the homeland. By that time there was a strong pro-Tito movement in America to which some Serbian groups and individuals also switched their support.

Thousands of American Serbs and Montenegrins joined the U.S. armed forces. Sergeant George W. Mirich was a "one-man army" during the Attu campaign in 1943. Singlehanded he cleaned out with machine gun and grenades seven Japanese pillboxes defending a strategic pass. He was awarded the Distinguished Service Cross. In 1944 Lieutenant Mitchell Page (Serbian name: Milan Pejić) of the Marines was awarded the Congressional Medal of Honor for his heroic action on Guadalcanal. These are but a few examples of heroism. At the same time thousands of Serbs on the home front did their share in essential industries.[10]

Captain George S. Wuchinich of Ridgeway, Pennsylvania, son of Serbian immigrants, was attached to the Office of Strategic Services (predecessor of C.I.A.) in 1942. He was parachuted to Tito's partisans in occupied Slovenia in November 1943 and remained there until July 1944. In November 1944 he was given the Distinguished Service Cross "for extraordinary heroism" for his mission. Ironically, this same man who later became very active in the American Slav Congress, a pro-Soviet and Communist front organization, was subject to hearings in Washington and denounced after the war as a Communist stooge. His case is typical and reveals the whole dilemma of many Serbs during and after World War II.[11]

As already discussed, under the influence of the All-Slav Committee in Moscow, the American Slav Congress was established in late 1941 as a pro-Soviet movement. The Serbian representatives participated in the preliminary discussions, the actual founding, and its several congresses. The Serbian Vidovdan Congress and Serbian National Federation became a part of the American Slav Congress and its president, Zarko M. Nuncick, became one of its national officers. After the war the Serbian Vidovdan Congress was cited by U.S. authorities as "subversive and Communist." The American Serbian Committee for Relief of War Orphans in Yugoslavia was also labeled a Communist-front organization. The same label was attached to the Serbian Progressive Club Karageorge in Gary, Indiana. and to the Serbian Fraternal Society, an affiliate of the International Workers Order.[12] Six months after its formation (April 1942) the American Slav Congress denounced Draža Mihajlović and his movement in Yugoslavia and reiterated its support for Tito.

However, the Serbian National Federation continued its support for Mihajlović and King Peter in whose government in exile Mihajlović served as minister of defense and commander of all royal armed forces. The organ of the Serbian National Federation was the paper *Srbobran*. This was the publication that Adamic had in mind when he wrote in his wartime book *A Nation of Nations*: "In Pittsburgh a Serbian language paper pursues a course I can describe only as Balkan medievalism gone corrupt in the service of dark forces in America and abroad." The inclusive United Committee of South Slavic Americans formed in 1943 was joined also by some Serbian representatives. The Serbian Vidovdan Congress joined Adamic's United Committee. It, too, was later denounced by United States authorities as a Communist-front organization. Adamic openly advocated a future Soviet Balkan Federation, in which

Serbia would be one of the republics. This stand and his opposition to King Peter made Adamic one of the most hated men among the American Serbs.

They were even more infuriated when in 1943 he published his book *My Native Land* and denounced the "pan-Serbian propaganda" in the United States, naming all the leading diplomats and their collaborators who waged anti-Croatian campaigns of slander. In a chapter "The Yugoslav Nightmare Invades America" Adamic described the details, including the fact that the Serbian National Federation, its daily *Srbobran*, and Bishop Dyonisie of the Serbian Orthodox Church in America were closely connected with and paid by Fotich, King Peter's ambassador to Washington. Stoyan Pribichevich, writer and journalist, working for *Fortune* magazine, collaborated with Adamic in trying to calm down the tensions. According to Adamic, Nikola Tesla, the famous inventor—a Serb born in Croatia—before his death in January 1943 "protested against the activities of the Yugoslav legation's stooge organization, the Serbian National Defense, which had presumed to make him its honorary president."[13]

On January 1, 1944, the executive board of the Serbian National Federation, as the largest Serbian fraternal organization with some twenty-three thousand members, issued a resolution in Pittsburgh. It announced its withdrawal from the American Slav Congress and condemned its "sinister influences" by which Adamic and others tried "to put across their progressive, foreign views."[14]

One Serbian paper that opposed the nationalistic press campaign was *Slobodna Reč* (Free Word). Its editorial offices were at 1916 East Street, Pittsburgh. In later investigations it was branded as a Communist paper which "has consistently indicated to the American Serbians that only the Communist Party has been constantly right" and has steadily attacked the American domestic and foreign policies. Among its editors were several men who after the war returned to Yugoslavia and became high officials in Belgrade. One of them was Stefan Dedijer, a brother of Vladimir Dedijer, one of Tito's close friends.[15] The paper supported the policies of the American Slav Congress.

This Congress, the United Committee of South Slavic Americans, and other elements supported by the U.S. official policy of aiding Tito's National Liberation Front, saw their goals realized when Yugoslavia became a Communist-ruled federal republic. Serbia became one of the six republics, Montenegro was another, and monarchy was abolished.

The "Yugoslav nightmare" slowly disappeared in America. Its aftermath was still felt until the early 1950s. By this time thousands of Serbian displaced persons, many former officers and soldiers who spent four years in German prisoner-of-war and concentration camps, came to this country to start new lives. They had refused to return to a Communist-dominated homeland.

By late 1947 among many other Slavic organizations which denounced the American Slav Congress and expressed their support of the American domestic and foreign policy, was the American Serbian Council. It consisted of the Serbian National Federation, Serbian National Defense, and several others.[16] When in 1948 Stalin and the Cominform broke off relations with Tito, a majority of the South Slavic leftists took a pro-Cominform stand. One of them was the former war hero, Captain George S. Wuchinich who was among Tito's partisans in 1943–1944.

V   The Serbian Contribution

The great inventor Nikola Tesla was born on July 10, 1856, in the village of Smiljan, near Gospić, district of Lika in a part of Croatia that formed the Austrian Military Frontier. His father was an Orthodox priest. Throughout his life Tesla always declared himself a Serbian born in Croatia. After completing gymnasium (high school) in Karlovac and studies in electrical engineering at the Universities of Graz and Prague, he worked for a while in Budapest and Paris. He arrived in New York a penniless immigrant in mid-1884.

He had been fascinated by electricity from childhood and his mind was filled with fantastic ideas. Thomas Edison gave him a job immediately, but they soon parted, because Edison could not be made to recognize the importance of alternating current. In 1887, with the backing of some financiers, the Tesla

Electric Company was founded. In the same year Tesla registered several important inventions with the U.S. Patent Office.
He made it possible to deliver electricity inexpensively from
powerhouses over vast distances.[17]

Tesla, who never married, achieved international fame. His
inventions changed the life of America. However, his brilliant
career was stormy and he was often driven to despair. He
was as talented as he was impractical and he lacked business
sense. His complex personality caused him to lose friends and
the support of many of his business associates. In a competitive
society his inborn Balkan peasant honesty could not compete
with the shrewd tycoons by whom he was surrounded. In 1888
and 1889 he received a million dollars from George Westinghouse in Pennsylvania for his inventions. In a typical grand
gesture he saved Westinghouse from financial ruin by giving
up millions of dollars in royalties. And then they parted.

Tesla patented a system of electrical transmission of power,
an electromagnetic motor, a system of electrical distribution, a
dynamo electric machine, a regulation system for alternating
current motors, a method of operating arc lamps, an induction
motor that moved everything on wheels. He discovered the
nature of cosmic rays. He produced the first bolt of man-made
lightning. He harnessed Niagara Falls. His revolutionary but
practical inventions staggered the American mind. He was hailed
in all newspapers, magazines, and scientific journals. The *Electrical Experimenter* stated "Nikola Tesla ... is conceded to be
the greatest inventor of all time." He lectured in America and
Europe. He had more inventions (some seven hundred) to his
credit than any other man in history. His discoveries were
described as "having no equals in the annals of the world."[18]

According to some sources he refused the Nobel Prize for
all these discoveries. According to others he was never offered
it. Some people considered him a modest man, "to whom money
and public renown had no meaning ... a sort of scientific
saint, an inspired poet-physicist." Some who knew him compared him to Leonardo da Vinci, and called him "the greatest
man of the Industrial Era." An eccentric, a dreamer, and a
mystic, he was pirated and eventually ignored.

Mark Twain and many other prominent Americans were his

friends. In later years he befriended Ivan Meštrović who made a bust of Tesla for the homeland. America, which had benefited enormously from Tesla's genius, refused for a long time to recognize his worth. A perfect gentleman, a humanitarian, and a citizen of the world, Tesla was truly an unusual personality. Perhaps this explains why he would not involve himself in his old country's politics.

In the words of another famous immigrant, David Sarnoff, "Tesla was a highly imaginative and original thinker, and many of his ideas were far ahead of the technical resources of his day." The present modern apparatus of high-voltage electrical engineering "is based on his early triumphs with the alternating current motor.... In his later years, many of his ideas verged upon the fantastic, even by the standards of the present."[19]

In his autobiography Ivan Meštrović writes about Tesla: "Once after we had supper, he talked to me extensively about his inventions as well as about the fact that Edison and Marconi, and in the end Pupin too, stole his inventions. Here he looked as a hero from Greek dramas."[20]

Ignored and forgotten by the public except for occasional interviews by the press, Tesla lived on an honorary pension of $7,000 a year granted by the government in Belgrade. He died at the age of 87 on January 7, 1943, in the Hotel New Yorker. The posthumous tributes and new books about him claim that radar, high-frequency currents, wireless, every power-house, every dynamo, every vehicle that uses his coils are a lasting monument to him. This greatest contributor among Serbs—and among all Slavs—remained ignored by the American people and by scientists.

Finally in the U.S. Bicentennial year 1976 the long-overdue tribute to him was awarded. On July 23, on Goat Island of the Niagara Frontier State Park, a monument of Tesla was unveiled. The site overlooks the scene of his greatest triumph, the power plant at the foot of the Horseshoe Falls which harnessed Niagara Falls in 1895.

The statue is a nine-foot bronze sculpture by the Croatian artist Frane Kršinić. It is a gift of the Yugoslav government and a delegation from the old country was present at the ceremonies. Assisting in this tribute to Tesla were officials of the

Niagara Mohawk Power Company and the Westinghouse Electric Corporation, both of which played a significant role in the scientist's life.

Michael Pupin (1855–1935) was a native of Idvor, Banat, in southern Hungary, which now belongs to Yugoslavia. Son of Serbian peasants, he had talent and the ambition to educate himself. He came to New York in 1874 alone from Germany and after a long struggle was graduated from Columbia University in 1883. After more studies in Cambridge, England, and in Germany, he returned to the United States to become a distinguished teacher at Columbia University, researcher, and inventor. As an electronics engineer of high quality, Pupin, according to Sarnoff, greatly extended the range of long-distance telephone by the invention of the telephone repeater ("Pupin coil"). He was "one of the first to recognize the importance of Marconi's experiments with wireless."[21]

At the Peace Conference at Paris in 1919, he was a member of the American delegation and was also honored by the Yugoslav government for his services to the Serbian cause. In the United States he served till 1922 on the National Advisory Committee for Aeronautics and was a friend of President Wilson. In 1923 Charles Scribner published Pupin's autobiography for which he won the Pulitzer Prize.[22]

Tesla's nephew and student Nikola Terbo (Trbojević) was an inventor who contributed many patents important to the automobile industry. It is interesting that a new generation of Serbian scientists is participating in projects envisioned by Tesla many years ago. Several national magazines reported in 1972 that seven Serbian scientists were working in the Apollo space program.

In the arts, the sculptor John David Brcin (born in 1899 in Gračac, Lika) resembled Meštrović in his style of execution. He arrived in the U.S. in 1912 and by 1926 held his first exhibit at the Chicago Art Institute. Among his many fine busts are portraits of Mark Twain, Presidents Lincoln and Woodrow Wilson. Dudley Craft, the art critic, stated that Brcin's works "have an American realism, a Slavonic decorativeness and a Greek beauty."[23]

Vuk Vucinich was a painter and sculptor. Savo Radulovich, a

native of Montenegro, served during World War II in General Mark Clark's army and drew many scenes from the battlefront. Many of his drawings appeared in *Life* and other magazines.

Among the noted singers were Danica Ilić, a soprano from Belgrade who appeared at the Metropolitan Opera, and Mia Novich (Bosiljka Mijanović), born of Serbian parents in Chicago. Novich, a dramatic soprano, has given concerts in many large cities of this continent.

Dr. Paul Radosavljevich, professor and chairman of the Department of Experimental Education, New York University, was also the author of the pioneering work in Slavic Studies *Who are the Slavs?* (Boston, 1910). The Serbians have contributed to all areas of humanities and natural sciences. The list is long and it includes dozens of men and women teaching at the universities and working in institutes and laboratories all over the country. Among the historians is Michael B. Petrovich (a native of Cleveland), a writer and translator of several works of Djilas.

Stoyan Pribichevich, of a well-known Serbian family from Croatia, settled in America in 1935. He eventually joined *Time* and *Fortune* magazines, worked as a war correspondent, and wrote several books on the Balkans. Mladin Zarubica, whose parents came from Montenegro, was a lieutenant in the U.S. Navy during 1941–1945, and commanded a PT boat in the Pacific. During the 1960s he published several successful novels. William Jovanovich, born in Colorado, had a Montenegrin father and a Polish mother. He, too, spent four war years in the U.S. Navy. In 1947 he joined Harcourt, Brace and Co., as a salesman. At the age of thirty-four he became the president of this big publishing company which now includes his name. In 1964 he published his *Now, Barabbas* (Harper).

The last wife of Frank Lloyd Wright, America's greatest architect, was Olga J. Lazovich, beautiful daughter of a Montenegrin Supreme Court Justice. Wright called her Olgivanna. A devoted wife from 1927 until her husband's death in 1959, she was "a refuge to which Wright could fly when all the world seemed to be against him."[24]

A most successful post-World War II immigrant is Milan Panić, now in his late forties. He came in 1955. He is the

Chairman of the International Chemical and Nuclear Corporation with headquarters in Pasadena, California. It is a healthcare complex with some 5,000 employees and 1,000 salesmen. Their sales in 1971 amounted to $136 million. Panić's yearly salary is $300,000.[25]

Among those holding important federal jobs was Donald R. Perry (Dragoslav Perušić), who was assistant commissioner of the Immigration and Naturalization Service, Department of Justice. In October 1969 Helen Delich Bently (of Serbian origin), a long-time newspaper woman for the Baltimore *Sun*, was appointed Chairman of the Federal Maritime Commission. Madam Commissioner stated on one occasion: "This is a great nation, this America of ours. It is not Utopia, it is the closest approach to it that man has achieved throughout the whole history of his existence." This message of a remarkable woman expresses the South Slavic achievement in America.[26]

VI *The Split in the Church*

The most important problem the Serbians face today is still the split within their Orthodox Church in America. By 1961 there were some seventy-three Serbian churches with 130,000 members.[27] Some sources put the membership as high as 250,000, while the *World Almanac and Book of Facts* for 1967 lists some 200,000 Serbian Orthodox.

Two bishops have been involved in the struggle between the mother church in Yugoslavia and the American-Canadian Serbian Orthodox Diocese: Bishop Iriney and Bishop Dionysius (Dionizije). Bishop Iriney, the vicar bishop, claims the dictatorial government of Yugoslavia has turned the Serbian Orthodox Church in Belgrade into a puppet of the state. He regards the year 1958 as the date when the Serbian Patriarch Gherman and his church organization were overcome by the Tito government. Iriney explained his position on several occasions in *The Diocesan Observer*, a national periodical of the church in Libertyville, Illinois, whose editor-in-chief is Milan Karlo. The struggle between the church in the old country and in America resulted in a division between the faithful in the United States and Canada. The conflict broke out into the open when Bishop Dionysius issued a statement in June 1962 demanding that the diocese become independent of the mother church in Belgrade. Some of the clergy opposed this move. Then Bishop Dionysius stated that the diocese still would remain a canonical part of the Serbian Orthodox Church whose head is Patriarch Gherman. This, however, did not end the controversy that split the Serbian Church wide open all across the country. According to Bishop Iriney, Bishop Dionysius was slandered and discredited by the Communists in an attempt to defrock him—because since 1944 the bishop had consistently opposed the regime in Belgrade and sent letters to the U.S. government opposing its recognition of Tito's government. Official newspapers in Yugoslavia declared Bishop Dionysius an enemy of the people.

Since the summer of 1963 Bishop Dionysius has been involved "in a cruel and costly court battle with the Church in Belgrade and another faction of Serbian Orthodox in Southern California which refuses to recognize the Illinois-based Diocese." Headquarters in Libertyville severed all ties with the mother church in Yugoslavia.[28]

Generally most of the old and American-born Serbs recognized the authority of the patriarch in Belgrade. Most of the postwar immigrants reject his authority and side with the separate diocese in Libertyville. One of the most violent and emotional struggles—which made occasional headlines—existed for years in St. Sava Church, Cleveland, Ohio. The dispute was finally settled out of court in March 1975 when members loyal to the mother church retained possession of the beautiful church, now called a cathedral, at Broadview Road in Parma, a Cleveland suburb. After several outbreaks of physical violence the church was padlocked by authorities. The members loyal to Bishop Dionysius, who was ousted by the church in Belgrade, and consisting mostly of post-World War II immigrants, were given property at West Wallings Road, Broadview Heights. Similar partitions took place in other cities. Those who formed separate parishes claimed that "the main issues are the attempt on the part of the Communist Party of Yugoslavia to dominate the religious life of the Serbian Orthodox Church members in America and Canada and to control their parish properties." Judging from the looks of the beautiful St. Sava in Parma, the church buildings alone are quite valuable.[29]

In a way the struggle between the two factions of the Serbian Church reflects the gap between two generations. The problem also involves nationalism. Most of the opponents of the patriarch in Belgrade are ardent nationalists and monarchists. They are not ready to quit their old loyalties. They are staunch anti-Communists. They also accuse Patriarch Gherman of capitulating to the regime in Belgrade by agreeing to establishment of a separate Macedonian Church in Yugoslavia. When Peter Karageorgevich, the last king of Yugoslavia, died in November 1970 in a Los Angeles hospital at the age of 47, his passing was mourned by his supporters in America. Before his death he worked in New York City.

The Serbian Orthodox Church finally split into three dioceses. The dispute reached even the U.S. Supreme Court. On June 21, 1976 it ruled that civil courts should not interfere in internal church disputes. The 7–2 ruling apparently ended the thirteen-year church fight over control of the Serbian Orthodox Church in America. The Supreme Court overturned a ruling of the Illinois Supreme Court to which the independent diocese centered in Libertyville, Illinois, had appealed. The decision stated that "the Yugoslav based church could govern its own affairs in America, and that churches which have their own hierarchy of rulers should not seek to settle disputes in the court." The justices said the Illinois court's intervention had violated the constitutional guarantee of religious freedom. The decision puts an end to litigation between factions of the Serbian church in the United States (ruled by the patriarch) and the efforts of a deposed bishop to be restored to leadership (Dionysius Milivojević).

The members of the patriarch-ruled church were pleased with the Supreme Court decision. Reverend Branko Skaljac, the pastor of St. Sava cathedral in Parma, said that it was the proper solution of the problem. Reverend George Majeric, pastor of St. Sava Church in Broadview Heights could not be reached for comment.[30]

Besides the division within their own church, there is friction between the Serbs on one side and the Bulgarians and Croatians on the other. There is less friction between the American-born Serbs and the rest of the South Slavs. In many settlements hardly any contact occurs between the Serbs and Croatians and Bulgarians. The Serbian, Croatian, and Macedonian papers are engaged in constant disputes and attacks and continue to perpetuate feuds from the old country.

Wynar's *Directory* of ethnic newspapers lists six Serbian papers with a circulation of thirty-two thousand. Both figures are probably much too low. The most widely read is *Amerikanski Srbobran—The American Serb Defender*, founded in 1929 and printed in Pittsburgh. Sponsored by the Serb National Foundation, it appears three times a week with a circulation of some ten thousand. Its purpose is "to keep alive traditions and ideals of the Serbian people and to promote hundred percent Americanism." The weekly *Sloboda—Liberty*, founded in 1952 in Chicago, is the organ of the Serbian National Defense Council of America. Its circulation is over two thousand.

Srpska Borba—The Serbian Struggle, a weekly formed in 1946 in Chicago—one of the major centers of the postwar immigrants— is printed in Serbian and English and has a circulation of some sixteen thousand. Its editor is Dr. Slobodan Draskovich, well known among the Serbian activists. The paper supports the Serbian Cultural Club St. Sava which was originally organized in Belgrade during the 1930s. Many of its members are Serbian intellectuals, supporters of the royalist and Chetnik movement. The club is in fact a Pan-Serbian movement which held its twentieth congress in May 1971.

The organ of the Serbian Chetniks is *Serbia*, founded in 1960 in Gary, Indiana, as a bi-monthly. It is the "Voice of Serbian Freedom Fighters," and is edited by Momchilo Djujich, a Chetnik leader. The known circulation was 3,500. *Srpske Novine* of Chicago-Gary is another nationalistic paper. The oldest Serbian newspapers are *Radnička Borba* of Cleveland (Socialist, founded in 1907) and *Jugoslavenski Amerièki Glasnik —Yugoslav American Herald*, appearing in California since 1909. These two differ in tone from the before-mentioned papers.

The *Diocesan Observer* and *Eparhijski Glasnik* are published by the Serbian Orthodox Diocese in Libertyville, Illinois. These are religious publications and organs of the diocese. There have been other papers, periodicals, bulletins, most of which had a short existence. On the whole, the press remains an important factor in the Serbian political activities. Many newcomers read the newspapers and magazines printed in the homeland which are shipped by air freight and can be purchased in many places all over the country.[31]

America has maintained close relations with the government of Yugoslavia. It has given it economic and military aid in excess of four billion dollars and has exchanged visits by highest dignitaries. Both Presidents Richard Nixon and Gerald Ford visited Yugoslavia. Twice President Tito was an official guest in this country. On both occasions Serbian demonstrators protested against his visit. In November 1971, Bishop Iriney led the protestors on their march and demonstration in Washington, D.C. The bishop still claims that Tito and his Communist regime have split the Serbian Orthodox Church in America.

The Yugoslav authorities try to keep as close a watch on the immigrants in America as possible. Besides the embassy in Washington they have consuls in several major cities: New York, Cleveland, Pittsburgh, Chicago, and San Francisco. Yugoslavia regards as her citizens all immigrants born in that country and even their children unless they are stricken from the lists of citizens. The process involves a lot of red tape and high fees; it can also mean a humiliating experience for an applicant. Naturalized American citizens who were born in Yugoslavia thus have dual citizenship. In many instances American citizens who went to visit their native land in Yugoslavia experienced harsh treatment by authorities. Many were interrogated by the secret police; several were jailed. The Yugoslav press constantly attacks the activities of several exile organizations, including several Serbian ones.

As a result of the immigrants' influx after the late 1940s the life of the Serbian ethnic group in this country has been revived in many areas. In folklore, culture, social and political activities, and in religious life the American Serbs show great vitality. Thousands of former refugees, prisoners of war, after working in factories for years, have established themselves in better jobs and professions. Because of their economic success it was possible for the Serbs, through generosity and dedication of many individuals, to bring about a real renaissance of Serbian life in America.

By enumerating some organizations in one of the strongest Serbian ethnic centers—Cleveland, Ohio—one can get an idea of the organizations all over the country. In Cleveland are two parishes, one around a beautiful and valuable church. Both are named after St. Sava. Affiliated with the church are also St. Sava Pensioners Club and American Serbian Women's Club. The Serbian National Defense Council has a chapter. There are six radio and television programs, and a bi-monthly publication. There exist also five singing and dancing groups; one sports soccer club "Karageorge"; a Council of Serbian Organizations of Greater Cleveland; Ravna Gora Serbian Chetniks-Cleveland Chapter; Royal Yugoslav Army Combatant Association "Draža Mihajlović"; St. Petka Serbian Sisters' Circle; St. Sava Serbian Cultural Club; Serbian Historical and Cultural Association "Njegoš"; Serbian Republican League of Ohio; American Association of War Veterans of the Kingdom of Yugoslavia. Among fraternal organizations are: Serbian Brothers' Help, Inc.; Serbian National Federation, Lodges No. 15 and No. 108 with patriotic names "Bratska Sloga" and "St. Sava" respectively.[32]

As members of separated families, relatives, and friends keep joining those who were here already, the number of Serbs kept increasing. The attendance at many gatherings, celebrations, manifestations, cultural and sports events is usually very high. National conventions held in several cities attract several thousand people. At the end of April 1976 the 37th Annual Serb National Federation's basketball tournament, held in Cleveland, was attended by some five thousand people with a large proportion of young men and women. The welcome dance was held in the largest facility of the city, the Public Hall. Judging from this and many other Serbian gatherings, in spite of the painful split within the church and political failures, the future life of the Serbian ethnic group in America seems secure for many years to come.

The preservation of their national heritage is also boosted by close ties with the homeland. While many Serbs visit the old country, many visitors come every year from Yugoslavia to visit their Serbian relatives and friends here. Matica Iseljenika, an official emigrants' organization, exists in the Serbian Republic in Yugoslavia. It tries to keep contact with the immigrants and through propaganda to win them over to support the present regime. A similar organization also exists in the republic of Montenegro. Both are devoted to the goal of preserving the national heritage of the Serbian and Montenegrin immigrants respectively. Some Serbian and Montenegrin immigrants, after retirement, return to the homeland to spend the last years of their life. One reason for their return is that they do not want to be buried in a foreign land.

The official emigrants' societies and the Federal Conference of the Socialist League of Yugoslavia organized the First Yugoslav Symposium on Emigration under the title "Emigration of the Peoples and Nationalities of Yugoslavia and Its Relationship with the Native Country." It was held in the Emigrants' Home in Zagreb during December 2–4, 1976. Several American South Slavic scholars were invited and participated. American and Yugoslav scholars have also held joint symposia in the United States in honor of Pupin and Tesla.[33]

CHAPTER 18

The Bulgarians and Macedonians

T HE smallest of the South Slavic ethnic groups in America
are the Bulgarians. One branch of them are the Macedonians.
Even though they were the last to join the migration from
the Balkans to the North American continent, one of them was
among the sailors of Columbus when he discovered America in
1492. His name was Dragan. He was a native of the town
of Ohrid, an important center of Bulgarian culture and religion
which is now located in the Macedonian Republic, Yugoslavia.
Dragan belonged to the Bogomil sect which was regarded as
heretical by both Catholic and Orthodox churches. He made
his way to Spain, but was discovered as a religious dissenter
and was condemned by the authorities to die on the stake in
Salamanca. He was saved from certain death by Columbus who
was gathering his motley crew before sailing to America. Dragan
who was an experienced gunner thus became a valuable member
of Columbus' crew.

Following the discovery—before Columbus returned to Spain—
Dragan was left with forty-two other sailors at the newly built
fortress La Navidad. Subsequently he survived the Indian
massacre. "Drahan da Lihnida" is mentioned in contemporary
eyewitness accounts in the Spanish court. Lihnida is the old
name for Ohrid.[1]

I The Role of the Americans

Even before the liberation of Bulgaria from Turkish rule in
1878, numerous Bulgarians migrated to other countries in
Europe and the Near East. Some worked as seasonal laborers,
merchants, tradesmen, and gardeners. A great majority were
peasants. Over seventy-five percent of all Bulgarian immigrants

were from Macedonia which was under Turkish rule until 1912.

Between 1899 and 1920 U.S. immigration authorities lumped together Bulgarians, Serbs, and Montenegrins. After 1920 they listed Bulgarians as a separate nationality. However, at no time did our immigration authorities list Macedonians as a distinct nationality. Some Bulgarians came from the Balkan provinces of Thrace and Dobruja, outside the Bulgarian state. Some emigrated to America by way of Rumania, Greece, and even Austria.

After the middle of the last century American Protestant missionaries became increasingly active in several provinces of the Ottoman Empire. In 1860 the American Board of Commissioners for Foreign Missions of the Congregational Church founded a college in Plovdiv, Bulgaria, then under Turkish rule. Congregational missionaries became active in all Bulgarian provinces. Robert College was established under the same auspices in 1863 in Constantinople, the Turkish capital. Some Orthodox Bulgarians became converts to Protestantism. A considerable number received their first education from the American Protestants. Over the years many young Bulgarians were sent to various Protestant colleges in the United States to complete their education. A few of them became Protestant ministers, teachers, and physicians. Some remained in America. In Bulgaria the work of the missionaries and the reputation of those who returned as educated people aroused interest in America. This in turn contributed to an increase in immigration to the United States.[2]

The Methodist Episcopal Church also started its activities in Bulgaria as early as 1857. The Methodists worked primarily in the northern parts of the country. In 1878 the American Bible Society published the complete Bible in the Bulgarian language. The translation was done by Dr. Elias Riggs, an American missionary and linguist, who chose the Thracian Bulgarian dialect for his work. By 1905 Methodist congregations existed in Sofia and eighteen other towns.[3]

A different kind of missionary was the American journalist Januarius A. MacGahan (1844–1878) who was born in Ohio of Irish immigrant parents. After covering the Franco-Prussian War of 1870 and the Russian military actions in Turkestan, he returned to London during the time of the Bulgarian revolt and the Turkish massacres of 1876. The London *Daily News* sent him to Bulgaria. There he witnessed the destruction committed by the Turks and his reports sent to the *Daily News* during July and August 1876 aroused public indignation in Great Britain. MacGahan's reports resulted in Gladstone's writing of *Bulgarian Horrors* and an official investigation. Finally, Russian intervention brought about liberation of Bulgaria. On account of his contribution to their cause the Bulgarians called MacGahan "the Liberator of Bulgaria." On June 9, 1878, he died near Constantinople of typhoid. In 1884 his remains were moved to New Lexington, Ohio. The inscription on his tomb monument reads "MacGahan, Liberator of Bulgaria." For many years the Bulgarian envoys in Washington made ceremonial visits to his grave and the American Bulgarian papers still pay him tribute.

From the 1860s until the 1920s American Protestant missionaries founded and maintained schools in Bulgaria from kindergarten through junior college, including an agricultural school. These educational and charitable projects were organized and carried on by people of the highest integrity. The consequence was that America was held in high esteem by many Bulgarians.

Students sent by missionaries for further study in America, generally returned to Bulgaria after 1878, to help build the new country. Almost all of them were sons of peasants or small shopkeepers. At the time over ninety percent of the Bulgarians belonged to the peasant class; they were engaged in agriculture, forestry, the raising of sheep, and cattle.[4]

The city population was low. The country on the whole was backward because of five centuries of Turkish rule, neglect, and exploitation. Though poor, the peasantry still was better off than in most parts of the Balkans. There were no large landowners and every peasant owned at least a small plot of land. Over ninety percent of all Bulgarian immigrants between 1890 and 1914 were peasants or common laborers. Before 1914 the number of educated people, especially university graduates, was very small. Hundreds of young Bulgarians studied abroad: Western Europe, Russia, and at the University of Zagreb in Croatia.

Heavy taxation and low living standards as well as the rising dissatisfaction of the people with the government bureaucracy spurred emigration. In 1908 the yearly salary of King Ferdinand was $200,000, four times higher than that of the President of the United States. With a standing army of 53,000 and a reserve of 322,000 the burden of military service was heavy. By the 1900s Socialists were very active. The number of their followers increased in the homeland and especially in the Bulgarian colonies in America.[5]

II Suffering Macedonia

The bulk of these immigrants came from Macedonia's Vilayet (Turkish province) of Monastir (Bitola). In western Macedonia, in the town of Resan, the Macedonian patriots founded in 1893 the Internal Macedonian Revolutionary Organization. The IMRO, as it was popularly known, fought for liberation of the three predominantly Macedonian vilayets. A great majority of its leaders insisted that an independent Macedonia should join the mother country, Bulgaria.

As Turkish oppression became unbearable the Macedonian patriots started a revolt on St. Elias Day, August 2, 1903. Over thirty thousand armed rebels, organized in many *chetas* (companies) scored initial successes against the Turks. This "Ilinden Uprising" won considerable sympathy in the West. Western politicians, missionaries, writers, and journalists responded with innumerable reports, articles, and books in favor of the Macedonian cause. The Macedonian problem became a serious concern of diplomats in the West (including the United States) and in St. Petersburg.

Some two hundred thousand Turkish soldiers crushed the revolt. Hundreds of patriots were killed in numerous engagements. About five thousand innocent civilians were massacred, 10,000 homes were burned, and over fifty thousand people were made homeless. Altogether two hundred villages were destroyed. The main strength of the IMRO was broken.[6]

Even though IMRO opposed the emigration of Macedonians, thousands of people now decided to leave for America while their *comitadjis* (guerrilla fighters) still remained in the mountains. Columns of young men journeyed to the port of Salonica

for their voyage across the sea. One of them was Stoyan Christowe, a future writer in America.[7]

A great number of these refugees came from one small district
in Monastir vilayet, Kostur, where the fighting during the revolt
was especially fierce. The immigrants listed by United States
authorities as "Bulgarian, Serbian and Montenegrins" jumped
in number from 204 in 1900 to 6,500 in 1903 when Macedonia
was in revolt. In 1904 some 4,500 and in 1905 over 5,800 of
this group came to America. The number climbed to almost
12,000 in 1906, and 27,000 in 1907. In 1908, when Stoyan
Christowe reached this country, 18,000 of the group—most of
them Macedonians—came to our shores.[8]

The year 1908 was also the year of the Young Turk Revolt,
a serious crisis in the Balkans, and of Bulgaria's proclamation
of complete independence from Turkey. Among the thousands
of Bulgarians flocking to the midwestern United States, were
also people from Bulgaria proper, especially from the district of
Tirnovo. This region "had long been overpopulated, and emigration began across the Danube into Rumania, where the
Bulgarians first came into contact with Macedonian refugees,
and were incited by them to leave for America."[9]

These Bulgarian immigrants were better schooled than those
from Macedonia, as "this latter province had been woefully
neglected in educational matters by the Turks, while the Bulgarians had the advantage of fundamental education." The
continued persecution by the Greek Orthodox Church, which
was opposed to the existence of an independent Bulgarian
Church, and the closing of Greece as a market for Macedonian
labor also had an impact on the rising emigration to America.[10]

III   *Earlier Bulgarian Immigrants*

In the first years of the twentieth century a few Bulgarian
colonies existed on the East Coast, notably in Philadelphia and
Alfred, New York. When young Peter D. Yankoff, the future
physician, arrived in 1905 in New York City, he joined a group
of his countrymen in the brickyards of Alfred. Here as in many
parts of the country the Bulgarians constituted a predominantly
male society. From the East, after earning some money, they

moved to the Midwest. They established strong settlements in southern Illinois. The largest before 1914 was Granite City. Here at times some ten thousand Bulgarians worked in various industries. They were also recruited into railroad labor gangs.

In St. Louis, too, a large Bulgarian colony was established, while many were spreading to different parts of the Midwest and adjacent regions. Young Yankoff went in the summer of 1906 to the Methodist Park College in Parkville, Missouri. He mastered the difficult English language and by working his way through college he obtained his B.A. in 1914. He then attended the Medical School at Lawrence, Kansas, to become one of the first Bulgarian physicians educated in America.[11]

The Bulgarians also founded their settlements in towns of Pennsylvania, especially in Pittsburgh and vicinity where they joined other South Slavs. They established smaller or larger groups in Ohio; Michigan (with a large number in Detroit); Indianapolis, Indiana; Minneapolis and St. Paul, Minnesota; Butte, Montana; South Dakota; Seattle, Washington; and elsewhere. Thousands were railroad workers who built tracks from the Midwest to the Pacific. They loved this kind of work under open skies, living in railroad cars and eating their hearty dishes prepared by their own cooks. After a few months they would return with their earnings to Granite City, St. Louis, or to some other place which was their home in America.

Coming from a country that for centuries had struggled against oppressors, these immigrants were anything but passive and submissive. On April 8, 1908 the Chicago newspapers reported a very interesting incident: some six hundred unemployed and starving Bulgarians marched on the city hall demanding work. The demonstration was a rare occurrence for that time. It was as harmless as it was ineffective, but it aroused considerable interest on the part of some concerned Americans. The League for Protection of Immigrants investigated this case and interviewed 106 Bulgarians who participated in the march on the city hall. Subsequently, the League published reports that shed light on the background, social conditions, life, and work, as well as on causes of immigration for the Bulgarians.[12]

Some educated Bulgarians in Chicago tried to help their countrymen who numbered a few thousand in 1908. One was

P. D. Vasileff, a Methodist minister. He secured the help of influential Americans in Chicago and Illinois. Together they appealed to Governor Denee of Illinois who was sympathetic to the Bulgarians in distress and did intervene in Chicago to help them obtain employment. Another was Ivan Doseff who had come to America in 1902 and studied at the University of Chicago. He was widely known in college circles as the star tackle of the 1907 football season. During the winter of 1908–1909, when hundreds of Bulgarians were starving, Doseff spent all his savings and a lot of his time to help his unfortunate countrymen.[13] The American Socialists, very active among the Slavs, also tried to help the Bulgarians as much as they could.

In 1910 close to fifteen thousand Bulgarians lived as steel workers in the ghastly town of Hungry Hollow, Illinois. Thousands were single men, their ages ranging from the teens to the late forties, who lived under most primitive conditions. Hungry Hollow, like several other Balkan immigrant settlements, was worse than any present-day slum in America.[14]

The main Bulgarian base remained Granite City, Illinois. Its population was highest during the winter months when there was no seasonal work on the railroad lines. Eventually these migrations stopped, many Bulgarians did not return to the city, and their population decreased sharply.

In 1909, Albert Sonnichsen, considered an expert on the Bulgarians, served as agent for Bulgarians on the U.S. Immigration Commission. He wrote a book on the revolutionary struggle in Macedonia entitled *Confessions of a Macedonian Bandit*. In his opinion there were forty thousand immigrants from Bulgaria and Macedonia, one fourth of whom were working on the railroad lines in Montana, the Dakotas, Iowa, and Minnesota in 1909. Sonnichsen told Emily Balch: "I hope you are not making any racial distinction between Bulgarians and Macedonians. . . . The distinction between the Bulgars from Bulgaria and those from Macedonia is purely political. Many of those who are registered as Greeks are so in church affiliation only, being Slavic by race and tongue."[15]

In 1909 Sonnichsen visited ten large gangs of Bulgarian railroad workers, each group averaging fifty men. Over ninety percent of them were from Macedonia. He made these interesting comments: "I have been quite surprised at the similarity between the speech of the Bulgarians and Croatians (Horvats). I found I could converse quite freely with them, and that they took me for a Horvat coming from a different province from their own.... I am especially interested in the Slavs. I have great faith in their virility as a race, in proportion as they are unmixed with Turkish or Greek blood."[16]

Besides living in their main settlements, the Bulgarians were also scattered in every state and territory, including Alaska and Hawaii. Somewhat surprised, Miss Balch exclaimed: "Such a dissemination of the peoples of the earth sometimes fills one with amazement. How did 110 Servians [*sic*] and Bulgarians happen to ... go to Alaska, or 116 to Oklahoma, or 137 to New Mexico, one wonders."[17]

And Grace Abbott who studied the Bulgarians of Chicago remarked: "These Bulgarians are splendid material for skilled workers, strong, quiet, sober, intelligent and eager to work. There should be some way by which they could be turned more quickly and with much less suffering into the valuable citizens they are sure to become."[18]

IV *It Was a Long Struggle*

In spite of their good traits the Bulgarians had a difficult time on their long road to success and recognition. To a people who survived five centuries of Turkish rule and had to fight against all neighbors in modern days to preserve its independence, constant struggle is a way of life. When the Bulgarians in Macedonian villages heard about America, there was a new hope for many of them. The letters from America played an important role in the life of the villagers and in stimulating their emigration to the land across the ocean.

When the letters arrived in Stoyan Christowe's Macedonian village from compatriots in St. Louis, they "struck the village like a comet." Such a letter usually contained a check. And it was "that magic slip of paper, more than wonders which the letter narrated, that started the exodus to America and changed the life of Selo [village] and the neighboring villages." The contents of those letters "exaggerated and distorted, were passed from mouth to ear until all manner of queer beliefs and opinions about America came into being."[19]

For a young Bulgarian, either from Macedonia or Bulgaria proper, emigration was a heartbreaking step. He left a village where his ancestors had lived for many generations. Going to faraway America in most cases meant leaving forever. When villagers of Macedonia were departing, they were accompanied for miles by their parents, relatives, and friends. It was on such occasions that the brave peasant women, who had experienced much tragedy in their past, cried aloud, wailing as if lamenting the dead.

After the tearful farewell (usually at a mountain top) the prospective emigrants walked the long distance to the railroad station. From there a train took them to the port of embarkation. Stoyan Christowe and his Macedonian fellow travelers, bound for Cherbourg, wore a red button with a white star upon it, to identify them to agents as passengers on the ship *Oceanic* that would take them to New York. It carried a thousand steerage passengers.[20]

Some Bulgarians who traveled by way of Germany had a nightmarish experience that they remembered for many years. How they fared in an emigrant train, in the German emigrant station in Leipzig, on the trip to Hamburg and its detention camp was dramatically described by Peter Yankoff in his autobiography. He claims that life in such emigrant camps for "Bulgarians, Serbians, Montenegrins, Russians and other nationalities" proved to be "much worse than even that of prison."[21] For a young teen-aged boy, who was lonely and without any relatives to accompany him, this phase before reaching the destination in America was real agony.

According to Bulgarian eyewitness accounts, the crossing of the Atlantic was for these Balkan peasants the most dreadful experience. They feared it more than the uncertainty of the strange world that awaited them. The sight of the Statue of Liberty was therefore the moment of great relief. Before entering America, one had to pass through the "Island" (Ellis Island) about which they had heard so much. Everybody feared it. For it was here that some people were refused admission into the land of hope. Some had mortgaged their fields and houses to raise the needed money for their journey only to be returned from the "Island" when they were within sight of the skyscrapers of New York. There were also stories of "people jumping overboard rather than to return to their villages."[22]

Those Bulgarians that passed through the "Island" and came eventually to their settlement in St. Louis, Missouri—as Christowe did—usually joined a group of their countrymen. In one apartment twelve of them lived sharing six beds during two different shifts. The place was filthy with dirty blankets and no sheets on the beds. Shano, the Bulgarian, was the majordomo of the group. He presided over it "with patriarchal authority and had to be consulted about everything." All the men did their share of work in rotation. The hard economy which they practiced and the toil in the shops had imprinted themselves on "their drawn and haggard faces." As for their toil, in St. Louis the erstwhile Balkan plowmen "cleaned the noses of groaning locomotives, emptied carloads of ashes from their cylindrical bellies and stuffed their yawning jaws with coal." They did it for twelve hours every day including Sundays. Their daily wage was $1.50.[23]

Other jobs were not much better and they took their toll in health and lives. The conditions were similar in all large industrial cities. In Pittsburgh and vicinity, for instance, the Bulgarians lived under equally appalling conditions. In 1908 in West Homestead twenty homes held some three hundred Bulgarians. There were only *three women* among them! The men cared little about how they lived as long as they lived cheaply. They were industrious men, all bent on saving money in order to be able to return to the old country as men of property. In one apartment of two rooms and a kitchen lived the "boarding boss," his wife, two babies, and twenty men.

At this time Slavs in metropolitan Pittsburgh performed the most hazardous and difficult work. In 1907–1908, only twenty-three percent of them received a daily wage of $2.50 to $5.00, which was considered very good. Only five percent of them received above $5.00 a day, regarded as unusual earnings. However, the Bulgarians in West Homestead were making only from $9.00 to $12.00 a week. Out of this sum they paid three dollars a week for a place to sleep, their laundry, and their food. The boarding boss worked in the steel mill and ran the boarding house. In this way he accumulated considerable sums of money. On Saturdays they all had plenty of beer to drink. Though fights broke out and often the police had to be called in, one officer said that in general these men were good natured and easy-going. In his nine years of experience he had never arrested a sober "Hunkie" as he called these Slavs.[24]

Those Bulgarians who saved a few hundred dollars and decided to stay here dreamed of establishing a little restaurant of their own, or a grocery, or even having a farm. Many, however, did not remain but went back to the homeland. Hundreds returned in 1912 and 1913 when the Balkan Wars broke out. They responded to the call of their mother country. In late 1912 the first Balkan War as a war of liberation was started by Bulgaria, Montenegro, Serbia, and Greece against Turkey. In the summer of 1913, after Turkey had been defeated, Bulgaria went to war against her former Balkan allies because of Macedonia. Bulgaria lost the war. After five centuries of harsh Turkish rule Macedonia was partitioned between Serbia and Greece and only a small section was awarded to Bulgaria. In Macedonia the long Turkish oppression was now exchanged for Serbian and Greek oppression. To all the returned emigrants who had joined the Bulgarian troops the loss of Macedonia was the most painful disappointment of their lives. These returned volunteers either settled in Bulgaria or came back to the United States to continue their political struggle for liberation and unification of Macedonia.

Some Bulgarians who returned from the Balkan struggle to America in late 1913 encountered another kind of struggle. It was the labor struggle in the West, in Colorado where nine thousand miners struck against the Colorado Fuel and Iron Company. The miners and many of their families lived in their tent settlement in Ludlow near Trinidad. When, on October 31, the National Guard arrived under the command of General Chase they were greeted by friendly strikers. Chase reported later that among those lining the road "many of the men were in strange costume of the Greek, Montenegrin, Servian and Bulgarian armies; for the colony numbered among its inhabitants many returned veterans of the Balkan wars." The little children were dressed in white, carried small American flags, and sang union songs. This friendly atmosphere changed later. In clashes between the strikers and the guardsmen (infantry, cavalry, and field artillery) at least a dozen men were killed on both sides.

The culmination of violence was reached on April 20, 1914. The guardsmen opened fire against the tent colony and later burned it. According to one version, twenty-one people, including eleven children, were massacred by the Guard. Another estimate was "sixty-five people . . . forty-three of whom were women and children."[25] Among the strikers, besides the Bulgarians and other South Slavs, there were Italians, Mexicans, Anglo-Saxons, Negroes, and Japanese. The Ludlow Massacre was but one of many incidents in which the Bulgarians participated.

CHAPTER 19

World War I and After

THE Bulgarians had not yet recovered from the defeat in the Balkan Wars when they had to face the dilemma of the World War that broke out in late 1914. In October 1915 Bulgaria joined the Central Powers: Germany, Austria-Hungary, and Turkey. The main reason for the decision of King Ferdinand's government was Macedonia. Ferdinand, a native of Germany, was convinced that after a victorious war he would be able to gain Macedonia that had been taken away from him by Serbs and Greeks.

When by the end of 1915, the Bulgarian armies occupied Serbia, the Bulgarians in America were happy. However, the response of a majority of those who joined the Bulgarian army was less than enthusiastic because of bad experiences only two years earlier. Many Bulgarian Socialists, who were especially strong in the Midwest, followed the general anti-war line taken by their American comrades.

The Bulgarians in America, especially those who had not become citizens, did not fare well. It was probably because "their continued opposition to Serbian and Greek rule in Macedonia was looked upon [by U.S. authorities] with distrust." Moreover, "the Greek and Serbian colonies also conducted their campaign against them." In spite of these obstacles "the Macedonian revolutionary group continued its activities, and in 1918, a large Macedonian conference was held in Chicago, and passed a resolution in favor of liberty of Macedonia."[1]

One of the enemies of Bulgarian aspirations was the Serbian scientist and scholar, Professor Michael Pupin, who also served as an honorary Serbian consul in New York. In his speeches and articles he constantly advocated a Great Serbia in which Macedonia was to be merely Southern Serbia. All the Bulgarians who were not American citizens were regarded by American authorities and many influential people as German allies and enemies, especially after April of 1917. It was difficult to be a Bulgarian in America during World War I.

One of the outspoken Bulgarians at the time was Todor Cvetkov, a Bulgarian Socialist who arrived in Chicago at the end of 1908. Cvetkov had left Bulgaria for political reasons and lived for a while in the Croatian capital Zagreb which traditionally attracted many young Bulgarians. Cvetkov was a former theology student and in Zagreb he learned fluent Croatian, having experienced his conversion to Socialism. In Chicago he became the editor of the Croatian Socialist weekly *Radnička Straža* (Workers' Sentinel) that started to appear in December 1907. Later on Cvetkov finished his studies in the Law School at Valparaiso University, Indiana, where many South Slavs received their degrees.

Cvetkov became attorney-at-law and then worked among the Croatians and Bulgarians and wherever his help was needed. A dedicated Socialist, he was for years a friend and adviser to many people in need. During the war Cvetkov was in the forefront of those that denounced war. He also attacked the activities of the South Slav movement and even engaged in public debates with some of its leaders. As an editor of *Radnička Straža* Cvetkov aroused the ire of U.S. authorities. In the fall of 1917 they prohibited the publication of his paper because of its anti-war stand. Later on the paper continued for a while under several different titles always adhering to its radical Socialist ideas.[2]

The Socialists were strong among the Bulgarians and very active in publishing newspapers and periodicals. Until 1930 there were in the United States close to thirty such publications. Because the Bulgarian language uses the Cyrillic alphabet all were printed this way. As a majority of Bulgarians were uneducated and illiterate, many learned to write and read in America. One of the primary goals of the Socialist Bulgarian press was to educate its readers, to inform them about events in the homeland and in America, to report the activities of Bulgarian and other Socialist workers, and to help them adapt to their new life in America.

In New York City the *Robotnik* (The Worker) was started in 1906. In September of 1907 the first Bulgarian daily *Naroden Glas—The National Herald* came into existence in Granite City, Illinois, at the time the main and largest Bulgarian colony in America.[3]

I   After the War Was Lost

For his principles of self-determination which he had publicly announced, President Wilson was hailed by several of the Slavic peoples in Europe. However, after the end of the war in which hundreds of thousands of Balkan soldiers had perished, self-determination was denied to several Slavic nations. One of them was Bulgaria. In the autumn of 1918 the Allies defeated the Bulgarian armies. The victors then imposed on Bulgaria the peace treaty of Neuilly on November 27, 1919. Bulgaria lost Macedonia in the west and the access to the Aegean Sea which she had gained in 1913. King Ferdinand abdicated in favor of his son Boris. Alexander Stambuliski, an agrarian politician, formed the new government. The country suffered a great deal from the consequences of the war and the punitive peace treaty which also limited its army to a minimum.[4] But most of all, the Bulgarians suffered emotionally from the loss of Macedonia. It was again placed under the harsh rule of Belgrade and Athens. Between 1918 and 1941, the Serbs and Greeks treated Bulgarian-speaking Macedonians as enemies and mercilessly suppressed any signs of Bulgarian nationalism, forced the people to change their family names, abolished their schools, subjugated their Orthodox Church, arrested men by the thousands, declared an open season on all patriots, liquidated large numbers, and on the whole treated the Macedonians worse than the Turks had done. As the Macedonians had many friends among the former Western Protestant missionaries (most of whom were expelled by the new conquerors) and among the scholars, a great deal of publicity in the West followed.

Thus the Bulgarian defeat and loss of Macedonia caused bitter feelings among the Bulgarians and Macedonians in America. During and after the war a few thousand Bulgarians returned to the homeland. Some again made the trip back to America alone or with their families. Many wives and children, after 1919, joined the immigrants in America. There were now many more women among them than before 1914. And a new American-born generation was now making its appearance. Also, there was an increasing number of educated people and professionals.

II The Religious Life

Over ninety percent of all Bulgarians and Macedonians belong to the Bulgarian Orthodox Church which is administered by the Patriarch in Sofia. In America the first Bulgarian Protestant group was organized in Chicago around 1905. Its leader was P. D. Vassilef. An evangelical mission was started in the Methodist church on Monroe Street. Gradually there were established Methodist, Congregational, Presbyterian, and Baptist missions among the Bulgarians in Granite City and Madison, Illinois, and in Battle Creek, Michigan. Most of the books the ministers used were in the Bulgarian language.[5]

The only Bulgarian parochial school in the United States at that time was in Steelton, Pennsylvania. There were, however, evening schools for the children and grown-ups in Granite City and Madison, Illinois; Indianapolis, Indiana; Detroit and Battle Creek, Michigan; Toledo and Lorain, Ohio; Homestead and Johnstown, Pennsylvania; and Lackawanna, New York.

The first Bulgarian Orthodox church in America, that of Sts. Cyril and Methodius, was established in 1909 in Granite City, Illinois. Other churches were founded in Steelton, Pennsylvania (1910); St. Stephen, Indianapolis (1915); St. Clement Ohridsky, Detroit (1929); St. Trinity, Madison, Illinois (1929); and one in Lorain, Ohio, in 1934. The number of registered parishioners was approximately eight thousand at the end of the 1920s.

As an administrative body, the Bulgarian Church began its official activities in 1920 as the Bulgarian Orthodox Mission under the jurisdiction of the Holy Synod of the Bulgarian Exarchate in Sofia. (In 1953 it was elevated to the Patriarchate.) The first head of the mission was Reverend Dr. K. Tsenoff. The center for the mission for the entire United States and Canada was in Indianapolis, Indiana. In 1937 it was named the Bulgarian Eastern Orthodox Church, Diocese of the United States and Canada.[6]

In 1947 a canonical conference in Buffalo, New York, under the Chairmanship of Metropolitan Leonty, Primate of the Russian Orthodox Metropolia, elected Bishop Andrey Velitcki as the administrator of the diocese. The conference severed ties with the Holy Synod in Bulgaria "due to the takeover by the communists." However, in 1963 "for unjustified reasons, Bishop Andrey subordinated himself to the administrative orders of Sofia ... without the knowledge and against the will of the entire clergy and elected representatives of the parishes." As a result the diocese experienced many difficulties.

In 1963 another canonical conference convened in Detroit and decided not to accept the administrative orders from Sofia even though continuing "a spiritual relationship with the Mother Church." The Holy Synod then reorganized its structure in the United States "to settle the problems of church life as determined by the conditions of this country." The Holy Synod of Sofia recently instructed Bishop Andrey to limit his activities to the city of New York. In the rest of the United States and Canada the head of the Bulgarian Church is still Bishop Kyril, who does not recognize the patriarch in Sofia.

There are twenty-five parishes in America and Canada served by full-time clergy. As Bishop Kyril says: "We are blessed with beautiful churches, educational buildings, social halls, choirs, and a very normal religious life." The headquarters of Bishop Kyril are in Toledo, Ohio. He was consecrated as bishop in the Russian Orthodox Monastery, Holy Trinity, Jordanville, New York, in August 1964. He refused to recognize the recently created Macedonian Church with the see at Ohrid, Macedonian Republic of Yugoslavia. In his statement in the *Macedonian Tribune* Bishop Kyril also said:

We, the Bulgarians, regardless of place of birth, are true Orthodox believers. We love and hold dear our traditions and national customs. But at the same time, we are very devoted and thankful to be citizens of this great country of America—to worship, preach and teach without being disturbed by any outside sources.[7]

While a great majority of the members of the diocese before the 1950s were the immigrants from Macedonia and their descendants, hundreds of newcomers from Bulgaria, mostly refugees from the Communist rule, became new members during the last twenty years. They were also joined by the immigrants from the Yugoslav Macedonian Republic whose center is in Skopje.

The split within the Bulgarian Church in America and Canada is still wide open, causing a lot of bitter feelings on both sides. The controversy goes on in the same fashion as in the American Serbian Orthodox Church. It remains to be seen how and when—if ever—it will be resolved.[8]

III *Bulgarians and Americanization*

Even though a Balkan immigrant may not be a regular churchgoer, the church always played a great role in his life. Basically, most old-timers—the peasant immigrants from Bulgaria—were conservative. In America many changed their views. In fact, some Bulgarians came as Socialists from the old country or from a stopover in Europe. Bulgarians like all other Slavic peasants possessed a lot of natural intelligence and inherited from the long time of struggle against the Turks an inborn sense of distrust, suspicion, and shrewdness.

It is interesting that the *Dictionary of Races and Peoples* of the Reports of the Immigration Commission (1910–1911) described the Bulgarians "less warriors in spirit" than some of their neighbors, and "more settled as agriculturists" due to their traditional skill in horticulture.[9] While the assertion about Bulgarians as being less warlike may not be true, their ability as farmers and gardeners has been well known for a long time.

Surprisingly, many educated Bulgarians embraced Americanization eagerly and deliberately severed all ties with their mother country. This was, for instance, the case of the Bulgarian Stoyan Christowe, a fairly successful American writer. Born in 1898 in Konomlady, Macedonia, he came to the United States as a young lad and was educated at Valparaiso University, Valparaiso, Indiana. He described, in his autobiography, how eagerly he embraced Americanization. To him this was not "the shock of alienation." Christowe claims that, while visiting in Bulgaria in the spring of 1928, during the audience with King Boris in Sofia it was easier for him to talk with the king in English than in his native Bulgarian. He felt that "America, my America, stretched her arms across the distance so that I might hold on to her hand." So poignant was his nostalgia for America that he could hug a Ford car just because it was made there. He was afraid that after a few months he might become "re-Balkanized" and was happy when his friends told him: "You belong to America. America belongs to you. You don't know how fortunate you are."[10]

John Gunther, the American writer, who visited Bulgaria during the 1930s calls the Bulgarians "poor, clean, intensely honest, ... the best people in the Balkans." These are high compliments by a writer who traveled all over Europe at the time and met many other peoples. Gunther was impressed with the beauty of the Bulgarian country and the modesty of its king. Appropriately he called Bulgaria "the unfortunate little country . . . mercilessly chopped asunder . . . by the peace treaties."[11]

Reuben Markham, who spent years in Sofia as a correspondent of *The Christian Science Monitor*, also highly praised the Bulgarians and was their true friend. In 1931 he published a book *Meet Bulgaria* which reflected his intimate knowledge of the subject. The work was considered the best general discussion of Bulgaria in the English language.

The people that Gunther called "the best . . . in the Balkans" have had, like the rest of the Slavs, their share of problems in experiencing adjustment, alienation, and assimilation in America. Christowe (who partly anglicized his Bulgarian family name) after all his eager attempts to become a true American reflected in one of his writings upon some problems that Bulgarians experienced in the process of becoming Americans. "While I am not a whole American, neither am I what I was when I first landed here; that is, a Bulgarian," he wrote. His inherited native traits barred him "forever from complete assimilation." As a visitor in Bulgaria he "felt like a foreigner and was so regarded." While in Bulgaria he was not wholly a Bulgarian, in the United States he was not wholly an American. Thus he had to go "through life with a dual nationality." In America he longed for the sleepy villages and the intimate life of the Balkans. When he was in the Balkans he dreamed of America day and night. "Yet I cannot leave America," he writes, "though I am but half American."[12]

Christowe modified his views later on. At least to a certain degree this is how many educated Bulgarians felt about the problem. Millions of immigrants reacted differently in each individual case. Many even second and third generation ethnics have in a way dual personalities. They are torn apart by two loves: one for America, one for the country of their ancestors. Many Bulgarian immigrants, their children, and grandchildren have remained "half Americans." Indeed it can be said that millions of other ethnics feel the same way.

IV *The Macedonian Struggle*

The activities of the church, press, and political organizations contributed to the making of many Bulgarians "half Americans." Most of the Bulgarian political activities in this country were caused and prolonged by the Macedonian problem. The situation in Serbian and Greek controlled parts of divided Macedonia remained precarious. During the 1920s and 1930s the American and Western press kept reporting about the fighting in mountains and valleys in the heart of the Balkans: between the troops and gendarmes on one side and the guerrillas of the Internal Macedonian Revolutionary Organization on the other side. IMRO's leader was Ivan Mihajlov, popularly known as Vanča. The armed struggle in Yugoslavia went on for years. Mihajlov directed his struggle against Belgrade from his hideouts in Sofia and the Bulgarian part of Macedonia.

The American Macedonians reacted vehemently against the despotic rule, against the terror, killing, tortures, and burning in their native land. Their postwar organization in America was the Union of Macedonian Political Organizations. In October 1922 it convened in a congress in Fort Wayne, Indiana. Delegates represented the organizations from some fifteen cities. The result of this gathering was the creation of the Macedonian Patriotic Organization, a union of all Macedonian patriotic organizations "under one standard and with one ideal: the liberation and unification of Macedonia." The president of the Central Committee was Anastas Stephanoff of Fort Wayne; its secretary was Atanas Lebanoff. The center of the MPO moved to Indianapolis, Indiana.

The MPO claims to be the political spokesman of the American and Canadian Macedonians and has generally supported the goals and activities of the homeland IMRO. In its official creed the Macedonians are regarded as an integral part of the Bulgarian nation and the Macedonian language as a Bulgarian dialect. Since its founding the MPO has undertaken numerous activities and printed papers, memoranda, pamphlets, books, and almanacs in English and Bulgarian on the Macedonian struggle. It has tried to attract the interest of congressmen and senators in Washington and has appealed to several U.S. Presidents to intervene diplomatically in favor of Macedonians outside Bulgaria. It has also held yearly congresses at which many American and foreign scholars have spoken in sympathy with and in support of the Macedonian cause.

On February 10, 1927, the first issue of *Makedonska Tribuna—The Macedonian Tribune*, a weekly organ of the MPO, appeared in Indianapolis. It has been published ever since. It also serves as the voice of the Macedono-Bulgarian Orthodox Church in the United States and Canada. For fifty years it has been an interesting chronicle of the lives of Macedonians and other Bulgarians on this continent and in the homeland. It is printed in both Macedonian (with Cyrillic letters) and English.[13]

Out of the movement that was founded by patriotic Macedonians during the 1920s has developed a well-concerted effort by a large number of Macedonians in America and foreign lands. Their goals are described by the leader of the IMRO, Ivan Mihailoff, in his book in English, *Macedonia: A Switzerland of the Balkans.*

When he was a young revolutionary leader in the mountains of the Balkans, and his name was mentioned in whispers in Yugoslav Macedonia, he received Stoyan Christowe in his mountainous hideout in Bulgaria. Christowe as correspondent of the *Chicago Daily News* was the first foreign correspondent to be granted such an opportunity by Mihailoff. John Gunther who then worked for the same paper was refused an interview by "Vanča." The *Daily News* and scores of other American papers featured Christowe's articles on Mihailoff and the Macedonian revolutionary struggle in the Balkans. Later on Christowe wrote his book *Heroes and Assassins* on the same subject. However, the book was a great disappointment to the Macedonians. His hosts in the mountains expected him "to be a Macedonian first, a writer and an American afterward."[14]

CHAPTER 20

In Controversial Battles

THE involvement of American Slavs in leftist causes was proportionately high in relation to their number. Documents of book length resulting from hearings and investigations in Washington after World War II reveal strong Bulgarian participation during the late 1930s and early 1940s. In order to comprehend better the reasons for the enthusiasm shown by the Bulgarians in these controversial battles it should be pointed out that many of them believed in Slavic solidarity and that traditionally they were friendly to Russia because she had liberated their country from the Turks in 1878. In addition, during some twelve years, the famous Bulgarian Communist revolutionary Georgi Dimitrov had been at the helm of the Communist International (Comintern) in Moscow.

The Communist Party of the U.S.A. paid a great deal of attention to Slavic immigrants. For years the Croatian Frank Borich had headed the South Slav Bureau of the Communist Party of U.S.A. Its organ was the *Daily Worker* in New York.[1] This paper had reported on all South Slavic radical activities for many years and had printed articles by many leading South Slavic radicals.

In 1923 the left-wing Socialists led by the Bulgarian Todor Cvetkov seceded from the South Slav Section of the C.P.U.S.A. Together with the Croatian Djuro Kutuzović, he formed the Yugoslav Educational League in Chicago. They appealed to the Bulgarians and all South Slavs. Also trying to gain audience among them during the late 1920s was a New York monthly *Slavjanski Jug—The Slavonic South*.[2]

All Bulgarian organizations and papers, from the extreme right to the extreme left, denounced the royal dictatorship in Yugoslavia. In opposing King Alexander's policies many Bulgarians and Croatians formed a common front in America. Among them the Socialists were especially active during the 1930s. The Socialist Labor Party of America, during these years of Depression, tried to gain the support of the Bulgarians. It published numerous books and pamphlets in Bulgarian and in other South Slavic languages. They were often translations from Karl Marx, Friedrich Engels, and other Socialist ideologists. The party sponsored a Bulgarian weekly *Rabotnicheska Prosveta* (The Workers' Enlightenment) in Granite City, Illinois.

A majority of these Socialists shunned Communist influence and leadership. The leading Bulgarian Communist in America was George Pirinsky whose real name was George Zaikoff. Many of his articles appeared in the radical Bulgarian press signed George Nicoloff. In an article that was printed in the summer of 1935, Pirinsky quoted a letter from G. Dimitrov dated May 13, 1934, which is very important because it presented the official line of the Soviets in favor of Macedonian independence.[3]

On October 9, 1934 in Marseilles, France, a Macedonian revolutionary, Vlade Chernozemsky, assassinated King Alexander of Yugoslavia shortly after he landed at the port for an official visit. Another who was killed was Louis Barthou, the French Minister of Foreign Affairs. The assassin was a member of Mihailoff's Internal Macedonian Revolutionary Organization. The *attentat* was organized by the Croatian revolutionary Ustasha movement which operated from Italy. The fact that a Macedonian killed the Serbian king was interpreted as a revenge of the Macedonians for the king's brutal rule in Macedonia. The event gained wide publicity in the American and international press and was debated at the League of Nations in Geneva. Chernozemsky who was killed on the spot by a French officer was hailed by Macedonians in America as a hero and martyr.

The violent end of a Balkan dictator resulted also in strained relations between several ethnic groups. Louis Adamic, who in his writings had predicted such an end for King Alexander, was attacked by the king's defenders, particularly by some Serbian and Yugoslav-oriented papers. Some of these papers were subsidized by the Belgrade government.[4]

I The "Popular Front" in America

In 1935 the Comintern in Moscow ordered all Communist parties in the world to start collaborating with all anti-fascist groups and individuals. Georgi Dimitrov, the leader of the Comintern, having established relations with the leading American leftists, instructed them to utilize services of sympathizers, particularly the left-wing writers.[5]

Dimitrov especially praised the work of George Pirinsky. This was publicized in the *Daily Worker*; in its issue of August 31, 1935, Pirinsky appealed to American Bulgarians to heed the call for action by their countryman Dimitrov. The weekly *Narodna Volya* (People's Will) an organ of Pirinsky's Macedonian American People's League, frequently writing about Dimitrov, constantly appealed for creation of a Popular Front in America. In 1937 Pirinsky was held under deportation warrant by the U.S. Department of Justice on a charge of illegal entry, but the charge was subsequently dropped.

By 1939 the Communist Party of Yugoslavia also embarked on a Popular Front policy and started to pay increased attention to its active supporters among the immigrants in America. On the eve of World War II the Yugoslav Communist Party, led by Josip Broz Tito, was well organized and became more active abroad. Immigrants in the United States and Canada were instructed to collaborate with the Bulgarian and other Slavic Communist organizations and leftist groups. When in late August 1939 the Soviet government signed a pact with Nazi Germany (which had been the main target of attack by the Popular Front), the Communists in America were caught by surprise. Now they adopted a new line, namely that America should remain strictly neutral in the European war that broke out in September 1939. On December 3, 1939, a conference of delegates of many Slavic organizations, with a generous sprinkling of Communists, took place in Pittsburgh to discuss future actions. In all such gatherings the Bulgarians were well represented.[6]

II World War II Period

In early April 1941 Hitler's armies, together with their allies, swept into Yugoslavia and Greece. The Bulgarian army marched into Macedonia and parts of Serbia proper. It seemed that the old dream of uniting all of Macedonia was finally a reality. Bulgaria as a member of the Axis powers annexed Yugoslav and Greek Aegean territories. Remembering the fate of their fatherland at the end of World War I, the Bulgarians in spite of their joy over the liberation of Macedonia were apprehensive. The Serbian and Greek ethnic press immediately started a vicious campaign against the American Bulgarians, branding them as supporters of Nazi Germany and Fascist Italy.

In late June 1941 the Germans began their invasion of the Soviet Union and in his battle for the survival of the Soviet state Stalin appealed for help from Communist and Popular Front members in Europe and in America. Tito and his Communist partisans started to wage a guerrilla war against the Germans and Bulgarians in Yugoslavia, and he included under his sponsorship the Communists in Macedonia. In America the Bulgarian and Macedonian leftists formed a common front with all other pro-Tito South Slav groups.

Soviet General Alexander Gundorov, president of the All Slavic Committee in Moscow, appealed to the American Slavs to get organized and help the Soviet Union which was fighting for survival. A mass meeting of various Slavic representatives was held in Gary, Indiana, on September 2, 1941. The Macedonians were also present. The principal speaker was George Pirinsky.[7]

These activities received a boost when after December 1941 the United States entered World War II and began to send massive military aid to its new ally, the Soviet Union. A huge All-Slavic Congress convened in Detroit on April 25 and 26, 1942. Some twenty-five hundred delegates represented all Slavic ethnic groups. The congress received telegrams from the president of the Soviet Union, Mikhail Kalinin, and from President Roosevelt who assured the delegates that "America is proud of its Slavic citizens." To this the delegates responded with an enthusiastic telegram claiming to speak in the name of "fifteen million Americans of Slavic descent."[8]

It was in Detroit on this occasion that the American Slav Congress was founded. Its purpose was to operate as a powerful pressure group in behalf of Soviet foreign policy within the

United States. Its organ became *The Slavic American*. The American Slav Congress was actually a subsidiary of the All Slavic Committee in Moscow. Members of the American Slav Congress were the Macedonian-American People's League and the Bulgarian-American People's League whose president was Victor Sharenkoff. The president of the ASC was Leo Krzycki (of Polish descent) while the secretary general became George Pirinsky. He was for years the most active of all the leaders of this movement. He showed fanatical devotion to the cause.

The cause prospered in America because of America's alliance with the Soviet Union. Pirinsky and a host of other Bulgarians spared no effort in getting the support of the Slavic masses for the Soviet Union and Communist-led liberation movements in the homelands. To show this support some sixty thousand Slavic Americans in Soldiers Field in Chicago answered the call of the American Slav Congress on July 19, 1942. The Bulgarians and Macedonians were also present and "outstanding Americans were induced to sponsor this and other meetings of the American Slav Congress in line with the spirit of American-Soviet cooperation at the time."[9]

A great majority of Bulgarians in America were loyal to the U.S. government and supported the war effort. Thousands of them joined the armed forces and fought with distinction. Hundreds were killed and wounded on many fronts. On the home front among the Slavic workers, who comprised fifty-three percent of the work force in the heavy and essential industries, thousands were Bulgarians.

During the weekend of July 17–18, 1943, the Michigan Slav Congress held a mass gathering of Slavs in Detroit. A meeting of some five thousand people was also held at Keyworth Stadium in Hamtrack and the left-oriented Bulgarians and Macedonians came together to discuss their wartime actions. The principal speaker at the stadium was George Pirinsky.[10]

III   *The Dilemma Goes On*

The delegates of the Macedonian left participated also on August 7, 1943, in the mass gathering at the Slovenian National Home in Cleveland where Louis Adamic and Zlatko Baloković founded the United Committee of South Slavic Americans. Adamic was elected its president while several Bulgarians and Macedonians joined its national board. The main purpose of the Committee was to promote the cause of a Communist Yugoslav federation under Tito. One of its republics would be Macedonia.

In the same year Adamic's *My Native Land* was published. It was hailed by the *Daily Worker* and other Communist and leftist papers. In this controversial book Adamic advocated the establishment of a Yugoslav or Balkan federation which would be "a republic within the Soviet Union, and would most likely be headed by Tito or Dimitroff." Or, as he wrote, "there may be a number of small Soviet republics: Slovenia, Croatia, Serbia, Macedonia, Bulgaria, etc."[11]

The role of Adamic, Baloković, and Pirinsky was gratefully acknowledged by the Second Session of the Anti-Fascist Council of the National Liberation of Yugoslavia which met at the Bosnian town of Jajce in Communist-controlled territory on November 29, 1943. This event is regarded as the beginning of the Communist Yugoslav Republic. The Council sent a message of thanks to the South Slavic leaders in America. Tito himself later, in March 1944, sent a letter addressed to Adamic and a message to "dear brothers across the ocean."[12]

By the end of November and beginning of December 1943 during the Teheran Conference (Roosevelt, Churchill, Stalin attending) the U.S. government recognized Tito's National Liberation Front and pledged his fighting partisans military and diplomatic support. This encouraged leftist sentiment among the South Slavs in America even more and increased the dilemma of many Bulgarians and other non-Communist South Slavs. Various leftist organizations and hundreds of tireless activists collected large sums of money, great amounts of food, clothing, and medicine for the partisans in Yugoslavia. Baloković headed the American Committee for Yugoslav Relief for the people in the homeland and in Allied refugee camps. Mrs. Eleanor Roosevelt was the honorary president of this relief committee. Over $750,000 were collected in the United States in cash and millions of dollars worth of material aid. A substantial amount was donated by American Bulgarians and Macedonians.[13]

Closely related to the American Slav Congress was the International Workers Order, a Communist front organization with some 160,000 members. It had special sections for the Bulgarian and individual South Slavic groups. The Bulgarians were well represented at the second congress of the American Slav Congress assembled (with some twenty-five hundred delegates) in Pittsburgh during September 23–24, 1944. The South Slavs comprised a majority. They met in an atmosphere of jubilation over the victories of the advancing Soviet armies in East Europe. Again the speakers stressed that the Congress represented fifteen million Slavs. The entire war industry depended on them. One million Slavs were fighting in the U.S. armed forces. The guest speakers included Harold I. Ickes, the Secretary of the Interior.[14]

With their mother country fighting on the side of Germany, loyal non-leftist Bulgarians who abstained from all pro-Soviet activities found themselves in a difficult position. The Bulgarian and other leftist papers labeled them pro-German and anti-American. The Macedonian Patriotic Organization still advocated the cause of an independent and united Macedonia "where all the nationalities will have equal rights and duties." As expressed in their weekly, the *Macedonian Tribune*, they continued to oppose the aims of Greece and Yugoslavia to retain parts of Macedonia and the goal of the Bulgarian government to absorb all Macedonia within Bulgaria.

The non-leftist Bulgarians were disturbed by the whole campaign of defamation that was waged against them. They tried to explain to the American public why Bulgaria under King Boris sided with the Axis powers. Thus the Bulgarian Bureau of Information in Oak Park, Illinois, attempted in various publications to defend the cause of a free non-Communist Bulgaria.[15] On the other hand, leftist publications like *Narodna Volya* and *Trudova Macedonia* and the Bulgarian Telegraphic Agency propagated establishment of a Communist Bulgaria. They supported the pro-Tito Macedonian Liberation Front in occupied Yugoslavia which fought for a Macedonian republic within a Yugoslav federation.

In September 1944 the Soviet army overran Bulgaria. A Communist-dominated coalition government was installed in Sofia and it declared war on Germany. A few months later the whole of Yugoslav Macedonia came under Tito's rule. After his victory in May 1945, a federal republic was proclaimed in Belgrade in November of the same year and Macedonia became one of its six federated republics with a capital in Skopje. Tito and his Macedonian collaborators now claimed that the Macedonian question was solved once and for all.

During the summer of 1945 the Macedonian Patriotic Organization printed a book *The Case for an Autonomous Macedonia*. The old Macedonian problem was presented entirely through the eyes of foreigners: French, English and American scholars, missionaries, and writers. This publication came out at the time when many South Slavs and Americans protested against the bold leftist pro-Soviet campaign and the authorities in Washington became apprehensive about the rising leftist anti-American propaganda.

The third American Slav Congress convened at Manhattan Center in New York during September 20–22, 1946, with some seventeen hundred delegates present. George Pirinsky, the executive secretary of the ASC, delivered the keynote speech in which he sharply criticized American foreign policy and the alleged American "intervention" in Bulgaria and Yugoslavia. The main speakers included the Soviet general Gundorov and the Bulgarian Communist from Sofia, Tsola Dragoicheva. She brought the greetings of Georgi Dimitrov who now ruled Bulgaria, having returned from Moscow after many years of absence. The Yugoslav Communist delegates were denied entry to New York by U.S. authorities; the relations between the United States and Yugoslavia were at a low point after Tito's forces had shot down two U.S. airplanes over Slovenia, killing several Americans. Stalin sent his greetings in a telegram to this congress and *Izvestia* in Moscow on September 24 published a very favorable account of the congress quoting Pirinsky, Adamic, and others who in their speeches denounced the U.S. "imperialist" policies.[16]

This was the time of the "Cold War" between the United States and the Soviet Union. In September 1946 Bulgaria was proclaimed a People's Republic and the young King Simeon was expelled from the country. The relations between Bulgaria—now a docile Soviet satellite—and the United States became very strained and for a long time there were no diplomatic relations. In Bulgaria many Bulgarians were accused of being American spies and condemned by "People's Courts" to death or years of imprisonment, while thousands of anti-Communists were either liquidated or sent to concentration camps. As in Yugoslavia, all political opposition was eliminated. By violating wartime agreements, the Russians gained strict control of the Balkans, and while U.S. authorities started to investigate the leftist activities during and after the war, Pirinsky and his men would not cease their determined course of action. Thus on the occasion of Dimitrov's sixty-fifth birthday, the *Narodna Volya* devoted its June 20, 1947 issue to him. The paper reported that the Bulgarian-American People's Union sent him a letter stating: "We Bulgarians in the United States wish you health and a long life to lead the Bulgarian people...."[17]

The Bulgarians in America were by various means induced to send food parcels, clothing, and other items to the homeland. The extent of this aid is evident from the report of the U.S. Department of Commerce which made public the fact that between July 1, 1947 and June 30, 1948 alone $3,747,000 worth in parcels was sent to Bulgaria. The value of parcels sent to Yugoslavia during the same period was $4,427,000. Considering the fact that there are more than ten times as many immigrants from Yugoslavia as there are from Bulgaria, the amount of this kind of aid to Bulgaria was indeed substantial.

In May 1948, the Committee on Un-American Activities of the House of Representatives and the U.S. Attorney General branded the American Slav Congress and its affiliates as "a Moscow inspired and directed federation of Communist-dominated organizations" seeking by methods of propaganda to influence the ten million people in this country of Slavic birth or descent. Its aim was, they claimed, "to utilize Slavic organizations in the United States as a pro-Soviet fifth column."[18]

In June 1948 Stalin expelled Tito and his Communist Party from the ranks of Cominform (which replaced the defunct Comintern) and this Soviet-Yugoslav break caused a split within the Communist ranks in the United States. A majority of their organizations in the United States sided with Stalin and took an anti-Tito position. Neither this split nor the condemnations by U.S. authorities could deter the American Slav Congress from holding its fourth congress in Chicago during September 24–26, 1948. However, shortly before that Pirinsky was arrested. The Soviet government sent a telegram to the American Slav Congress protesting Pirinsky's arrest and hailing him as "the fighter against fascism, and for peace and democracy." The congress stood up for Henry Wallace as the presidential candidate on the ticket of the Progressive Party. The speakers and various papers supporting the American Slav Congress accused the United States of planning a new war against the Communist states in Europe. Pirinsky was later released and, while fighting deportation, continued his campaign against American foreign policy. And on March 14, 1949, the Bulgarian Home Service radioed from Sofia that "the American Slav Congress condemned the Atlantic Pact project." It quoted Pirinsky still as the "general secretary" of the ASC who denounced NATO and American goals.[19]

During the years of investigation and hearings in Washington, the reports and documents printed in the course of what sometimes seemed a "witch hunt" against the radical activists, included all details of activities and published names of all the people involved. Among the several Bulgarian and Macedonian left-front organizations mentioned was the Bulgarian-American Committee for Protection of Foreign Born. Along with various Slavic committees for the protection of the foreign born it was a part of the nationwide American Committee for the Protection of Foreign Born. The authorities labeled it a hard-core Communist front movement whose main purpose was to prevent deportation of leftist activists. In spite of these efforts some South Slavic leftists were either deported or left the country voluntarily. In fact, immediately after the war many relinquished their American citizenship to assume government posts in Communist-ruled countries.[20]

Many American Bulgarians and their fellow Slavs were perplexed by the investigations. Except for hard-core activists, hundreds of them were far from being Communists and had only followed what had been in wartime the official American policy of alliance with the Soviets. A historian of immigration may be surprised to find even the name of the old friend of Slavic fellow citizens, Emily Greene Balch, on a list of left-front activists.[21]

CHAPTER 21

The Present and Future

AMONG the Bulgarian and Macedonian anonymous immigrants the women deserve special recognition. They appeared on the scene considerably later than their husbands. Beset by innumerable hardships and grueling household chores, they lived in constant fear of industrial accidents, strikes, and violence.

Ever since the 1890s when the Bulgarians started to arrive in larger numbers, they—both men and women—have been giving their energy to the building of America. In America's wars of this century, as well as in steel mills, mines, and factories hundreds died or were maimed. This was their supreme sacrifice, their contribution in blood to America.

The earliest Bulgarian contributors in the late 1800s and in the early twentieth century were doctors and educators. They were sponsored by the Protestant missionaries. Unfortunately, the names of these contributors fell into obscurity.

Stephen Panaretoff, a former professor at the well-known American-established Robert College in Constantinople, served as the Bulgarian Minister to the United States between 1914 and 1924. Others taught philosophy, history, engineering, biology, and other disciplines. George Dimitroff worked for years at the Harvard Observatory. Assen Jordanoff, a former World War I pilot, served as technical adviser to prominent aircraft manufacturers and airlines. The roster of the more outstanding Bulgarians includes scholars, inventors, sculptors and writers, a prominent architect, and a noted photographer among others.

Assen Nicoloff finished the American High School in Samkov, Bulgaria, came to America in 1927, earned degrees from Oberlin College and Northwestern University, and returned to Sofia in 1930. When he came back to the United States, he received more degrees and worked as a librarian and scholar. He is the author of several books on Bulgarian history and literature.

Atanas Katchamakoff was a sculptor, illustrator, and writer who, under the pseudonym Monica Shannon, published the novel *Dobry*. It won the John Newbery Medal in 1935 "for the most distinguished contribution to American literature for children."

Of the Bulgarian singers in the Metropolitan Opera in New York, the best known is Ljuba Welitsch, a soprano who made her American debut in February 1949. Other "Met" stars were Lubomir Vishegonov and Boris Christov.

Among the most successful writers has been Stoyan Christowe mentioned elsewhere in this book. Besides *This Is My Country*, he published five other books. He moved to Vermont in the late 1930s and served in its state legislature for twelve years (until 1972). Now 77, he lives with his wife in a house he built himself sixteen years ago. On the occasion of the U.S. Bicentennial he expressed in his statement for *Newsweek* (of July 4, 1976) his great love and belief in the future of his adopted country.

As educators and scientists the Bulgarians have contributed more than their share. Dr. Stefan Stojanoff is eminent in research in antibiotics. Others have excelled in business, sports, engineering, organized labor, and federal jobs. Their gifts to the folklore are varied and colorful. Nicholas Jordanoff is one of the leading men in the Duquesne University Tamburitzans, one of the best folklore groups in the country. Among the "Tammies" many young Bulgarians have over the last forty years helped in presenting, here and abroad, the Bulgarian folk dances, accompanied by Bulgarian music (including drums and flutes) and exhibiting beautiful national costumes of various regions of the homeland.

Many Bulgarians are today in the mainstream of American life. They can be identified if their last names end with "off" or "ov." However, others—like their other fellow South Slavs— are hidden behind their adopted Anglo-Saxon names.[1]

Because of the confusing way in which the U.S. Immigration Service classified entering immigrants, it is impossible to give an accurate number of the three generations of Bulgarians who live in America. According to some estimates, there are over 100,000 Bulgarians, born either in this country or in the Balkans, living in almost all fifty states. They are concentrated mostly in the Midwest and in Pennsylvania. A great majority of all

American Bulgarians came from Macedonia which is ruled now by Yugoslavia, Greece, and Bulgaria.

According to the official immigration statistics, 67,250 Bulgarian immigrants were admitted between June 1920 and June 30, 1973. As our Immigration and Naturalization Service classifies the immigrants by "the country or region of birth," it is difficult to count members of an ethnic or nationality group whose geographical origins vary. Between 1946 and 1974 under "Refugees Admitted by Country or Region of Birth" some 3,750 came from Bulgaria.[2]

In 1973 only 320, and in 1974 only 189 immigrants from Bulgaria were admitted, while in years preceding the 1970s there were usually less than 100. The number of immigrants from Bulgaria, all of Bulgarian nationality, is therefore one of the smallest of any nationality group in America. Apparently the People's Republic of Bulgaria does not permit any significant outflow of immigrants. Only a few hundred Bulgarians after a long struggle have been permitted to go to the United States, but even this number in the 1970s presents a considerable increase over the immigration during the quarter of a century between 1946 and 1970. The relations between the United States and Bulgaria are much more relaxed in this decade than before, and the ties between the Zhivkov government in Sofia and that in Washington have been normalized. The Bulgarians are trying to attract American tourists and many American magazines advertise the beautiful beaches on the Black Sea and other scenic parts of Bulgaria. More American scholars now visit Bulgaria, attend the international Slavists' congresses in Sofia, while more Bulgarians are allowed to visit the United States. The American Bulgarians hope that progressive relaxation of conditions in the homeland will result in more immigrants to America, especially those related to Bulgarians already here.

Some Bulgarian immigrants come from Greece, from the Macedonian settlements in so-called Aegean Macedonia. The largest number of Bulgarian immigrants now come from Yugoslavia, from the Macedonian Republic and from the autonomous region of Kossovo-Metohija (Kosmet). From the annual average number of some five thousand immigrants from Yugoslavia, about ten percent are Bulgarian-speaking Macedonians. Because of the impractical system of classification by our Immigration and Naturalization Service, all Bulgarian immigrants from Yugoslavia and other lands are *not* counted as Bulgarians but as Yugoslavs, Greeks, and others.

I *The Gulf between the Generations*

The Bulgarian immigrants after the last war differed in many ways from their ancestors who came before the 1920s. While the old immigrants were predominantly peasants, during the last thirty years the newcomers included a large number of educated and skilled people. This is especially true of those who have come to the United States during the last ten or fifteen years. Inevitably, there is a gulf between the old and new generations. A whole new, young generation of these and other Balkan immigrants grew up under Communism and even though many may not believe in it, they were inevitably affected by it in many ways. This, of course, creates animosities that result in separation and conflict. Many newcomers either don't care about the church and observance of religious practices, or if they attend church, they opt for the faction in the church that supports the patriarch in the old country in the continuing split within the Bulgarian Orthodox Church.

A recent reference book lists four Bulgarian-language papers with a circulation of some ten thousand. Some appeared in recent years and were of short duration.[3] The *Macedonian Tribune* (Makedonska Tribuna) is still going strong after fifty years of publication. As evident from its columns, it is generously supported by the readers and political organizations with donations in money and paid advertisements. The large size format with special enlarged issues for Christmas, the New Year, and Easter, and many advertisements offers still the best chronicle of Bulgarian life in this country. To bridge the gap between the old and new generations the *Tribune* frequently prints special English-language sections.

II *Partial Revival*

A fair number of Bulgarian immigrants and refugees—intellectuals, exiled politicians, professors, and other professionals—

have met with success in reviving Bulgarian culture and political life. The Macedonians are divided on the issue of Macedonia. There are certain animosities between those that came from Yugoslav Macedonia and those who came from Bulgaria and Greek-controlled southern Macedonia. The old Macedonian Patriotic Organization still holds very well attended yearly conventions with many political, social, and religious activities. The MPO is still against the regime in Belgrade and opposes the Communist regime in Sofia. The *Macedonian Tribune* as its organ still prints appeals, letters, and articles by the old leader of the Internal Macedonian Revolutionary Organization, Ivan Mihailoff. His memoirs (written in Bulgarian) are advertised by the paper and are avidly read. To many of the old and young, "Vanča" remains the symbol of the old revolutionary struggle and the guerrilla warfare in the mountains of the homeland.

The policy of the Macedonian Patriotic Organization remains unchanged: liberation and unification of Macedonia as a sort of Switzerland of the Balkans. As the Bulgarian government under Premier Zhivkov continues to raise its claims to the Macedonian Republic in Yugoslavia, the goals of the Macedonian patriots in exile and those of the government in Sofia are pretty much identical.

In 1976 Bulgarians and Macedonians everywhere commemorated the centenary of their revolt of 1876 against the Turks and the beginning of the liberation of Bulgaria. This centenary also affected Bulgarian politics in the old country and in immigrant colonies abroad. In 1977 the American Macedonians continue to stress the role of Macedonia in the Balkan vortex. The old slogan that was inscribed on the flags of the fighting Macedonian *komitadjis* (guerrilla fighters) "Svoboda ili smert!" (Liberty or death) is still repeated in the most recent issues of Macedonian publications.[4]

In their political activities the Macedonians have cordial relations with the Croatians. Usually some Croatian political delegates attend the annual MPO convention or are main speakers. In their press the Macedonians frequently write about the Croatian problem while the Croatians often refer with sympathy to the Macedonian struggle. To inform the English-speaking world of the problems of Macedonia, the Macedonians started in January 1967 the publication of a review in English called *Balkania*. It is an "International Quarterly on Balkan Affairs," printed in St. Louis and edited by Christ Anastasoff.

One individual who disappointed those Macedonians who are opposed to Belgrade's rule was the writer Stoyan Christowe. In 1953, when his compatriots lived in Macedonia under very harsh conditions, he went to Yugoslavia for a five months visit, was dined and wined by the authorities, and was received by Tito.[5] Macedonian patriots thought Christowe should have stayed away from such a visit. However, like him, many old immigrants, who have not seen the country for decades, visit the homeland. This does not necessarily mean that they condone Tito's rule in Macedonia. Trips to Macedonia as well as to Bulgaria are also undertaken by American-born Bulgarians and Macedonians.

A Yugoslav organization catering to returning emigrants, the "Matica," exists in the Macedonian republic. It publishes its monthly magazine and provides guided tours for American visitors through the republic and other parts of Yugoslavia. The authorities try to impress on the visitors the achievements of the Communist regime; the political activists in America denounce such trips as a betrayal of the national cause. They also object to the help American tourists give by bringing their dollars to the Communist regime. The jet age did bring Skopje much closer to the American Bulgarian immigrants.

There exists in America a Bulgarian National Front whose recent president was Dr. Ivan Docheff. It held its eleventh congress on March 7–8, 1970 in Washington, D.C., dedicated to "the heroes of the 25-year resistance against Communism and for the liberation of Bulgaria." The invocation was said by the Bulgarian Diocesan Prelate in Exile, H. E. Bishop Kyril. Congressman John Murphy and other distinguished Americans joined some eight hundred Bulgarians who attended. The twenty-fifth anniversary of the BNF was celebrated on March 18–19, 1972, also in Washington, D.C. The Bi-annual Congress was held at the same time.[6]

The leading Bulgarian democratic politician in exile was Georgi M. Dimitroff (no relation to his Communist namesake). In the homeland he was the president of the Bulgarian Peasant

Party. After escaping from Bulgaria, where he was sentenced to death, he found asylum in Washington, D.C. Like several others he was accused by the Red rulers as an American spy. He died in Washington in November 1972.[7]

Dimitroff, the exiled agrarian, and other politicians from Bulgaria disagreed with some of the issues of the Macedonian Patriotic Organization. Disagreements seem to exist even within the ranks of the MPO itself, as evident from a letter by the leader of the Internal Macedonian Revolutionary Organization, Ivan Mihailoff, which was printed in the *Macedonian Tribune*, issue of April 1, 1971. Mihailoff refers to "Communist attempts in America to break the MPO." One of those attempts was made by George Pirinsky who—as we learn here—was later deported by the United States for his leftist activities.

Constant efforts are being made to preserve the Macedonian heritage, especially among the younger generation. This is evident from special English-language issues of the *Macedonian Tribune* dedicated to the young Macedonians. The Macedonian Patriotic Organization has a special Youth Section which stimulates various activities. The Ladies Section of the same organization makes similar efforts. At its Fifteenth Annual Conference held in Indianapolis in May 1972, Mrs. Zhivka Tsafarova of Toronto delivered the main speech under the title "The Women in the Macedonian Liberation Movement, Past and Present." Indeed, the role of women in the MPO as well as throughout the Macedonian struggle has been very important. Some women died as revolutionary heroines with rifles in their hands or were tortured to death by enemy police.[8]

III   Ethnic Pride

The feelings of the young Macedonians are well described in an issue of the *Tribune*, in a short article written by Suzy Repplogle, whose father is German and mother is Macedonian (maiden name Lebanoff). In her article "I am Proud," Suzy writes that she has always looked upon herself "as being Macedonian." Her two brothers and she were "raised as Macedonians." She participates in a folklore group performing at annual conventions of the MPO. She likes the *Macedonian Tribune* which arrives at their home every weekend. She cannot read Bulgarian, but she enjoys the English page. She is a member of the Youth Section of the MPO and thus keeps in touch with her "blood brothers—Macedono-Bulgarians," as she calls them. In conclusion she adds: "Our family is proud to be called Macedonians! Even my dad considers himself a Macedonian at heart. My mother did a great job indoctrinating us all. I still remember my brother Dan, crying as if his heart was broken when he realized that he was only half Macedonian. This is also the way I feel."[9]

This is the way many of the young generation feel. After a Ph.D. candidate from Fort Wayne, Indiana, gave a lecture on Macedonian folklore, a reporter of the *Tribune* wrote: "We discussed our Macedonian heritage with emphasis on our church beliefs, weddings, name days, and unique customs. It was a most enjoyable opportunity for us to freely express our pride in being Macedonians."[10]

This pride was also evident when on January 28, 1972 Ivan Argire Lebanoff was sworn in as the thirty-eighth mayor of the same city, Fort Wayne. He is a Democrat, a prominent member of the MPO, and has been active in the local Orthodox parish and entire community. "Fort Wayne Macedonians stand tall and proud" because of their mayor, stated the *Tribune* on March 30, 1972.

Pride was expressed by the same paper in one of its recent issues when it published (along with a photograph) the news that John S. Kostoff, age 36, son of Draga Teodoroff and the late Richard M. Kostoff, was recently promoted to full professor of mathematics at Delta College, Bay City, Michigan. To the members of a small ethnic group such an event is important; its reaction reflects tremendous respect for education. It has been a long way from the steel mills and mines, where illiterate Balkan peasants worked, to the halls of academe where their grandsons, some of them doctors of philosophy, teach young Americans. But the two generations—set apart by some fifty years of long and painful struggle—are fatefully and inevitably linked. The grandparents prepared the road to success for the grandchildren.[11]

Many old-timers who fled the oppression of the Balkan rulers and brought with them the memory of the bloody risings and wars will soon completely disappear from the scene. The Bulgarian-Macedonian political leaders and activists are faced with the same problem that affects other South Slavs in this country: they are getting old while a new and, in many ways, different generation is emerging in the homeland as well as in their adopted country. Unlike other South Slavs whose number is augmented by a constant influx of thousands of immigrants, the Bulgarians—as already explained—are receiving few newcomers. If this very limited immigration from Macedonia and Bulgaria continues, within two or three decades, the Bulgarian ethnic group in America will dwindle down to a very small community.

IV *Conclusions*

According to the U.S. Census of 1960, there were 448,503 Americans whose country of origin is Yugoslavia. These statistics do not specify their ethnic composition. The Census of 1970 indicates 447,273 in the same group. Of those, 154,000 were born in the old country. Those who have one foreign-born parent are considered individuals of foreign extraction.

There are reasons to believe that these census statistics are unreliable and much too low. Thousands of people of the third and even fourth generation still identify themselves as members of one of the six South Slavic ethnic groups. This trend is understandable in this era of ethnicity and signifies a search for "roots."

To the question of who were the most outstanding individuals from among the peoples who have come from the Balkans, the author would name three. One is the Slovenian missionary, Bishop Frederick Baraga. Another is Nikola Tesla of Serbian nationality, the inventor and scientist. And the most recent one is the Croatian universal artist, Ivan Meštrović. Each of them was great in his own way. All three enriched America considerably. They left a memorable heritage to the descendants of the South Slavic peoples. Each one was of peasant background. They were similar in that they believed in the freedom and dignity of *all* men.

Even though the Bulgarians and Macedonians did not produce

a giant comparable to these three, Stoyan Christowe, who is still alive, can be singled out as the best representative of his people. The most significant contributors, however, among these people—and among all South Slavs—are still the anonymous immigrants—men and women. They helped to build modern America. Their descendants, living between the Atlantic and Pacific, still regard it as a land of opportunity, a land of the future. Each year approximately six thousand South Slavs come here in search of freedom and bread. They emigrate in fast jet planes, not on ships as the generations have done before. For them the "Golden Gates" to America are not Ellis Island, but usually Kennedy International Airport. These modern-age immigrants arrive under more favorable circumstances than those encountered by their forefathers. And they assert themselves much sooner.

Thousands of their countrymen form very active and live ethnic communities. New ethnic awareness, close contacts with the homeland, and a steady influx of thousands of new immigrants will undoubtedly prolong the existence of distinct Slovenian, Croatian, and Serbian communities for many years to come. However, the future of the Macedonian and Bulgarian community looks less optimistic if present trends continue.

The body of Bishop Baraga rests in the crypt of St. Peter's Cathedral in Marquette, Michigan. Thousands of American Slovenians come here each year to pray. Revered in his own day, Baraga's reputation for sanctity has been increasing. On September 19, 1970 the *New York Times* reported from Marquette that the Diocese of Marquette, having completed the long, prescribed proceedings, officially submitted the proposal to the Vatican's Congregation of Holy Rites for Baraga's beatification. After this the necessary steps will be undertaken for his canonization. If this ever happens, Baraga would be the first Slovenian and Slavic saint on American soil.

Shortly before his death, in the midst of a horrible war, Nikola Tesla stated in 1942:

Out of this war . . . a new world must be born . . . a world in which there shall be no exploitation of the weak by the strong, of the good by the evil; where there will be no humiliation of the poor by the violence of the rich; where the products of intellect, science and art will serve society for betterment and beautification of life, and not the individual for achieving wealth. This new world shall not be a world of the down-trodden and humiliated, but of free men and free nations, equal in dignity and respect for man.[12]

If this dream of Tesla—and of his many fellow immigrants from the Balkans—has not yet become a reality, it is a worthy ideal for the future.

Ivan Meštrović, too, in his sculptures and in his writings expressed hope in the future and his respect for the freedom and dignity of man. Unlike Baraga and Tesla he is buried in his native soil. There he rests surrounded by a people who firmly believe in his ideals and who, like their immigrant brothers in America, want to live as free men.

Notes and References

Chapter One

1. On what has been done in this field see Charles Jelavich, ed. *Language and Area Studies: East Central and Southeastern Europe* (University of Chicago Press, 1969), 470 pp.; Thomas F. Magner, "Russia's 'Sputnik' Brought Slav Peoples to Forefront," *Zajedničar* (Pittsburgh), April 23, 1958, p. 8; Louis Adamic, "Foreigners are News in Cleveland," *My America* (New York, 1938), pp. 233–237; "Ethnic Heritage Revival Described," *The Plain Dealer,* February 18, 1972, p. 1-B. This manuscript was finished in 1976!

2. *Congressional Record,* Vol. 118, No. 96, June 14, 1972, one-page reprint distributed by U.S. Senator Richard S. Schweiker (R-Pa), "Ethnic Heritage Studies Bill Passes Congress."

3. Henry A. Christian, *Louis Adamic: A Checklist* (Kent State University Press, 1971). The titles of Adamic's works appear in the bibliography of this book; for detailed bibliographies on South Slavs see also: George J. Prpic, *The Croatian Immigrants in America* (New York, 1971), pp. 471–499.

4. Francis Dvornik, *The Slavs: Their Early History and Civilization* (Boston, 1956); Roger Portal, *The Slavs* (New York, 1969), translated by Patrick Evans; Joseph S. Roucek, ed. *Slavonic Encyclopedia* (New York, 1949); Oscar Halecki, *Borderlands of Western Civilization* (New York, 1952).

5. Ferdinand Schevill, *A History of the Balkan Peninsula from the Earliest Times to the Present Day* (New York, 1933); Christ Anastasoff, *The Tragic Peninsula* (St. Louis, 1938) emphasizes Bulgaria and Macedonia. René Ristelhueber, *A History of the Balkan Peoples* (Twayne Publishers, 1971).

6. Francis H. Eterovich and Christopher Spalatin, eds. *Croatia: Land, People, Culture* (University of Toronto Press, 1964), Vol. I, p. 8, and in Vol. II (University of Toronto Press, 1970), Stanko Guldescu, "Croatian Political History 1526–1918," pp. 3–118.

7. On the limits of the Balkans see also L. von Südland, *Die Südslawische Frage und der Weltkrieg* (Zagreb, 1944), pp. 151–153.

8. *Statistički Godišnjak SFRJ 1963* (Belgrade, 1963), Vol. X, p. 336; *Yugoslav Survey* (Belgrade, 1971), Vol. XII, p. 3; Stane Stanić,

257

"Nacije u popisu," *N. I. N.* (Belgrade), May 28, 1972, pp. 31–35. The population of Yugoslavia in 1976 was about 22.5 million.

9. Dominik Mandić, *Hrvatske zemlje u prošlosti i sadašnjosti* (Croatian Lands in the Past and Present) (Rome, 1972), pp. 9–11.

10. Ivo Baučić, *The Effects of Emigration from Yugoslavia and the Problems of Returning Emigrant Workers* (The Hague, 1972), 48 pp.

11. Ristelhueber, *A History of the Balkan Peoples*, "The Madedonian Question," pp. 172–182, and map on p. 360. Alan Palmer, *The Lands Between* (New York, 1970), pp. 104–106.

Chapter Two

1. Joseph Felicijan, *The Genesis of the Contractual Theory and the Installation of the Dukes of Carinthia* (Cleveland-Klagenfurt, 1967), 144 pp.

2. Stephen Gaži, *A History of Croatia* (New York, 1973), pp. 98–99.

3. John A. Arnež, *Slovenia in European Affairs* (New York, 1958), 204 pp.; Rudolf Čuješ, *This Is Slovenia* (Toronto, 1958), 221 pp. Louis Adamic wrote a great deal on all phases of Slovenian history, especially in his books *The Native's Return* (New York, 1934), *My Native Land* (New York, 1943), and *The Eagle and the Roots* (New York, 1952).

4. M. Pivec-Stelé, *La Vie Economique des Provinces Illyriènnes* (Paris, 1930); Hans Kohn, *Pan-Slavism* (New York, 1962), p. 60.

5. George J. Prpić, "French Rule in Croatia: 1806–1813," *Balkan Studies* (Salonica), Vol. 5 (1964), pp. 223–276.

6. Bogumil Vošnjak, *A Bulwark Against Germany* (London, 1917); many pages in Rebecca West's *Black Lamb and Grey Falcon* (New York, 1941) deal with the history of the Slovenians and other South Slavs.

7. Stanko Guldescu, *History of Medieval Croatia* (The Hague, 1964), pp. 11–106. Dominik Mandić, *Crvena Hrvatska* (Rome, 1973), new edition, 354 pp.

8. Robert A. Kann, "The Croats," in his *The Multinational Empire* (Columbia University Press, 1950), Vol. I, pp. 233–259; Stephen Gaži, *A History of Croatia* (New York, 1973), pp. 1–110. F. H. Eterovich and C. Spalatin, eds. *Croatia: Land, People, Culture* (University of Toronto Press, 1964), Vol. I, 408 pp. Dominik Mandić, *Bosna i Hercegovina* (Chicago, 1960), 487 pp.

9. George J. Prpić, *Tragedies and Migrations in Croatian History* (Toronto, 1973), 32 pp. Gunther E. Rothenberg, *The Austrian Military Border in Croatia: 1522–1747* (Urbana, 1960), 156 pp., and *The*

Military Border in Croatia, 1740–1881 (University of Chicago Press, 1966), 224 pp.

10. Ernest Bauer, *Glanz und Tragik der Kroaten* (Vienna-Muenich, 1969), 107 pp.; *Zwischen Halbmond und Doppeladler* (Vienna-Muenich, 1971), 191 pp.; *Drei Leopardenköpfe in Gold* (Vienna-Muenich, 1973), 302 pp.

11. The origin of the Vlachs is not certain. The Balkan Vlachs (*Vlasi* in Slavic languages) were nomadic shepherds. In Macedonia and Albania they still speak a Rumanian dialect. Most of them have been assimilated by their neighbors. A greater part of the Serbs in Croatian lands are of Vlach origin.

12. Chapter "Serbia" in S. Clissold's *A Short History of Yugoslavia* (Cambridge, England, 1968), pp. 87–134; Phylis Auty, *Yugoslavia* (New York, 1965), pp. 25–37; Portal, *The Slavs*, pp. 364–379; a large number of books in English dealing with Yugoslavia, discuss all aspects of Serbian history. See also Robert W. Seton-Watson, *The Rise of Nationality in the Balkans* (London, 1917); L. S. Stavrianos, *The Balkans Since 1453* (New York, 1958).

13. As quoted in Milovan Djilas, *Land Without Justice*, introduction and notes by William Jovanovich (New York, 1958), p. x. In this autobiography of his youth Djilas, a leading dissident in present Yugoslavia, gives a good analysis of his native Montenegro.

14. Sekula Drljević, *Balkanski sukobi: 1905–1941* (The Balkan Clashes) (Zagreb, 1944); and D. Mandić, *Crvena Hrvatska* (Chicago, 1957), pp. 248–255.

15. Djilas, *Land Without Justice*, p. xi.

16. Leon Sciaky, *Farewell to Salonica* (New York, 1946) pp. 132–155, 171–183, describes the life in Salonica, its cosmopolitan society, and the struggle of the Macedonian revolutionists.

17. Stephen Runciman, *A History of the First Bulgarian Empire* (London, 1930); Will A. Monroe, *Bulgaria and Her People: With an Account of the Balkan Wars, Macedonia and Macedonian Bulgers* (Boston, 1914); C. Anastasoff, *The Tragic Peninsula* (Saint Louis); Ivan Mihailoff, *Macedonia: A Switzerland of the Balkans* (St. Louis, 1950), 139 pp.; George B. Zotiades, *The Macedonian Controversy* (Salonica, 1961), 132 pp.; and Djoko Slijepčević, *The Macedonian Question* (Chicago, 1958), 267 pp. These reflect several views on Macedonia.

18. For additional information see also: Reuben M. Markham, *Meet Bulgaria* (Sofia, 1931); Elizabeth Barker, *Macedonia, Its Place in Balkan Power Politics* (London, 1950); and the recent Stephen E. Palmer, Jr. and Robert R. King, *Yugoslav Communism and the Macedonian Question* (Hamden, Conn., 1971).

Chapter Three

1. The definitive study of Dubrovnik is: Francis W. Carter, *Dubrovnik (Ragusa) a Classic City-state* (London, 1972), 710 pp.

2. G. J. Prpić, "Early Croatian Contacts with America and the Mystery of the Croatans," *Journal of Croatian Studies* (New York), Vol. I, 1960, pp. 6–24.

3. Vinko Foretić, "Činjenice i pretpostavke: veze starih Dubrovčana s novo-otkrivenim zemljama i njihovo iseljavanje" (Facts and Presuppositions: Relations of the Old Ragusans with the Newly-discovered Lands and Their Emigration), *Matica Iseljenički Kalendar za 1960* (Zagreb), pp. 143–156. Tias Mortidjija, "Die Kroatische 'Hansestadt' Dubrovnik," *Croatia*, Vol. VI (Zagreb, 1943), p. 54.

4. Foretić and Mortidjija, op. cit.

5. Josip Luetić, "1000 godina dubrovačkog brodarstva" (A Thousand Years of Ragusan Marine) (Zagreb, 1969), pp. 129–130; Adamic, *The Native's Return*, pp. 151–153.

6. W. F. Wingfield, *A Tour in Dalmatia, Albania and Montenegro; With a Historical Sketch of the Republic of Ragusa* (London, 1859), p. 290; R. West, *Black Lamb and Grey Falcon* (New York, 1941), p. 235.

7. He was Vicko Paletin (Vincentius Paletinus).

8. A. Zaninović, "Fra. Vicko Paletin," *Zbornik u povodu 700. obljetnice smrti Sv. Tome Akvinskoga* (Zagreb: Croatian Dominicans, 1974), pp. 195–199. The late Father Zaninović "discovered" Paletin for his countrymen. Nothing was written about him in the homeland until this study was published.

9. Prpić, "Early Croatian Contacts with America and the Mystery of the Croatans," pp. 14–15. In 1976 Captain Ivo Šišević published in Dubrovnik a 32-page booklet on the same topic, *Kroatski Indijanci,* with some interesting new discoveries.

10. Joseph S. Roucek, *One America,* (Englewood Cliffs, N.J., 1945), p. 158.

11. Francis L. Hawks, *History of North Carolina* (Fayetteville, 1956), Vol. I, pp. 80–92; Hamilton McMillan, *Sir Walter Raleigh's Lost Colony* (Wilson, N. C., 1888), p. 62.

12. Anon., "Das Ausgewanderte Kroatien," *Za Dom* (Zagreb), April 1, 1945, p. 5.

13. Ivan Mladineo, *Narodni Adresar-National Directory* (New York, 1937), p. xxii; L. Adamic, *A Nation of Nations*, p. 236; J. S. Roucek, *Our National Minorities* (New York, 1937), p. 247.

14. Adam S. Eterovich in "Croatians and the Salzburger Georgia Colony and Matija Gubec," *Zajedničar*, January 2, 1974, p. 2, presents final arguments: there were no South Slavs in Ebenezer!

15. Mladineo, *Narodni Adresar*, p. xvii.
16. Foretić, "Činjenice i pretpostavke," p. 152.

Chapter Four

1. G. J. Prpić, "Rev. Juan M. Ratkay, First Croatian Missionary in America, 1647–1683," *Studia Instituti Chroatorum* (Rome, 1971), Vols. III-IV, pp. 179–221.
2. *Der Neue Welt-Bott*. edited by J. Stoecklein (Augsburg and Graz, 1726), Vol. I, pp. 77–84; H. E. Bolton, *Rim of Christendom* (New York, 1936), pp. 51–55.
3. Prpić, op. cit., pp. 204–221; G. Decorme in his *La Obra de los Jesuitas Mexicanos*, 2 vols. (Mexico City, 1941), Vol. I, p. 410, calls Ratkay "a Croatian martyr."
4. M. D. Krmpotić, *Life and Works of the Reverend Ferdinand Konšćak, S.J.* (Boston, 1923), pp. 14–23.
5. P. M. Dunne, "Lower California, an Island?" *Mid America*, Vol. XXXV, No. 1 (January 1953), pp. 39–42.
6. P. M. Dunne, *Black Robes in Lower California* (Los Angeles, 1952), p. 375; Krmpotić, op. cit., pp. 6, 83–95.
7. Manuel P. Servin, *The Apostolic Life of Fernando Consag, Explorer of Lower California* (Los Angeles, 1968), p. 30.
8. Ibid., pp. 12–13.
9. B. J. Blied, "Leopoldinen Stiftung," *The New Catholic Encyclopedia*, Vol. VIII, p. 664; see also "Holy Men and Heathens" and "Trail Blazers All" in Gerald G. Govorchin, *Americans from Yugoslavia* (Gainesville, 1961), pp. 27–41.
10. Dunstan McAndrews, *Father Joseph Kundek* (St. Meinrad, Ind., 1954), 74 pp.; Prpić, *The Croatian Immigrants in America* (New York, 1971), pp. 51–55; *Katolički List* (Zagreb), March 27 and April 3, 1852.
11. Milos Vujnovich, *Yugoslavs in Louisiana* (Gretna, La., 1974), pp. 21–39 with excellent data on the early Croatians in the Gulf region and many names of those serving in the Confederate Army. A. S. Eterovich, "A Croatian Panorama of the West and South: 1700–1900," unpublished manuscript, p. 5.
12. Foretić, "Činjenice i pretpostavke," pp. 152–153; Prpić, *The Croatian Immigrants*, p. 24. See also most recent: Wayne Vucinich, ed., *Dubrovnik and American Revolution: F. Favi's Letters* (San Francisco, 1977).
13. Emily G. Balch, *Our Slavic Fellow Citizens* (New York, 1910), p. 194; T. H. Kane, *Deep Delta Country* (New York, 1944), p. 92; see his chapter "Dalmatia on the Mississippi," pp. 92–104.

14. Vujnovich, "Dalmatians In Louisiana," (unpublished study, 1971), pp. 4–5, and *Yugoslavs in Louisiana*, pp. 29.

15. Vujnovich, "Dalmatians...," pp. 1–2; Adam S. Eterovich, "Marco's Croatian Plantation," *Zajedničar*, March 20, 1974, p. 6.

16. Eterovich, *B.E.E.A.G.H.S.*, Vol. II, pp. 7, 11, 17–19; Eterovich, *Slavonic*, Vol. 1, No. 1 (June 1964), p. 7, from the microfilm on file in the New Orleans Public Library. Kane, *Deep Delta Country*, p. 93.

17. Ivan Krešić, "Industrija kamenica u Louisiani," *Danica Koledar za 1932* (New York), pp. 188–189.

18. Vujnovich, *Yugoslavs in Louisiana*, pp. 28, 29, 82.

19. Vujnović, "Jugoslaveni...," pp. 62–64.

20. John Badovinac, "Croatian Family listed Among Florida's Earliest Pioneers," *Zajedničar*, January 14, 1976, p. 2.

21. A. S. Eterovich, *Croatians from Dalmatia and Montenegrin Serbs in the West and South 1800–1900* (San Francisco, 1971), pp. 12–15; Vujnovich, *Yugoslavs...*, pp. 78–82, with the roster of the Cognevich Company.

22. Eterovich, *Croatians from Dalmatia...*, p. 14. Among those killed in Gettysburg was George Petrovich.

Chapter Five

1. L. D. Baldwin, *The Stream of American History* (New York, 1952), Vol. 1, pp. 710–715.

2. Adamic, *A Nation of Nations*, p. 239; Vjekoslav Meler, *Slavonic Pioneers in California* (San Francisco, 1932), p. 17; A. S. Eterovich, *Slavonic* (San Francisco, 1964), Vol. 1, No. 1, p. 9.

3. Eterovich, A. S. *Yugoslav Survey of California, Nevada, Arizona and the South, 1800–1900* (San Francisco, 1971), p. 57.

4. Eterovich, *B.E.E.A.G.H.S.*, Vol. II, No. 2, p. 6; Meler, *Slavonic Pioneers*, pp. 38–42.

5. Eterovich, A. S. "Croatian Pioneers on the Barbary Coast of San Francisco, 1849–1870," *Croatia Press* (New York), Vol. XVII (November 1963), p. 2.

6. Prpić, *The Croatian Immigrants*, pp. 62–64, with many names of the old pioneers.

7. Baldwin, op. cit., Vol. II, pp. 321–322, 339

8. John Badovinac, "A Story about Hawaii's Croatian 'King,'" *Zajedničar*, June 28, 1972; Vincent L. Knaus, "His Royal Highness, the Prince Consort John O. Dominis," *The American Croatian Historical Review* (Youngstown, Ohio), Vol. I, No. 2, August 1946, pp. 3–9.

9. Josip Splivalo, *Kruh sa sedam kora* (Bread with Seven Crusts) (Rijeka, 1966), p. 223. Mentions Captain Stephen Splivalo.

10. Eterovich, "Croatian Pioneers," pp. 2–3; Meler, *Slavonic Pioneers*, pp. 32–34.

11. Meler, op. cit., p. 34; Eterovich, A. S. *Croatian Cemetery Records of San Francisco, California 1849–1930* (San Francisco, 1964) reprints the records of buried people.

12. A. S. Eterovich, *Irish Slavonians in California 1849–1880* (San Francisco, 1964) lists hundreds of these "Irish Slavonians"; Meler, op. cit., pp. 42–43.

13. Eterovich, "Antonio Milatovich vs. the Republic of Mexico," *Croatians from Dalmatia*, pp. 33–35.

14. Prpić, *The Croatian Immigrants*, pp. 74–75; see quoted sources.

15. *Alaska Herald* (San Francisco), Vol. II, No. 39, August 15, 1869, p. 66. Courtesy of Adam S. Eterovich, San Francisco.

16. Eterovich, *Croatians from Dalmatia*, pp. 16–21.

17. *The Virginia Daily News*, September 20, 1864; *The Daily Territorial Enterprise*, January 10, 1863; A. S. Eterovich, "The Saga of Marco Medin," *Zajedničar*, January 15, 1964, p. 7; also "Saga of the Gunfight and Killing of Nikola Perasich," *B.E.E.A.G.H.S.*, Vol. II, No. 1 (January 1965), pp. 8–10.

18. Eterovich, *Croatians from Dalmatia*, "Geronimo and Mazzanovich," pp. 55–69; A. Mazzanovich, *Trailing Geronimo* (Los Angeles, 1931).

19. *Slavonic*, Vol. I, No. 1, p. 9; *B.E.E.A.G.H.S.*, Vol. II, No. 1, pp. 8–10.

20. *Slavonic*, Vol. I, No. 1, p. 8; Prpić, *The Croatian Imigrants*, pp. 82, 86–87.

Chapter Six

1. David Barton, "A Croatian Predecessor to Sir Francis Chichester," *BC Review* (London), Vol. III, No. 7 (March 1976), pp. 10–14.

2. Anon., "Pelješac," *Pomorska Enciklopedija* (Zagreb, 1960), Vol. VI, pp. 73–76.

3. Mladen Lorković, *Narod i zemlja Hrvata* (Croatian People and Land) (Zagreb, 1939), pp. 145–146; U.S. Immigration and Naturalization Service, *Annual Report 1957*, p. 16; Reports of the Immigration Commission, *Emigration Conditions in Europe* (Washington, 1911), p. 351; Immigration and Naturalization Service. *Annual Report 1966*, p. 29.

4. Philip Taylor, *The Distant Magnet: European Emigration to the U.S.A.* (New York, 1971), pp. 48–65.

5. Josip Lakatoš, *Narodna statistika* (Osijek, 1914), p. 64; Smail

264   SOUTH SLAVIC IMMIGRATION IN AMERICA

Balić, *Etičko naličje bosansko-hercegovačkih Muslimana* (Vienna, 1952), p. 62.

6. Oscar Handlin, *The Uprooted* (New York, 1951), p. 36.

7. Meler, *Slavonic Pioneers,* pp. 52–53.

8. Ibid., p. 53.

9. Jack London, *Valley of the Moon* (New York, 1914), pp. 363–366; Ante Kadić, "Jack London and Croatian Settlers in Watsonville," *Croatia Press,* Vol. IX, No. 146 (February 1955), pp. 6–7.

10. Frank Zaitz, ed. *American Family Almanac 1931* (Chicago), p. 127.

11. Paul E. Vendor, *History of Fresno County* (Los Angeles, 1919), pp. 1621–1624.

12. Ibid., pp. 1623–1624.

13. Meler, *Slavonic Pioneers,* p. 56; E. A. Ross, *The Old World in the New* (New York, 1914), p. 203.

14. N. Sestanovich, *Slavs in California* (Oakland, 1937), pp. 20–24.

15. Eterovich, *B.E.E.A.G.H.S.,* Vol. II, No. 2 (June 1965), pp. 52–53.

16. *Narodni List* (New York), January 28, 1899; Većeslav Holjevac, *Hrvati izvan domovine,* (Zagreb, 1968), pp. 85–89.

17. M. Bartulica, "Dalmatinska Zora," *Hrvatska Enciklopedija* (Zagreb, 1942), Vol. IV, p. 496.

18. Michele Veltri, "Croatians and Slovenians in Crested Butte," *Zajedničar,* Vol. 68. No. 14 (April 1971), p. 2.

19. Ivan Senica, "Hrvati u Gallup, New Mexico," *Croatian Voice,* August 24, 1968, p. 4.

20. Ibid.; A. S. Eterovich, *Yugoslav Survey of California, Nevada, Arizona and the South* (San Francisco, 1971), pp. 137–138.

21. Adamic, *From Many Lands,* pp. 55–67.

22. Prpić, *The Croatian Immigrants,* pp. 121–122.

23. Ibid, pp. 369, 382.

24. Balch, *Our Slavic Fellow Citizens,* pp. 255–258. In Cleveland, Ohio among the early settlers around 1890 there were immigrants from the hilly district of Žumberak.

25. Stephen Gazi, *Croatian Immigration to Allegheny County: 1882–1914* (Pittsburgh, 1956), pp. 24–26.

26. Balch, op. cit., 271.

27. Boniface Soric, *Centennial* (McKeesport, Pa., 1947), p. 41; Prpić, op. cit., pp. 123–127.

28. Gazi, op. cit., pp. 29, 31-32; Croatian Fraternal Union, *Kratki pregled povijesti Hrvatske Bratske Zajednice* (Pittsburgh, 1949), p. 180.

29. Bosiljko Bekavac, "Prva hrvatska župa u U.S.A. u North Side,

Pittsburgh, Pa.," *Naša Nada Kalendar 1930* (Gary, Ind., 1929), pp. 57–92, and "Povijest hrvatske župe u Millvale, Pa.," *Danica Koledar 1929* (New York, 1928), pp. 161–195; *Danica Koledar 1928*, pp. 21–25; Mirko Kájić, "Hrvatska kolonija i osnutak hrvatske rk, župe u Johnstown, Pa.," *Naša Nada Kalendar 1923*, pp. 144–152; *Zajedničar*, April 8 and 15, 1970.

Chapter Seven

1. John Petelin, "The Saga of Anaconda," *Zajedničar*, June 5, 1963; Vujnovich, "Dalmatians in Louisiana," pp. 13–14.

2. Vujnovich,*Yugoslavs in Louisiana*, pp. 130–143, gives the best account of this tragedy; also *Danica Koledar 1934*, pp. 77–78.

3. S. Radić, *Moderna kolonizacija i Slaveni* (Zagreb, 1904), p. 321.

4. Sorić, *Centennial*, p. 69; Govorchin, *Americans from Yugoslavia*, pp. 115–116.

5. B. Sorić, *Croatian Almanac for 1950*, pp. 101, 105.

6. Ivan Krešić, in *Danica Koledar 1927*, pp. 17–26.

7. V. Meler, *Hrvati na dalekom sjeveru* (Calumet, Mich., 1929), p. 7; Victor D. Rogulj, *Souvenir Book of the Fortieth Anniversary of St. John the Baptist Church* (Calumet, 1941), no pagination.

8. S. Nemec, *A History of the Croatian Settlement in St. Louis, Mo.* (St. Louis, 1931), pp. 5–6, 10–11.

9. Prpić, *The Croatian Immigrants*, pp. 466–467.

10. Maude M. Holbach, *Bosnia and Herzegovina: Some Wayside Wanderings* (London, 1910), p. 15.

11. *Monthly Labor Review*, Vol. XVII (January 1924), p. 14; L. Kosier, *Srbi, Hrvati i Slovenci u Americi* (Belgrade, 1926), p. 33.

12. U. S. Treasury Department, *Letter from the Secretary of the Treasury*, 2 vols. (Washington, 1892), Vol. I, pp. 104, 120.

13. Immigration Commission, *Emigration Conditions in Europe* (Washington, 1911), pp. 361, 363–369.

14. Balch, *Our Slavic Fellow Citizens*, pp. 51–52.

15. Radić, *Moderna kolonizacija i Slaveni*, p. 339.

16. John R. Commons. *Races and Immigrants in America* (New York, 1920), pp. 109–111.

17. John Badovinac, "The Titanic Disaster," *Zajedničar*, August 23, 1972, p. 2. Walter Lord in his *A Night to Remember* (New York, 1955), 193–198, lists the names of all passengers.

18. Badovinac, *Zajedničar*, August 23, 1972, p. 2.

19. Steiner, *On the Trail of the Immigrant*, pp. 30–47.

Chapter Eight

1. F. J. Koch. "In Quaint Curious Croatia," *The National Geographic Magazine,* Vol. XIX (December 1908), p. 819; *Emigration Conditions in Europe,* pp. 351, 374–375.

2. Balch, *Our Slavic Fellow Citizens,* pp. 271–272.

3. Prpić, *The Croatian Immigrants,* pp. 141–148.

4. L. v. Südland, *Die Südslawische Frage* (Vienna, 1918), p. 505; Balch, op. cit., p. 196; Prpić, op cit., pp. 149–150.

5. M. S. Orenstein in *Survey,* Vol. XXIX (December 7, 1912), p. 211; Govorchin, *Americans from Yugoslavia,* pp. 81–108.

6. U.S. Immigration Commission, *Immigrants in Industries,* (Washington, 1910), Vol. I, pp. 329–418; Taylor, *Distant Magnet,* p. 203; Eilizabeth F. Crowell, "The Housing Situation in Pittsburgh," *Charities and the Commons,* February 6, 1909, pp. 871–881; ibid., A. F. Bacon, "The Housing Problem in Indiana," December 5, 1908, pp. 376–383.

7. Adamic, "Manda Evanich from Croatia," *From Many Lands* (New York, 1940), pp. 55–67.

8. See for instance *Hrvatska Zastava* (Chicago), April 14, 1908.

9. *Immigrants in Industries,* Vol. I, pp. 79, 96–97, 139, 148, 166, 277, 534–535, with numerous statistics and data on South Slavs in industries; U.S. Immigration Commission, *Immigration and Crime* (Washington, 1910), pp. 28, 31, 145.

10. Phillip Pribonic, "Newcomers to the Tube City," *Zajedničar,* July 27, 1967, p. 2.

11. John R. Commons, "Wage Earners of Pittsburgh," *Charities and the Commons,* March 6, 1909, p. 1051.

12. John A. Fitch, "Some Pittsburgh Steel Workers," *Charities . . . ,* January 2, 1909, p. 553; also ibid., Peter Roberts, "The New Pittsburghers," pp. 533–552; *Time,* November 8, 1963, p. 70, praising the immortality of Stella's works in Pittsburgh's steel mills.

13. *Immigrants in Industries,* Vol. I, pp. 322–323, 472–517; Crystal Eastman, "A Year's Work Accidents and Their Cost," *Charities . . . ,* March 6, 1909, pp. 1149, 1161–1162.

14. Eastman, op. cit., pp. 1161–1162; Marie Sabsovich Orenstein, "The Servo-Croats of Manhattan," *The Survey,* Vol. XXIX, No. 10 (December 7, 1912), pp. 277–286.

15. B. Koukol, "The Slav's a Man for A'That," *Charities . . . .* January 2, 1909, pp. 589–598.

16. Victor R. Greene, *Slavic Community on Strike* (Notre Dame, Ind., 1968), p. 137.

17. *Narodni List,* July 15, 17, 27, 1909; J. Badovinac, "A Visit to the Copper Country," *Zajedničar,* October 25, 1972, p. 2.

18. Badovinac, op. cit., p. 4.

19. Maldwyn A. Jones, *American Immigration* (Chicago, 1960), pp. 177–182.

20. Balch, op. cit., pp. 326, 338; Immigration Commission, *Abstract of the Report on Recent Immigrants in Agriculture* (Washington, 1911), pp. 17, 61, 64, which listed only 52 per cent of all South Slavs as engaged in agriculture; *Kažiput*, pp. 10–20.

21. Roucek, *One America*, pp. 14, 673.

22. M. Bartulica, "Braća Mirko i Stevo Seljan," *Matičin iseljenički kalendar za 1955* (Zagreb), pp. 142–144.

23. *Hrvastski Glasnik*, March 26, 1909; April 2, 1910; Prpić, *The Croatian Immigrants*, pp. 178–181.

24. *Croatian Almanac for 1950*, p. 250; *Zajedničar*, October 9, 1974, p. 4.

25. *Zajedničar*, September 21, 1912; *Hrvatski Svijet*, May 19, 1913 and many issues of *Hrvatska Zastava* through 1913 and 1914.

26. Vladko Maček, *In the Struggle for Freedom* (New York, 1957), pp. 24–57; *Hrvatski Svijet*, October 10 and 11, 1913 and its editorial of October 18, 1913 "S. Dojcic—American Croat" in English.

27. G. J. Prpić, "The South Slavs," in J. P. O'Grady, ed. *The Immigrants' Influence on Wilson's Peace Policies* (Lexington, Ky., 1967), pp. 173–176 and *passim*. Ivan Čizmić covers all these events in his book *Jugoslavenski iseljenički pokret u SAD i stvaranje jugoslavenske države* (Zagreb, 1974).

28. Milada Paulova, *Jugoslavenski Odbor* (Zagreb, 1925), pp. 236–247; Victor S. Mamatey's *The United States and East Central Europe* (Princeton, 1957); *Narodni List*, September 5, 1915.

29. Bogdan Raditsa, "Clash of Two Immigrant Generations," *Commentary*, Vol. XXI (January 1958), pp. 9–10; Mamatey, op. cit., pp. 117–118.

30. *Hrvatski Glasnik*, November 20–30, 1916.

31. *Narodni List*, December 6 and 7, 1916.

32. Prpić, "South Slavs," pp. 188–189; *Zajedničar*, July 18, 1917; *Hrvatski Glasnik*, November 17, 1917.

33. Prpić, "South Slavs," pp. 190–191.

34. *Hrvatski Glasnik*, July 6 and 20, 1918.

35. *Narodni List*, October 29, 1918; Mamatey, op. cit., p. 363.

36. Adamic, *My America* (New York, 1938), p. 193; C. Michael McAdams, "The United States Marines," *American Croat*, Vol. 10, 1976, p. 4.

Chapter Nine

1. Jerome Jareb, "LeRoy King's Reports from Croatia," *Journal of Croatian Studies*, Vol. I (1960), pp. 75–168; Prpić, *The Croatian Immigrants*, pp. 245–250.

2. "Voice of a People," in Govorchin's *Americans from Yugoslavia*, pp. 138–169.

3. Balch, *Our Slavic Fellow Citizens*, p. 387; *Golden Jubilee*, Saint Joseph's Croatian Church (St. Louis, 1954).

4. *Naša Nada Kalendar 1930* (Gary, Ind.), pp. 104–111; *Naša Nada* (bi-weekly), October 14, 1959, p. 4; *Croatian Catholic Messenger*, December 1968, pp. 372–376.

5. Smail Balić, *Etičko naličje Bosansko-Hercegovačkih Muslimana* (Vienna, 1952), pp. 58–63; Holjevac, *Hrvati izvan domovine*, p. 269; also Smail Balić, "Cultural Achievements of Bosnian and Herzegovinian Muslims," in Eterović-Spalatin, eds. *Croatia*, Vol. II, pp. 299–361.

6. All these facts are based on author's talks with many Moslem friends and many clippings and publications in his possession.

7. Balch, op. cit., pp. 370–371, 301.

8. Ibid., p. 169.

9. Steiner, *On the Trail of the Immigrant*, pp. 183, 196; Commons, *Races and Immigrants in America*, p. 81.

10. Reuben Markham, *Tito's Imperial Communism* (Chapel Hill, N.C., 1947), pp. 9–11.

11. *Literary Digest*, Vol. 61 (June 1919), p. 43.

12. Holjevac, op. cit., p. 50; *I. N. S. Report 1971*, p. 50; Kenneth L. Roberts, "Balkan Jottings," *The Saturday Evening Post*, February 11, 1922, pp. 16–17, 110, 113–114.

13. Holjevac, op cit., pp. 40–42; *I. N. S. Report 1966*, p. 56; Kosier, *Srbi, Hrvati i Slovenci u Americi*, p. 34.

14. *Jugoslavenski Svijet* (New York), March 20, 1920.

15. Issues of *Hrvatski Svijet* during the 1920s; Prpić, *The Croatian Immigrants*, p. 258.

16. Adamic, *My America*, pp. 240–244.

17. Holjevac, op. cit., pp. 153–156.

18. *Kratki pregled povijesti H.B.Z.*, pp. 180–181.

19. *Hrvatski List i Danica Hrvatska* 1928–1929 issues.

20. Josip Kraja, "The Croatian Circle, 1928–1946," *Journal of Croatian Studies*, Vol. 5–6 (1964–1965), pp. 145–204.

21. Edward Corsi, *In the Shadow of Liberty* (New York, 1935), pp. 224–226.

22. Henry A. Foley, *They Called Him King of the Grapes* (Porterville, Cal., 1975), pp. 1–96.

23. Ivan Senica, "Naši farmeri u Americi," *Koledar Hrvatski Svijet 1943* (New York), pp. 25–30; Vujnovich, *Yugoslavs in Louisiana*, pp. 61–62.

24. V. Maček, *In the Struggle for Freedom* (New York, 1957), pp. 176–260; Milovan Djilas, *Memoir of a Revolutionary* (New York, 1973), pp. 375–390.

25. *Hrvatski List i Danica Hrvatska*, October 30, 1941; *Kratki Pregled Povijesti H. B. Z.*, pp. 17–18.

26. *Navy Times*, March 27, 1963.

27. Adamic, *A Nation of Nations*, pp. 247–248.

28. *Uspjesi i zadaće Narodnog Vijeća Amerikanaca Hrvatskog Porijekla* (Pittsburgh, 1945). pp. 17–20; *Spomen Knjiga Američko-Hrvotskog Kongresa* (Pittsburgh, 1943); Holjevac, op. cit., pp. 265–266.

29. *Report on the American Slav Congress* (Washington, 1949), p. 15 ff.; *Kratka povijest H. B. Z.*, p. 87 ff.

30. Maček, op. cit., pp. 261–275; John Prcela and Stanko Guldescu, *Operation Slaughterhouse* (Philadelphia, 1970), 560 pp.

31. *Uspjesi i zadaće . . .*, pp. 30–33.

32. Raditsa described his experience in Yugoslavia in a dramatic book *Hrvatska 1945* (Croatia in 1945) (Barcelona, 1974).

33. *Croatian Almanac 1947* (Pittsburgh), p. 229, and reports in *Danica*.

34. J. Badovinac in *Zajedničar*, March 17, 1971, p. 2.

35. M. Cvetich, "I Posed as a Communist for the F.B.I.," *Saturday Evening Post*, July 15, 22, and 29, 1950; Bogdan Raditsa, "How Terror Rules Yugoslavia," *The Catholic Digest*, Vol. XI, No. 4 (February 1947), pp. 100–106; after his escape from Yugoslavia he wrote a series of articles for major American publications.

36. *New York Times*, September 27, 1948.

37. Committee on Un-American Activities, *Guide to Subversive Organizations and Publications* (Washington, 1951), p. 25.

Chapter Ten

1. The picture of "Immigrant Mother" in Prpić, *The Croatian Immigrants*, after p. 32.

2. *Hrvatski List*, September 19, 1922; *Danica Koledar 1924*, pp. 217–221.

3. Ben Franklin, "The Scandal of Death and Injury in the Mines," *New York Times Magazine*, March 30, 1969, pp. 25–27, 122–130.

4. *American Petroleum Institute Quarterly*, Vol. XV (January 1945), p. 9; *Who's Who in America 1897–1942* (Chicago, 1942), p. 751.

5. *The Sculpture of Ivan Meštrović* (Syracuse University Press, 1948), pp. 7–14; J. Lowe and D. Howard, "Meštrović, Man and Artist," *The Sign* (March 1958), pp. 40–44; L. Schmeckbier, *Meštrović, Sculptor and Patriot* (Syracuse N.Y., 1959), pp. 66, 200 illus.

6. Vladimir Markotić, *Biographical Directory of Americans and Canadians of Croatian Descent* (Calgary, Alberta, 1973), pp. 29, 63.

7. *Hrvatska Enciklopedija*, Vol. II, pp. 394–395; Vol. III, pp. 494–496; L. Adamic, "The Millvale Apparition," *Harper's Magazine* (April 1938), pp. 476–486; *Pittsburgh Sun Telegraph*, August 22, 1941; H. Kubly, "Pittsburgh," *Holiday* (March 1959), pp. 84–85.

8. Markotić, op. cit., p. 32.

9. *Narodni List*, December 23, 1899; "Od Kašmana do Ruždjaka," *Matica* (June 1964), pp. 177–179; *Znameniti Hrvati*, pp. 198, 267; E. K. Einstein, "Zinka Milanov: A Complete Discography," *Le Grand Baton*, Vol. 5, No. 2 (May 1968) p. 8.

10. Prpić, *The Croatian Immigrants*, pp. 360–361.

11. Adamic, *A Nation of Nations;* Govorchin, *Americans from Yugoslavia;* and Prpić, *The Croatian Immigrants*, pp. 361–361, quoting both.

12. *New York Times*, September 26, 1933; Prpić, op. cit., pp. 363–364.

13. Prpić, op. cit., pp. 364–366.

14. *Ibid.*, pp. 326–333; olso G. J. and Hilda Prpić, *Croatian Books and Booklets Written in Exile* (Cleveland, 1973), 100 pp.

15. Henry A. Foley, *They Called Him King of the Grapes*, pp. 355–385.

16. Prpić, op. cit., pp. 367–369.

17. *Time*, October 30, 1972; on Stepovich *Naša Nada*, July 9, 1959.

18. *Zajedničar*, January 1, 1975, and earlier articles.

19. Author's clippings from many papers.

20. Walter Kolar, *A History of the Tamburitza* (D.U.T.I.F.A., 1973), 28 pp.; Francis Owen, "The Saga of Joe Magarac Steelman," *Scribner's Magazine*, Vol. XC (November 1931), pp. 505–513.

21. Letter to author from Professor Stanko Guldescu, Fayetteville State College, June 6, 1960.

22. L. Adamic, "A Bohunk Woman," *The American Mercury*, Vol. XIX, No. 75 (March 1930), pp. 281–286.

23. Ivo Baučić, *The Effects of Emigration from Yugoslavia and the Problem of Returning Emigrant Workers* (The Hague, 1972), p. 12; also "Pet milijuna Jugoslavena i njihovih potomaka izvan Jugoslavije," *Vjesnik u srijedu*, April 3, 1968, p. 6.

24. "The New Americans—Where They're Coming From," *U.S. News & World Report,* June 14, 1971, p. 12.

25. *New York Times,* September 12, 1976, p. 1, and many other papers of the same and subsequent dates.

Chapter Eleven

1. Stanley Zele, "Dva slavna Amerikanca—potomca Slovencev". *American Family Almanac 1938* (Chicago), p. 32.

2. Ibid., pp. 33–37; Adamic, *A Nation of Nations,* p. 256.

3. E. Kovačič, "Pater Kapus, prvi slovenski misijonar v Severni Ameriki", *Ave Maria Koledar 1970,* pp. 89–91. A. I. Rezek, *History of the Diocese of Sault Ste. Marie and Marquette* (Houghton, Mich., 1906), pp. 18–19; M. Jezernik, *Frederick Baraga* (New York, 1968), p. 20; Joseph Gregorich, *The Apostle of the Chippewas* (Chicago, 1932), p. 24.

4. Edward Jacker, *Life and Services of Bishop F. Baraga* (Chicago, 1957), p. 15; Jezernik, op. cit., pp. 59–72.

5. W. Elliott, "Bishop Baraga, Apostle of the Chippewas," *Catholic World,* April 1901, pp. 76, 86; John G. Shea, *History of the Catholic Missions Among the Indian Tribes of the United States* (New York, 1957), p. 401.

6. C. Verwyst, "Baraga, Frederick," *The Catholic Encyclopedia* (New York, 1907), Vol. II, pp. 282–283.

7. J. M. Trunk, *Amerika in Amerikanci* (Klagenfurt, Austria, 1912), pp. 544–547; Adamic, *A Nation of Nations,* pp. 237–238.

8. Trunk, op. cit., pp. 578–590; Govorchin, *Americans from Yugoslavia,* pp. 33–34.

9. A. I. Rezek, "Mrak, Ignatius," *The Catholic Encyclopedia,* Vol. X, pp. 624–625.

10. Trunk, op. cit., p. 575.

11. Ibid., pp. 543, 559, 587–588.

12. Ibid., pp. 552–553.

13. Ibid., pp. 549–552.

14. Ibid., pp. 602–603; A. I. Rezek, "Vertin, John." *The Catholic Encyclopedia,* Vol. XV, pp. 377–378.

15. Trunk, op. cit., pp. 600–601; letter of Professor E. Gobetz, June 29, 1972.

16. Trunk, op. cit., pp. 554–556, 598–599, 591–592.

17. Marie Prisland, *From Slovenia to America* (Chicago, 1968), p. 123.

18. Anthony Kastelic, "California in njeni jugoslovanski naseljenci", *American Family Almanac 1931,* p. 126; Prisland, op. cit., p. 124.

Chapter Twelve

1. Mike W. Edwards, "Should They Build a Fence Around Montana?," *National Geographic*, May 1976, pp. 635–637.

2. Trunk, *Amerika in Amerikanci*, pp. 503–504.

3. His name was Jakob Župančič; Ivan Molek, "Zadnji pionirji," *Am. Family Almanac 1932*, pp. 70–75.

4. Trunk, op. cit., pp. 447–478.

5. Ibid., p. 478, 488–489; Prisland, op. cit., pp. 102–106. Balch, *Our Slavic Fellow Citizens*, p. 233.

6. Trunk, op. cit., p. 489–490.

7. Ibid., pp. 490–491, 492–493; *Am. Family Almanac 1939*, pp. 42–55; Prisland, op. cit., pp. 43, 110–115.

8. Trunk, op. cit., pp. 495–496.

9. Prisland, op. cit., pp. 116–123; Trunk, op. cit. pp. 496–497.

10. Trunk, op. cit., pp. 499–502, 505.

11. Prisland, op. cit., pp. 106–109; Anton Zaitz, "Forest City," *Am. Family Almanac 1940*, pp. 92–105.

12. Frank J. Turk, *Slovenski pionir* (Cleveland, 1955), pp. 47; Prisland, op. cit., pp. 124–131.

13. Trunk, op. cit., pp. 507–508; John Arnez, *Slovenci v New Yorku* (New York, 1966), p. 36.

14. Ivan Molek, "Rajska Dolina; odlomek iz zgodovine ameriških Slovencev," *Am. Family Almanac 1931*, pp. 32–42.

15. Prisland, op. cit., p. 63.

16. M. Veltri, "Croatians and Slovenians in Crested Butte," *Zajedničar*, Vol. 68, No. 14 (April 1971), p. 2; Anton Shular, "Dežela Solnčnih Rož" (Kansas)," *Am. Family Almanac 1937*, pp. 124–130.

17. A. Shular, "Podporna organizacija ki je ni več," *Am. Family Almanac 1933*, pp. 123–129.

18. Ibid., p. 151.

19. J. Chesarek, "Bogati trgovec," *Am. Family Almanac 1945*, pp. 143–155.

20. Joseph Snoy, "O naselbini Bridgeport," *Am. Family Almanac 1945*, pp. 158–162.

Chapter Thirteen

1. *Am. Family Almanac 1940*, pp. 92–105; Prisland, *From Slovenia to America*, p. 106; Trunk, *Amerika in Amerikanci*, pp. 560–588 and *passim*.

2. Trunk, op. cit., pp. 517–527.

3. Balch, *Our Slavic Fellow Citizens*, pp. 269–270, 271–272.

4. Ibid., p. 256.

5. "A Century of Immigration," *Monthly Labor Review*, Vol. XIII, No. 1 (January 1924), pp. 1–19.

6. *Am. Family Almanac 1937*, p. 153.

7. R. A. Schermerhorn, *These Our People* (Boston, 1949), pp. 366–367.

8. John Badovinac, "A Visit to the Copper Country," *Zajedničar*, October 25, 1972, p. 2.

9. *Am. Family Almanac 1945*, p. 82.

10. Prpić, "South Slavs," pp. 188–189.

11. *Foreign Relations of the United States: 1918*, Washington, D.C. Suppl. I, Vol. 1, pp. 828–831.

12. Adamic, *My America*, pp. 245–246; Govorchin, *Americans from Yugoslavia*, pp. 138–169; *Am. Family Almanac 1933*, p. 6; also its 1950 edition, pp. 78–160.

13. Balch, op. cit., p. 387, and author's clippings.

14. *Am. Family Almanac 1933*, p. 6; J. Poljak, *Almanak i statistika Južnih Slavena u S. D. Sj. Amerike* (Chicago, 1926), p. 199; Roucek, *One America*, pp. 172–173.

15. Markham, *Tito's Imperial Communism*, pp. 9-11.

16. Schermerhorn, op. cit., pp. 252–253.

17. Trunk, op. cit., p. 463.

18. *Cleveland News*, January 14, 1935.

19. *Am. Family Almanac 1931*, p. 20.

20. F. Zaitz, "Slovenska kulturna društva v Zedinjenih Državah," *Am. Family Almanac 1933*, pp. 60–99.

21. Ibid., p. 6.

22. Adamic, *My America*, pp. 244–245.

Chapter Fourteen

1. *American Slav Congress*, p. 45; Boris Furlan, "Slovenija v borbi," *Am. Family Almanac 1943*, pp. 24–52.

2. *American Slav Congress*, p. 40 and and ff. dealing in detail with Adamic and his activities.

3. Adamic, *A Nation of Nations*, pp. 247–248.

4. *Kratka povijest H.B.Z.*, pp. 87–88.

5. B. Raditsa, "How Terror Rules Yugoslavia," *The Catholic Digest*, Vol. XI, No. 4 (February 1947), pp. 100–106, was one of his many articles; Cvetich published his revelations in *The Saturday Evening Post* in the issues of July 15, 22 and 29, 1950.

6. Govorchin, *Americans from Yugoslavia*, p. 262.

7. Information supplied by Professor E. G. Gobetz of Kent State University, *The Sun Press*, June 20, 1974, p. A5.

8. Prisland, *From Slovenia to America*, p. 87.

274   SOUTH SLAVIC IMMIGRATION IN AMERICA

9. Ibid, p. 66.

10. Gobetz, *From Carniola to Carnegie Hall* (Wickliffe, Ohio, 1968), 103 pp.

11. Information supplied in several issues of *Slovenska Država*, a monthly in Toronto.

12. Tine Debeljak, "O slovenskoj emigrantskoj književnosti," *La Revista Croata*, Vol. XXI (March 1971), pp. 28–47.

13. Govorchin, *Americans from Yugoslavia*, pp. 241–245; Adamic, *A Nation of Nations*, p. 246; *U. S. News and World Report*, November 4, 1955, p. 72.

14. Govorchin, op. cit., pp. 245–247; Prisland, op. cit., pp. 82–83.

15. *The Sun Press*, June 20, 1974; Prisland, op. cit., p. 83.

16. The long list of names of Slovenians in education and all other fields is printed in the study by Professor E. G. Gobetz of Kent State University.

17. Prisland, op. cit., pp. 83–84; Govorchin, op. cit., pp. 251–253.

18. Lubomyr R. Wynar, *The Encyclopedic Directory of Ethnic Newspapers* (Littleton, Colo., 1972), pp. 184–186.

19. *Slovenska Država*, November 1975, pp. 1–2; information supplied by Dr. E. Gobetz: his Slovenian Research Center publishes a *Newsletter*. I also made use of his unpublished paper "Slovenian Contribution to America."

Chapter Fifteen

1. A. S. Eterovich, *Croatians from Dalmatia and Montenegrin Serbs in the West and South 1800–1900* (San Francisco, 1971), pp. 12–15 and ff.

2. Nikola R. Pribić, "George Šagić-Fisher: Patriot of Two Worlds," *The Florida State University Slavic Papers*, Vol. I, 1967, pp. 35–47.

3. Information supplied by Peter J. Divizich, a wealthy Croatian rancher from Delano in San Joaquin Valley.

4. Eterovich, *Croatians from Dalmatia*, pp. 5–6, 10–11, 108.

5. Ibid., p. 37.

6. Information supplied by C. Michael McAdams of Stockton, California.

7. Govorchin, *Americans from Yugoslavia*, p. 41.

8. Eterovich, *B.E.E.A.G.H.S.*, Vol. II, pp. 55–62.

9. John R. Palandech, "The Life and Work of an American Missionary, the Very Reverend Archimandrite Sebastian Dabovich," *B.E.E.A.G.H.S.*, Vol. II, No. 2, pp. 39–59.

10. *Slavonic*, Vol. I, No. 1, p. 8.

11. Paul Vendor, *History of Fresno County* (Los Angeles, 1919), pp. 1621–1624.

Chapter Sixteen

1. Balch, *Our Slavic Fellow Citizens,* p. 256.
2. Govorchin, *Americans from Yugoslavia,* pp. 79, 117–118; Kosier, *Srbi, Hrvati i Slovenci u Americi,* p. 222; *Am. Family Almanac 1932,* p. 224.
3. Balch, op. cit., p. 199.
4. U. S. Immigration, *Annual Report for 1907,* p. 22; Balch, op. cit., pp. 200, 200–201.
5. Kosier, op. cit., p. 34.
6. Djilas, *The Land Without Justice,* p. 34.
7. Commons, *The Races and Immigrants in America,* p. 108.
8. About Maksim Slijepčević see *The Canadian Srbobran,* March 19, 1970, p. 2.
9. Djilas, op. cit., p. 55.
10. Kosier, op. cit., pp. 34–35.
11. Steiner, *On the Trail of the Immigrant,* p. 180; Adamic, *The Native's Return,* p. 131.
12. Michael Pupin, *From Immigrant to Inventor* (New York, 1938), pp. 34–42.
13. Balch, op. cit., pp. 271–272.
14. Alvin R. Sunseri, "The Ludlow Massacre," *American Chronicle,* I. (January 1972), p. 24.
15. Paul Vendor, *History of Fresno County* (Los Angeles, 1919), pp. 1621–1624.
16. D. Radojević, "Problemi crnogorske historije oko prvoga svjetskog rata," *Kritika* (Zagreb), Vol. IV, No. 16 (January-February 1971), pp. 65–87; M. Paulova, *Jogoslavenski Odbor* (Zagreb, 1925), pp. 207, 236.
17. F. Šišić, *Dokumenti o postanku Kraljevine Srba, Hrvata i Slovenaca* (Zagreb, 1920), pp. 74–80.
18. *Foreign Relations of the United States, 1917,* Suppl. II (Washington, 1932), Vol. I, p. 590.
19. *Crnogorski Glasnik,* No. 3, June 15, 1917, pp. 1–2.
20. Radojević, op. cit., p. 75.
21. Prpić, "South Slavs," pp. 190–191.
22. Victor S. Mamatey, "The United States and the Dissolution of Austria-Hungary," *Journal of Central European Affairs.* Vol. X (October 1950), pp. 256–270.
23. *Foreign Relations: 1918,* op. cit., pp. 828–831.

Chapter Seventeen

1. *Matica Kalendar 1958,* pp. 67–74.

2. Govorchin, *Americans from Yugoslavia*, pp. 153–154; 161–167; Eterovich, *B.E.E.A.G.H.S.*, June 1965, p. 50.

3. Govorchin, op cit, pp 202–203; U. S. Bureau of Census, *Religious Bodies: 1916*, p. 263.

4. *Ustav Srpske Pravoslavne Crkve* (Belgrade, 1931 and 1947); *The Constitution of the Serbian Orthodox Diocese of the United States of America and Canada* (Pittsburgh, 1929).

5. *Spomenica: 1963–1969*, a souvenir book published by the Serbs in Cleveland that oppose the patriarch in Belgrade.

6. Adamic. *The Native's Return*, p. 236.

7. Pupin, *From Immigrant to Inventor*. pp. 4–9 and *passim*.

8. K. Bercovici, *The Incredible Balkans* (New York, 1938), p. 67.

9. *Danica*, April 27, 1960, p. 2; M. Djilas, *Memoir of a Revolutionary* (New York, 1973), pp. 375–390.

10. Adamic, *A Nation of Nations*, pp. 247–248.

11. Ibid., p. 248; *Report on the American Slav Congress* (Washington, D.C., 1949), pp. 54–56.

12. *Report on the American Slav Congress*, pp. 5, 12–13, 24a; *Guide to Subversive Organizations* (Washington, D. C., 1951), pp. 30, 151.

13. Adamic, *My Native Land*, pp. 81–83 (where he mentions also "the pan-Serbian slaughter of the Croatians"), pp. 399–414.

14. *Report on the American Slav Congress*, p. 18.

15. Ibid., pp. 56–60.

16. Ibid., pp. 18–19.

17. John J. O'Neill, *Prodigal Genius* (New York, 1944), pp. 55–59, 70–72; Cecyle S. Neidle, *Great Immigrants* (New York, 1973), pp. 133–161; Prpić, *The Croatian Immigrants*, pp. 346–349, 380–381.

18. Quoted in *Zajedničar*, April 11 and 18, 1956.

19. L. Adamic. *Americans from Yugoslavia*, reprint of the January 1945 issue of *Woman's Day*, p. 2; D. Sarnoff's letter to Professor Raditsa, March 21, 1966, *Journal of Croatian Studies*, Vols. VII–VIII (1966–1967), pp. 164–166; Eugene Lyons, *David Sarnoff* (New York, 1966), pp. 64, 71, 206.

20. Meštrović, *Uspomene . . .*, p. 192.

21. Raditsa, Sarnoff's Letter, p. 164.

22. Pupin, op. cit., p. 386. In his extensive book Pupin doesn't mention Tesla at all even though they were countrymen and lived in the same city.

23. A. Radaković, "Sculptor from Lika," *Review* (Belgrade, September 1968), pp. 14–15.

24. H. Jacobs, *Frank Lloyd Wright* (New York, 1965), p. 109.

25. *Signature*, September 1972, pp. 34–37.

26. "Washington Front," *America*, July 11, 1970, p. 5.

27. National Council of Churches, *Yearbook of American Churches*, 1962, p. 258.

28. Doug Nassif, "Serbs Fight to Save Church from Tito," *Twin Circle*, pp. 3, 9–10.

29. "Statement of Facts—St. Sava Church of Cleveland, Ohio," 4 pp. supplied by Mr. Risto Janjić of Willowick, Ohio; also *Spomenica* (Chicago, 1969), 176 pp.; "Fists, Chairs Fly in St. Sava Dispute," *The Plain Dealer*, January 18, 1968, p. 1.

30. *The Plain Dealer*, June 22, 1976, p. 4A

31. Wynar, *Encyclopedic Dictionary of Ethnic Newspapers*, pp. 178–179; *Srpska Borba*, May 19, 1971.

32. *Greater Cleveland Nationalities Directory 1974* (Sun Newspapers, 1974), pp. 131–133.

33. *Matica* (Zagreb), January 1977, p. 20.

Chapter Eighteen

1. Ivan Mazov, "Makedonac medju mornarima Kristofa Kolumba," *Zajedničar*, February 3, 1971, p. 9.

2. Macedonian Patriotic Organization, *The Truth About Macedonia: American Missionaries' Testimony* (Indianapolis, 1964), pp. vii, 4, 7; Will S. Monroe, *Bulgaria and Her People: With an Account of the Balkan Wars, Macedonia and Macedonian Bulgars* (Boston, 1914), pp. 222, 323–335.

3. Anon., "The American Bible Society," *Macedonian Tribune*, August 26, 1966, p. 1; *The Truth About Macedonia*, pp. 4, 6, 7; R. Markham, *Meet Bulgaria* (Sofia, 1931), pp. 357–373; Anon., "The American Missionaries Among the Bulgarians," *Macedonian Tribune*, August 27, 1965, p. 3.

4. Joseph S. Roucek, *The American Bulgarians* (Bridgeport, Conn., 1971), p. 15, and "Bulgarian Americans," in F. J. Brown and J. S. Roucek, *One America* (New York, 1960), pp. 176–184. *Dictionary of American Biography* (New York, 1933), Vol. VI, pp. 45–46.

5. Benjamin C. Marsh, "The Bulgarian at Home," *Charities and the Commons*, January 9, 1909, pp. 649–650. This is the same Dr. Marsh, a Protestant missionary in Bulgaria, mentioned by Peter D. Yankoff in his book *Peter Menikoff* (New York, 1928).

6. Liuben Dimitroff, *Ilinden 1903–1953* (Indianapolis, 1953), p. 220; J. S. Roucek, *Balkan Politics* (Stanford University Press, 1948), p. 148.

7. S. Christowe, *This Is My Country* (New York, 1938), pp. 11, 15; Brown and Roucek, *One America*, p. 178.

8. Balch, *Our Slavic Fellow Citizens*, p. 273.

9. Roucek, *The American Bulgarians*, p. 3.

10. Ibid.

11. Yankoff, *Peter Menikoff*, p. 294.

12. Grace Abbott published a valuable and illustrated study "The Bulgarians in Chicago," *Charities and the Commons*, Vol. XXI, January 9, 1909, pp. 653–660.

13. Ibid., pp. 654, 660.

14. M. A. Jones, *American Immigration*, p. 220.

15. Balch, op. cit., pp. 274–275.

16. Ibid., p. 276.

17. Ibid.

18. Abbott, op. cit., p. 660.

19. Christowe, op. cit., pp. 7, 10–11, 22.

20. Ibid., pp. 6, 148.

21. Yankoff, op. cit., pp. 123, 141–148.

22. Ibid., pp. 154–155; Christowe, op. cit., pp. 28, 32–36.

23. Christowe, op. cit., pp. 55, 58.

24. Margaret F. Byington, "The Mill Town Courts and Their Lodgers," *Charities and the Commons*, February 6, 1909, pp. 916–920; Taylor, *The Distant Magnet*, p. 202.

25. Alvin R. Sunseri, "The Ludlow Massacre," *American Chronicle*, Vol. I, No. 1, (January 1972), p. 24; Cecyle S. Neidle, *America's Immigrant Women* (New York, 1975), p. 122.

Chapter Nineteen

1. J. S. Roucek, "Bulgarian Americans," *One America*, p. 179.

2. P. Stanković "Teodor Cvetkov," *Croatian Voice*, March 27 and April 3, 1965.

3. Roucek, *The American Bulgarians*, p. 10; also author's various clippings.

4. L. S. Stavrianos, *The Balkans Since 1453* (New York, 1959), pp. 569–570, 644–647. See also C. Anastasoff, *The Tragic Peninsula* (Saint Louis, Mo., 1938), 369 pp.

5. Roucek, *The American Bulgarians*, pp. 9–10.

6. Ibid., and Bishop Kyril's statement in the *Macedonian Tribune*, April 8, 1971, p. 1.

7. *Macedonian Tribune*, April 8, 1971, p. 1.

8. Bishop Kyril, "The Bulgarian Orthodox Church Under Communism," *Balkania*, Vol. 1, No. 1 (St. Louis, Mo., January 1967), pp. 3–5; *Macedonian Tribune*, November 16, 1967, pp. 1–2.

9. Vol. V of the *Reports*, p. 26.

10. *This Is My Country*, pp. 268, 272, 284–286.

11. Gunther, *Inside Europe* (New York, 1938), pp. 409–411.

12. S. Christowe, "Half an American," *Outlook and Independent,* Vol. CLIII (December 1929), pp. 531, 557.

13. Dita Atzeff, "Constituent Congress of the MPO," *Macedonian Tribune,* June 10, 1971; Ivan Mihailoff, "The Newspaper Macedonian Tribune," *Macedonian Tribune,* March 8, 1973, p. 1, and many author's clippings from the *M. T.*

14. Mihailoff's book was published by Pearlstone Publishing Company in St. Louis, 1950. Christowe, op. cit., pp. 279–281.

Chapter Twenty

1. Committee on Un-American Activities, U.S. House of Representatives, *Report on the American Slav Congress and Associated Organizations* (Washington, 1949), p. 36; hereafter cited as *Report on the American Slav Congress.*

2. Author's clippings and issues of old South Slavic papers.

3. *Report on the American Slav Congress,* pp. 31–32.

4. A detailed discussion—very much in favor of the King—is: Stephen Graham, *Alexander of Yugoslavia* (New Haven, Conn., 1939), 329 pp. L. Adamic discussed it in his books, articles, and a pamphlet *Struggle.*

5. Committee on Un-American Activities, *Communist Political Subversion* (Washington, 1957), p. v.

6. Holjevac, *Hrvati izvan domovine,* pp. 143–144.

7. *Report on the American Slav Congress,* pp. 12–13.

8. *Kratka povijest Hrv. Bratske Zajednice,* pp. 21–24, 74–77.

9. *Report on the American Slav Congress,* p. 15.

10. Ibid., p. 43.

11. Adamic, *My Native Land,* pp. 447, 449, 465.

12. Holjevac, op. cit., pp. 276–277.

13. *Kratka povijest Hrv. Bratske Zajednice,* pp. 87, 120–121; Holjevac, op. cit., pp. 272–277.

14. *Daily Worker,* September 23 and 25. 1944; Holjevac. op. cit., p. 264.

15. Roucek, *One America,* p. 182.

16. *New York Times,* September 22, 1946; *Time,* September 30, 1946, p. 31; *Report on American Slav Congress,* pp. 24–25.

17. *Report on American Slav Congress,* p. 64.

18. Ibid., pp. 1–11.

19. Ibid., pp. 8, 10, 26–29.

20. *Guide to Subversive Organizations and Publications,* p. 25; *Communist Political Subversion,* pp. 1–12.

21. *Communist Political Subversion,* p. 15.

Chapter Twenty-one

1. Roucek, *American Bulgarians*, p. 15, and *One America*, p. 184; clippings in author's possession from the *Macedonian Tribune*. *Newsweek*, July 4, 1976, pp. 51–52.

2. Immigration and Naturalization Service, *Annual Report 1974* (Washington, 1975), p. 36; also *Annual Report* 1973, pp. 42, 55.

3. Lubomyr R. Wynar, *Encyclopedic Directory of Ethnic Newspapers* (Littleton, Col., 1972), pp. 30–31.

4. *Macedonian Tribune*, April 29, 1976, p. 1.

5. *Matica* (Zagreb), May 1972, p. 170.

6. *ABN Correspondence* (Muenchen), Vol. XXI, No. 3 (May-June, 1970), pp. 42–43, and (May-June 1972), pp. 38–39.

7. "Georgi M. Dimitrov," *Croatian Voice*, December 13, 1972, p. 7.

8. *Macedonian Tribune*, April 1, 1971, p. 1, and May 18, 1972, p. 1.

9. Ibid., December 30, 1971, p. 8.

10. Ibid., April 1, 1971.

11. Ibid., July 11, 1974, p. 3.

12. Adamic, *A Nation of Nations*, p. 249.

Selected Bibliography

United States Immigration and Ethnicity—General

1. Books and Articles

ADAMIC, LOUIS. *My America: 1928–1938*. New York: Harper, 1938.
————. *From Many Lands*. New York: Harper, 1940.
————. *Two-Way Passage*. New York: Harper, 1941.
————. *What's Your Name?* New York: Harper, 1942.
————. *A Nation of Nations*. New York: Harper, 1944.
ANDRICA, THEODORE, ed. *Greater Cleveland Nationalities Directory*. Cleveland, Ohio: The Sun Newspapers, 1974.
BROWN, FRANCIS J. and ROUCEK, JOSEPH S., eds. *One America: The History, Contributions, and Present Problems of Our Racial and National Minorities*. 3d ed. New York: Prentice-Hall, 1952.
CHRISTIAN, HENRY A. *Louis Adamic: A Checklist*. Kent, Ohio: Kent State University Press, 1971.
COMMONS, JOHN R. *Races and Immigrants in America*. New York: Macmillan, 1920.
CORSI, EDWARD. *In the Shadow of Liberty: The Chronicle of Ellis Island*. New York: Macmillan, 1935.
DUNNE, PETER M. *Black Robes in Lower California*. Los Angeles: University of California Press, 1952.
EATON, ALLEN H. *Immigrant Gifts to American Culture*. New York: Russell Sage Foundation, 1932.
FRANKLIN, BEN. "The Scandal of Death and Injury." *New York Times Magazine*, March 30, 1969, pp. 25–27, 121–30.
HANDLIN, OSCAR. *The Uprooted: The Epic Story of the Great Migrations that Made the American People*. New York: Grosset & Dunlap, 1951.
JONES, MALDWYN ALLEN. *American Immigration*. Chicago: University of Chicago Press, 1960.
MCWILLIAMS, CAREY. *Brothers Under the Skin*. Boston: Little, Brown, 1951.
MILLER, KENNETH D. *Peasant Pioneers*. New York: Friendship Press, 1925.

281

NEIDLE, CECYLE S. *The New Americans*. New York: Twayne Publishers, 1967.

————. *Great Immigrants*. New York: Twayne Publishers, 1973.

————. *America's Immigrant Women*. New York: Twayne Publishers, 1975.

NOVAK, MICHAEL. *The Rise of Unmeltable Ethnics*. New York: Macmillan, 1972.

PARK, ROBERT. *The Immigrant Press and Its Control*. New York: Harper, 1922.

SCHERMERHORN, R. A. *These Our People*. Boston: D. C. Heath, 1949.

STEINER, EDWARD A. *On the Trail of the Immigrant*. New York: Fleming H. Revell, 1906.

————. *The Immigrant Tide*. New York: Fleming H. Revell, 1909.

TAYLOR, PHILIP. *The Distant Magnet: European Emigration to the United States*. New York: Harper, 1971.

WITTKE, CARL. *We Who Built America: The Saga of the Immigrant*. New York: Prentice-Hall, 1939.

WYNAR, LUBOMYR N. *Encyclopedic Directory of Ethnic Newspapers and Periodicals in the United States*. Littleton, Colo.: Libraries Unlimited, 1972.

2. Official Documents

Secretary of Labor, "A Century of Immigration." *Monthly Labor Review* 18, no. 1 (January, 1922), pp. 1–19.

U.S. Congress, House Committee on Un-American Activities, *Report on the American Slav Congress and Associated Organizations*. Washington, D.C.: Government Printing Office, 1949.

————. *Guide to Subversive Organizations and Publications*. Washington, D.C.: Government Printing Office, 1951.

U.S. Congress, Senate. Reports of the Immigration Commission. *Dictionary of Races or Peoples*. Washington, D.C.: Government Printing Office, 1911.

————, *Emigration Conditions in Europe*. Washington, D.C.: Government Printing Office, 1911.

————, *Immigrants in Industries*, pt. 2, vol. 1, *Iron and Steel Manufacturing*. Washington, D.C.: Government Printing Office, 1911.

————, *Immigration and Crime*. Washington, D.C.: Government Printing Office, 1911.

————, *Immigrants in Cities*. 2 vols. Washington, D.C.: Government Printing Office, 1912.

U.S. Department of Justice, Immigration and Naturalization Service, *Annual Reports*. Washington, D.C.: Government Printing Office, 1955–1975.

U.S. Office of Strategic Services, *Foreign Nationality Groups in the United States.* Washington, D.C.: O.S.S., 1945.

Slavic Immigrants and Their Background

BALCH, EMILY GREENE. *Our Slavic Fellow Citizens.* New York: Charities Publications Committee, 1910.

CVETICH, M. "I Posed as a Communist for the F.B.I." *Saturday Evening Post,* July 15, 22, 29, 1950.

DVORNIK, FRANCIS. *The Making of East Central Europe.* London: Polish Research Centre, 1949.

GREENE, VICTOR R. *The Slavic Community on Strike.* Notre Dame, Ind.: University of Notre Dame Press, 1968.

HALECKI, OSCAR. *Borderlands of Western Civilization.* New York: Ronald Press, 1952.

JELAVICH, CHARLES. *Language and Area Studies: East Central and Southeastern Europe, A Survey.* Chicago: University of Chicago Press, 1969.

KOLAR, WALTER. *A History of the Tamburitza.* Pittsburgh: Duquesne University, 1973.

KOUKOL, ALOIS B. "The Slav's a Man for A' That." *Charities and the Commons* 21 (January 2, 1909), 589–98.

MAMATEY, VICTOR S. *The United States and East Central Europe, 1914–1918.* Princeton: Princeton University Press, 1957.

MELER, VJEKOSLAV, ed. *The Slavonic Pioneers of California.* San Francisco: Slavonic Pioneers of California, 1932.

MILOŠEVIĆ, BOŽO, ed. *Americans of Slav Ancestry.* New York: "Slavia," 1936.

RADIĆ, STJEPAN. *Moderna kolonizacija i Slaveni.* Zagreb: Matica Hrvatska, 1904.

RADOSAVLJEVICH, PAUL R. *Who Are the Slavs?* Boston: R. G. Badger, 1910.

ROBERTS, PETER. "The New Pittsburghers: Slavs and Kindred Immigrants in Pittsburgh." *Charities and the Commons* 21 (January 2, 1909), 533–52.

ROSS, EDWARD A. "The Slavs in America." *The Century Magazine* 88 (August, 1914), 590–98.

ROUCEK, JOSEPH S., ed. *Slavonic Encyclopedia.* New York: Philosophical Library, 1949.

SESTANOVICH, S. N., ed. *Slavs in California.* Oakland, Calif.: Slavonic Alliance, 1937.

SUNSERI, ALVIN R. "The Ludlow Massacre." *American Chronicle* 1, no. 1 (January, 1972), 23–25.

WARNE, F. J. *The Slav Invasion and the Mine Workers: A Study in Immigration*. Philadelphia: J. B. Lippincott, 1904.

The Balkans and Southeast Europe—General

Balkania: An International Quarterly Magazine on Balkan Affairs. St. Louis, Mo. Since 1967.

BERKOVICI, KONRAD. *The Incredible Balkans*. New York: Putnam, 1932.

CLISSOLD, STEPHEN. *Whirlwind*. London: Cresset Press, 1949.

DURHAM, MARY EDITH. *Twenty Years of Balkan Tangle*. London: Allen and Unwin, 1920.

GEWEHR, W. M. *The Rise of Nationalism in the Balkans, 1800–1930*. New York: Holt, 1931.

KANN, ROBERT A. *The Multinational Empire. Nationalism and National Reform in the Habsburg Monarchy, 1848–1918*. 2 vols. New York: Columbia University Press, 1950.

LENDVAI, PAUL. *Eagles in Cobwebs: Nationalism and Communism in the Balkans*. Garden City, N.Y.: Doubleday, 1969.

McCULLOCH, JOHN I. B. *Drums in the Balkan Night*. New York: Putnam, 1936.

PALMER, ALAN. *The Lands Between: A History of East-Central Europe since the Congress of Vienna*. New York: Macmillan, 1970.

PRIBICHEVICH, STOYAN. *World Without End*. New York: Reynal and Hitchcock, 1939.

ROBERTS, KENNETH L. "Balkan Jottings." *The Saturday Evening Post*, February 11, 1922, pp. 16–17, 110, 113–14.

RISTELHUEBER, RENÉ. *A History of the Balkan Peoples*. New York: Twayne Publishers, 1971.

ROUCEK, JOSEPH S. *Balkan Politics*. Stanford, Calif.: Stanford University Press, 1949.

SETON-WATSON, HUGH. *Eastern Europe Between Wars, 1918–1941*. Cambridge: Cambridge University Press, 1945.

SETON-WATSON, ROBERT W. *The Rise of Nationality in the Balkans*. London: Constable, 1917.

STAVRIANOS, L. S. *The Balkans Since 1453*. New York: Rinehart, 1958.

SÜDLAND, L. VON. *Die Südslawische Frage und der Weltkrieg*. Zagreb: Matica Hrvatska, 1944.

TAYLOR, A. J. P. *The Habsburg Monarchy: 1815–1918*. Rev. ed. London: Hamish Hamilton, 1949.

WOLFF, ROBERT LEE. *The Balkans in Our Time*. Cambridge, Mass.: Harvard University Press, 1956.

Yugoslavia—Historical Background and Immigrants

ADAMIC, LOUIS. *The Native's Return.* New York: Harper, 1934.
—————. *My Native Land.* New York: Harper, 1943.
—————. *The Eagle and the Roots.* Garden City, N.Y.: Doubleday, 1952.
ARMSTRONG, HAMILTON FISH. *Tito and Goliath.* New York: Macmillan, 1951.
AUTY, PHILIS. *Yugoslavia.* New York: Walker, 1965.
BAUČIĆ, IVO. *The Effects of Emigration from Yugoslavia and the Problems of Returning Emigrant Workers.* The Hague: M. Nijhoff, 1972.
BOMBELLES, JOSEPH T. *Economic Development of Communist Yugoslavia.* Stanford, Calif.: Hoover Institution, 1968.
BROWN, ALEC. *Yugoslav Life and Landscape.* London: Elek Books, 1954.
BYRNES, ROBERT F., ed. *Yugoslavia.* New York: Praeger, 1957.
CLISSOLD, STEPHEN, ed. *A Short History of Yugoslavia: From Early Times to 1966.* Cambridge: Cambridge University Press, 1966.
DJILAS, MILOVAN. *The New Class.* New York: Praeger, 1957.
—————. *The Unperfect Society: Beyond the New Class.* New York: Harcourt, Brace, 1969.
ETEROVICH, ADAM S. *Yugoslav Survey of California, Nevada, Arizona and the South, 1800–1900.* San Francisco: R. and E. Research Associates, 1971.
FISHER, JACK. *Yugoslavia—a Multinational State.* San Francisco: Chandler, 1966.
FOTICH, CONSTANTINE. *The War We Lost.* New York: Viking, 1945.
GOVORCHIN, GERALD G. *Americans from Yugoslavia.* Gainesville, Fla.: University of Florida Press, 1961.
GRAHAM, STEPHEN. *Alexander of Yugoslavia.* New Haven: Yale University Press, 1939.
HINKOVIĆ, HINKO. *The Jugoslav Problem.* New York: Yugoslav Committee, 1918.
HOPTNER, J. B. *Yugoslavia in Crisis: 1934–1941.* New York: Columbia University Press, 1962.
KADIĆ, ANTE. *Modern Yugoslav Literature.* Berkeley: University of California Press, 1956.
KERNER, ROBERT J., ed. *Yugoslavia.* Berkeley: University of California Press, 1949.
KOSIER, LJUBOMIR ST. *Srbi, Hrvati i Slovenci u Americi: Ekonomosko-socijalni problemi emigracije.* Belgrade: Biblioteka "Bankarstva," 1927.

LEDBETTER, ELEANOR S. *The Jugoslavs of Cleveland.* Cleveland: The Cleveland Americanization Committee, 1918.

MARKHAM, REUBEN H. *Tito's Imperial Communism.* Chapel Hill: University of North Carolina Press, 1947.

MATICA ISELJENIKA HRVATSKE. *Rodnoj Grudi: Iseljenici Jogoslavije svom "Starom Kraju."* Zagreb: Matica Iseljenika Hrvatske, 1951.

Matica, monthly and yearly almanacs: 1955–1976 (Zagreb).

MLADINEO, IVAN. *Narodni Adresar—The National Directory of the Croat-Slovene-Serb Organizations, Institutions; Business, Professional and Social Leaders in the United States and Canada.* New York: By the author, 1937.

MARJANOVIĆ, MILAN. *Jugoslavija.* New York: Jogoslavenska Biblioteka, 1916.

MILJEVICH, JUNE N. "The Yugoslav People in Michigan." *Michigan History Magazine* 25, nos. 3–4 (Autumn, 1941), 358–64.

MILOŠEVIĆ, BOŽO N. "Yugoslavs of Cleveland." *Slavia* (New York) (Summer, 1939), 61–69.

MIRTH, KARLO. "U.S. Census of Population: Americans Whose Country of Origin Is Yugoslavia." *Croatia Press* 19, nos. 4–6 (July–December, 1965), 2–15.

NILAND, BILLYANNA. "Yugoslavs in San Pedro, California: Economic and Social Factors." *Sociology and Social Research* 26, no. 1 (September–October, 1941), 36–44.

OSTOVIĆ, PAVLE D. *The Truth About Yugoslavia.* New York: Roy Publishers, 1952.

PAULOVA, MILADA. *Jugoslavenski Odbor.* Zagreb: Prosvjetna Nakladna Zadruga, 1925.

POLJAK, J., ed. *Alamanak i statistika Južnih Slavena u Sjedinjenim Državama Amerike.* Chicago: By the author, 1925.

POTOČNJAK, FRANKO. *Iz Emigracije: U Americi.* Vol. 3. Zagreb: Tipografija, 1927.

PRPIĆ, GEORGE J. "The South Slavs." In *The Immigrants' Influence on Wilson's Peace Policies,* edited by Joseph P. O'Grady. Lexington: University of Kentucky Press, 1967, pp. 173–203.

————. "Communism and Nationalism in Yugoslavia." *Balkan Studies* 10, no. 1 (1969), 23–50.

ROUCEK, JOSEPH S. "The Yugoslav Immigrants in America." *American Journal of Sociology* 40 (March, 1935), 602–11.

ŠIŠIĆ, FERDO. *Dokumenti o postanku Kraljevine S.H.S.* Zagreb: Matica Hrvatska, 1920.

STANOYEVICH, M. S. *The Yugoslavs in the United States of America.* New York: Yugoslav Section of America's Making, 1921.

TOMASICH, DINKO. *National Communism and Soviet Strategy.* Washington, D.C.: Public Affairs Press, 1957.

VUJNOVIĆ, MILOŠ. *Yugoslavs in Louisiana.* Gretna, La.: Pelican Publishing Co., 1974.

WEST, REBECCA. *Black Lamb and Grey Falcon.* 2 vols. New York: Viking Press, 1941.

Bulgarians and Macedonians

1. Bulgarians

ABBOTT, GRACE. "The Bulgarians of Chicago." *Charities and the Commons* 21 (January 9, 1909), 653–60. The excellent publication contains throughout years extensive information on many immigrant groups including also the South Slavs.

ANASTASOFF, CHRIST. *Bulgaria.* Hicksville, N. Y.; Exposition Press, 1977.

BLAGOEVA, S. D. *Dimitrov.* New York: International Publishers, 1934.

CHRISTOWE, STOYAN. *This Is My Country.* New York: Carrick Evans, 1938.

—————. *The Eagle and the Stork.* New York: Harper, 1976.

DELLIN, L. A. D. *Bulgaria.* New York: Praeger, 1957.

EVANS, STANLEY G. *A Short History of Bulgaria.* London: Lawrence and Wishart, 1960.

GUNTHER, JOHN. *Inside Europe.* New York: Harper, 1938.

MANNING, CLARENCE A., and SMAL-STOCKI, ROMAN. *The History of Modern Bulgarian Literature.* New York: Bookman Associates, 1960.

MARKHAM, REUBEN H. *Meet Bulgaria.* Sofia: By the author, 1931.

MONROE, WILL A. *Bulgaria and Her People; With an Account of the Balkan Wars, Macedonia, and the Macedonian Bulgars.* Boston: The Page Company, 1914.

NEIDLE, CECYLE S. "Stoyan Christowe." In *The New Americans,* pp. 283–87. New York: Twayne Publishers, 1967.

NEWMAN, BERNARD. *Bulgarian Background.* London: R. Hale, 1961.

NICOLOFF, ASSEN. *Bulgarian Folklore and Fine Literature: A Selected Bio-bibliography.* Cleveland: By the author, 1971.

PETROFF, B. G. *Son of the Danube.* New York: Viking Press, 1940.

ROUCEK, JOSEPH S. "Bulgaria." In *Balkan Politics,* pp. 47–48. Stanford, Calif.: Stanford University Press, 1948. See also "Macedonians," pp. 147–68.

—————. "Bulgarian Americans." In *One America,* pp. 176–84. Englewood Cliffs, N.J.: Prentice-Hall, 1952. The author stresses that he considers the Macedonians as part of the Bulgarian nation.

————. *The American Bulgarians.* Bridgeport, Conn.: By the author, 1971.

RUNCIMAN, STEPHEN. *A History of the First Bulgarian Empire.* London: G. Bell, 1930.

SANDERS, IRWIN T. *Balkan Village.* Lexington, Ky: University of Kentucky Press, 1949.

YANKOFF, PETER D. *Peter Menikoff: The Story of a Bulgarian Boy in the Great American Melting Pot.* New York: Children's Book Club, 1928.

2. Macedonians

ALLEN, H. B. *Come Over Into Macedonia.* New Brunswick, N.J.: Rutgers University Press, 1943.

ANASTASOFF, CHRIST. *The Tragic Peninsula: A History of the Macedonian Movement for Independence Since 1878.* St. Louis, Mo.: Blackwell Wielandy, 1938.

————, ed. *The Case for an Autonomous Macedonia: A Symposium.* Indianapolis, Ind.: The Central Committee of the Macedonian Patriotic Organizations, 1945.

Balkania, An International Quarterly Magazine on Balkan Affairs. St. Louis, Mo. Since 1967.

BARKER, ELIZABETH. *Macedonia, Its Place in Balkan Power Politics.* London: Royal Institute of International Affairs, 1950.

BRAILSFORD, H. N. *Macedonia.* London: Methuen, 1906.

DAKIN, DOUGLAS. *The Greek Struggle in Macedonia, 1897–1913.* Salonica, Greece: Institute for Balkan Studies, 1966.

DIMITROFF, LIUBEN. *Ilinden 1903–1953.* Indianapolis, Ind.: M.P.O., 1953.

MACEDONIAN PATRIOTIC ORGANIZATIONS. *An American Symposium on the Macedonian Problem.* Indianapolis, Ind.: M.P.O., 1941.

————. *The Truth About Macedonia: American Missionaries' Testimony.* Indianapolis, Ind.: M.P.O., 1946.

————. *How Our National Heroes Wrote.* Indianapolis, Ind.: M.P.O., 1956.

Makedonska Tribuna–Macedonian Tribune (Indianapolis), 1960–1976. A weekly.

MIHAILOFF, IVAN. *Macedonia: A Switzerland of the Balkans.* St. Louis, Mo.: Pearlstone Publishing Company, 1950.

SCIAKY, LEON. *Farewell to Salonica.* New York: Wyn, 1946.

SLIJEPČEVIĆ, DJOKO. *The Macedonian Question: The Struggle for Southeastern Serbia.* Chicago: The American Institute for Balkan Affairs, 1958.

ZOTIADES, GEORGE B. *The Macedonian Controversy.* 2d ed. Salonica: The Institute for Balkan Studies, 1961.

The Croatians

ADAMIC, LOUIS. *Cradle of Life.* New York: Harper, 1936.
––––––. "The Millvale Apparition." *Harper's Magazine,* April, 1938, pp. 476–86.
––––––. "A Bohunk Woman." *The American Mercury* 19 (March, 1930), 281–86.
BADOVINAC, JOHN. "A Story About Hawaii's Croatian 'King,'" *Zajedničar* (Pittsburgh), June 28, 1972, p. 2.
––––––. "The Titanic Disaster." *Zajedničar,* August 23, 1972, p. 2.
BALIĆ, SMAIL. *Etičko naličje bosansko-hercegovačkih Muslimana.* Vienna: Muslimanska Biblioteka, 1952.
BENKOVIĆ, THEODORE. *The Tragedy of a Nation: An American's Eyewitness Report.* Chicago: Franciscan Press, 1947.
BONIFAČIĆ, ANTUN F., and MIHANOVICH, CLEMENT S., eds. *The Croatian Nation in Its Struggle for Freedom and Independence.* Chicago: "Croatia" Publishing Company, 1955.
CARTER, FRANCIS W. *Dubrovnik (Ragusa) A Classic City-State.* London: Seminar Press, 1972.
Danica. Hrvatski Kalendar (Chicago), 1950–1976. A yearly almanac.
Danica–The Morning Star (Chicago), 1950–1977. A weekly.
ETEROVICH, ADAM S. *Croatian Cemetery Records of San Francisco, Calif., 1849–1930.* San Francisco: By the author, 1964.
––––––. *Croatians from Dalmatia and Montenegrin Serbs in the West and South 1800–1900.* San Francisco, Calif.: R. and E. Research Associates, 1971.
ETEROVICH, FRANCIS H., and SPALATIN, CHRISTOPHER, eds. *Croatia: Land, People, Culture.* 2 vols. Toronto: University of Toronto Press, 1964, 1970.
FOLEY, HENRY A. *They Called Him King of the Grapes: The Life of Peter J. Divizich.* Porterville, Calif.: By the author and P. J. Divizich, 1975.
GAZI, STEPHEN. *A History of Croatia.* New York: Philosophical Library, 1973.
GAŽI, STJEPAN. *Croatian Immigration to Allegheny County 1882–1914.* Pittsburgh: Croatian Fraternal Union, 1956.
GULDESCU, STANKO. *History of Medieval Croatia.* The Hague: Mouton, 1964.
––––––. *The Croatian-Slavonian Kingdom: 1526–1792.* The Hague: Mouton, 1970.

HILBERRY, HARY. *The Sculpture of Ivan Meštrović.* Syracuse, N.Y.: Syracuse University Press, 1948.

HOLJEVAC, VEĆESLAV. *Hrvati izvan domovine.* Zagreb: Matica Hrvatska, 1968.

HOLBACH, MAUDE. *Bosnia and Herzegovina: Some Wayside Wanderings.* London: J. Lane, 1910.

JAREB, JEROME. "LeRoy King's Reports From Croatia." *Journal of Croatian Studies* 1 (1960), 75–168.

KADIĆ, ANTE. "Jack London and Croatian Settlers in Watsonville." *Croatia Press* 9, no. 146 (February, 1955), 6–7.

————. "Croatian Emigré Writers." *Croatia Press* 8, no. 5 (1959), 2–7.

————. *Contemporary Croatian Literature, 1895–1959.* The Hague: Mouton, 1960.

————. *Croatian Reader with Vocabulary.* The Hague: Mouton, 1960.

————. *From Croatian Renaissance to Yugoslav Socialism.* The Hague: Mouton, 1969.

KANE, H. T. "Dalmatia on the Mississippi." In *Deep Delta Country.* New York: Duell, Sloan and Pearce, 1944, pp. 92–104.

KOSTELSKI, Z. *The Croats.* Floreffe, Pa.: "Kolo" Publishing Company, 1950.

KRAJA, JOSIP. "The Croatian Circle, 1928–1946: Chronology and Reminiscences." *Journal of Croatian Studies* 5–6 (1964–1965), 145–204.

KRMPOTIĆ, M. D. *Josip Kundek, Misionar u Jasperu, Dubois County, Ind.: Joseph Kundek, a Missionary in Jasper, Dubois County, Indiana.* Zagreb: By the author, 1925.

————. *Life and Works of the Rev. Ferdinand Konscak, S.J. 1703–1759, an Early Missionary in California.* Boston: Stratford Company, 1925.

LUPIS-VUKIĆ, IVO F. *Medju Našim Narodom u Americi: Among Our People in America.* Split: Leonova Tiskara, 1929.

MCANDREWS, DUNSTAN. *Father Joseph Kundek: 1810–1857 a Missionary Priest of the Diocese of Vincennes.* St. Meinrad, Ind.: A Grail Publication, 1954.

MAČEK, VLADKO. *In the Struggle for Freedom.* New York: Robert Speller, 1957.

MANDIĆ, DOMINIK. *Bosna i Hercegovina.* Chicago: The Croatian Historical Institute, 1960.

————. *Etnička Povijest Bosne i Hercegovine.* Rome: The Croatian Historical Institute, 1967.

MAROHNIĆ, JOSIP. *Popis Hrvata u Americi i kratki opis Sjedinjenih*

Država: Census of the Croatians in America and a Brief Description of the United States. Allegheny, Pa.: J. Marohnić, 1902.

Matičin Iseljenički Kalendar. Zagreb: Matica Iseljenika Hrvatske, 1955–1973.

MELER, VJEKOSLAV. *Hrvati u Americi; hrvatske kolonije u Chicagu i St. Louisu: The Croatians in America; Croatian Colonies in Chicago and St. Louis.* Chicago: Adria Printing Company, 1927.

————. *The Croatians of the Copper Country.* Calumet, Mich.: By the author, 1929.

MIHANOVICH, CLEMENT S. "Americanization of the Croats in Saint Louis, Missouri, During the Past Thirty Years." M.A. thesis, Saint Louis University, 1936.

NEMEC, SLAVKO. *Povijest hrvatske naseobine u St. Louisu, Mo., 1862–1931.* St. Louis, Mo.: By the author, 1931.

ORR, DOROTHEA. *Portrait of a People: Croatia Today.* New York: Funk and Wagnalls, 1936.

OWEN, FRANCIS. "The Saga of Joe Magarac: Steelman." *Scribner's Magazine* 10 (November, 1931), 505–13.

PANDŽIĆ, STEVEN. *A Review of Croatian History.* Chicago: "Croatia," 1954.

PRCELA, JOHN, and GULDESCU, S. *Operation Slaughterhouse.* Philadelphia: Dorrance, 1970.

PREVEDEN, FRANCIS. *A History of the Croatian People.* 2 vols. New York: Philosophical Library, 1955, 1962.

PRPIĆ, GEORGE J. "The Croats in America." Ph.D. dissertation, Georgetown University, Washington, D.C., 1959.

————. "The Croatian Newspapers in America Before 1918." *Croatia Press* 15 (December, 1961), 7–15.

————. "Maksimilijan Vanka: njegov doprinos umjetnosti Amerike." *La Revista Croata* 8, no. 2 (Summer, 1958), 129–60.

————. "Early Croatian Contacts with America and the Mystery of the Croatans." *Journal of Croatian Studies*, no. 1 (March, 1960), 6–24.

————. "Tisuće hrvatskih grobova: hrvatski doprinos Americi u krvi i životima." *La Revista Croata* 10, no. 4 (December, 1960), 741–59.

————. "Fernando Konschak, S.J. Misionero y Explorador en Baja California." *Studia Croatica* 3, no. 1 (March, 1962), 58–68.

————. "The Croatian Immigrants and the Americans from Yugoslavia." *Journal of Croatian Studies* 3–4 (March, 1965), 166–72.

————. *The Croatian Publications Abroad After 1939: A Bibli-*

ography. Cleveland: The Institute for Soviet and East European Studies, 1969.

————. *The Croatian Immigrants in America*. New York: Philosophical Library, 1971.

RADITSA, BOGDAN. "A West Coast Visit to Our Countrymen." *Croatia Press* 10 (October, 1956), 1–6.

————. "Clash of Two Immigrant Generations." *Commentary* 21, no. 1 (January, 1958), 8–15.

RADIĆ, STJEPAN. *Javna poruka hrvatskoj braći u Americi*. Zagreb: Slavenska Knjižara, 1913.

SANJEK, LOUIS. *In Silence*. New York: Fortuny's Publishers, 1938.

SCHMECKBIER, LAWRENCE. *Ivan Meštrović, Sculptor and Patriot*. Syracuse: Syracuse University Press, 1959.

SERVIN, MANUEL P., ed. *The Apostolic Life of Fernando Consag Explorer of Lower California*: By Francisco Zevallos. Los Angeles: Dawson's Book Shop, 1968.

SLISKOVICH, ANSELM, and ZUBACK, ANTHONY G. *50th Anniversary of the Life and Work of the Croatian People in the Shenango Valley*. Farrell, Pa.: The Croatian Historical Research Bureau, 1944.

SORIĆ, BONIFACE. *Centennial: 1847–1947; the Life and Work of the Croatian People in Allegheny County, Pennsylvania*. Pittsburgh: The Croatian Historical Research Bureau, 1947.

TOMASIC, DINKO. "Croatia in European Politics." *Journal of Central European Affairs* 2, no. 1 (April, 1942), 63–85.

TRESIĆ-PAVIČIĆ, ANTE. *Preko Atlantika do Pacifika: Život Hrvata u Sjevernoj Americi*. Zagreb: Dionička Tiskara, 1907.

VUKELIĆ, PHILIP, ed. *Kratki Pregled povijesti Hrvatske Bratske Zajednice, 1894–1949: A Short History of the Croatian Fraternal Union*. Pittsburgh: Croatian Fraternal Union, 1949.

Zajedničar, the weekly organ of the Croatian Fraternal Union (Pittsburgh, Pennsylvania). In 1975 in its seventieth year.

ZUBACK, ANTHONY G. *50th Anniversary of the Life and Work of the Croatian People in the Mahoning Valley*. Youngstown, Ohio: The Croatian Historical Research Bureau, 1946.

————. *Centennial: 1848–1948: The Life and Work of the Croatian People in Chicagoland*. Chicago: Croatian Franciscan Press, 1949.

The Montenegrins

BIHALJI-MERIN, OTO, ed. *Montenegro, Yugoslavia*. New York: A. Vanous, 1961.

DJILAS, MILOVAN. *The Land Without Justice*. New York: Harcourt, Brace, 1958.

————. *Montenegro.* New York: Harcourt, 1962.

————. *The Leper and Other Stories.* New York: Harcourt, 1964.

————. *Njegoš: Poet, Prince, Bishop.* Translated by M. B. Petrovich. New York: Harcourt, 1966.

————. *Wartime.* New York: Harcourt Brace Jovanovich, 1977.

DRLJEVIĆ, SEKULA. *Balkanski Sukobi: 1905–1941.* Zagreb: "Putovi," 1944.

JOVANOVICH, WILLIAM. *Now, Barabbas.* New York: Harper and Row, 1964.

LALIĆ, MIHAILO. *The Wailing Mountain.* New York: Harcourt, 1965.

ŠTEDIMLIJA, SAVIĆ. *Osnovi Crnogorskog nacionalizma.* Zagreb: Politička Biblioteka "Putovi," 1937.

WILES, JAMES W. *The Mountain Wreath of P. P. Nyegosh, Prince-Bishop of Montenegro, 1830–1851.* London: Allen and Unwin, 1930.

The Serbians

ADAMS, J. C. *Flight in Winter.* Princeton: Princeton University Press, 1942.

ANON. "Tesla Nikola." In *The Encyclopedia Americana,* vol. 26, pp. 542–43: New York: Americana Corporation, 1950.

ANON. *Spomenica borbe rodoljubnih Srba za očuvanje slobode srpske pravoslavne crkve Sv. Save u Klivlendu.* Cleveland: The Committee, 1969.

BEARD, A. E. S. "A Serbian-American Scientist—Michael Pupin." In *Our Foreign Born Citizens.* New York: Thomas Y. Crowell, 1939, pp. 283–89.

BIHALJI-MERIN, OTO, ed. *Serbia, Yugoslavia.* New York: A. Vanous, 1961.

BROWN, ALEC. *Mihailovitch and Yugoslav Resistance.* London: J. Lane, 1943.

GAKOVICH, ROBERT, and RADOVICH, MILAN. *The Serbs in the United States and Canada: A Comprehensive Bibliography.* St. Paul, Minn.: The Immigration History Research Center, 1976.

HALPERN, J. M. *A Serbian Village.* New York: Columbia University Press, 1958.

KADIĆ, ANTE. *Contemporary Serbian Literature.* The Hague: Mouton, 1964.

KOSIER, LJUBOMIR ST. *Srbi, Hrvati i Slovenci u Americi: Serbs, Croats and Slovenes in America.* Belgrade: "Bankarstvo," 1927.

MARTIN, DAVID. *Ally Betrayed.* New York: Prentice-Hall, 1949.

MARTIN, THOMAS C. *The Inventions, Researches and Writings of Nikola Tesla.* New York: The Electrical Engineer, 1894.

MATEJIĆ, MATEJA. *Pesme*. Munich: Iskra, 1964.

MATEJIĆ, MATEJA, and KARAPANDŽIĆ, BOR. M., eds. *Na stazama izbegličkim: srpsko pesništvo u izbeglištvu*. Melbourne, Australia, Srpska Misao, 1969.

NEIDLE, CECYLE S. "Michael Pupin." In *The New Americans*. New York: Twayne Publishers, 1967, pp. 163–66.

O'NEILL, JOHN J. *Prodigal Genius: The Life of Nikola Tesla*. New York: Ives Washburn, 1944.

PARMENTER, MARY F. *The Life of George Fisher*. San Francisco: R. and E. Research Associates, 1974.

POZZI, HENRI. *Black Hand Over Europe*. London: The Francis Mott Company, 1935.

PRIBIĆ, NIKOLA. "George Šagić-Fisher, Patriot of Two Worlds." *The Florida State University Slavic Papers* 1 (1967), 35–47.

PUPIN, MIHAILO. *From Immigrant to Inventor*. New York: Scribner, 1927.

RADAKOVIĆ, ACA. "Sculptor from Lika." *Review* (September, 1968), 14–15. On John David Brcin.

ROOTHAM, JASPER. *Miss-Fire*. London: Chattus and Windus, 1946.

SERBIAN ORTHODOX DIOCESE. *The Constitution of the Serbian Orthodox Diocese of the United States and Canada*. Pittsburgh: The Serbian Orthodox Diocese, 1929.

VRGA, DJURO J., and FAHEY, FRANK J. *Changes and Socio-Religious Conflict in an Ethnic Minority Group: The Serbian Orthodox Church in America*. San Francisco: R. and E. Research Associates, 1975.

VUCINICH, WAYNE S. *Serbia Between East and West*. Stanford, Calif.: Stanford University Press, 1954.

The Slovenians

ADAMIC, LOUIS. *Grandsons: A Story of American Lives*. New York: Harper, 1935. Adamic's book *Yerney's Justice*, a translation from the Slovenian by Ivan Cankar and almost all of Adamic's numerous short stories, articles, and books deal considerably with Slovenia and Slovenians.

ALESOVEC, JAKOB. *Ne v Ameriko! Povest Slovencem v poduk*. Ljubljana: By the author, 1883.

Ameriški Družinski Koledar—American Family Almanac. Chicago: Jugoslav Workmen's Publishing Company, 1925–1945.

ANDREJČKOV, JOŽE. *Amerika*. Novo Mesto: J. Krajec, 1885.

ARNEZ, JOHN. *Slovenci v New Yorku: Slovenians in New York*. Washington, D.C.: Studia Slovenica, 1966.

————. *Slovenia in European Affairs: Reflections on Slovenian Political History.* New York: League of S.S.A., 1958.

————. *Slovenian Community in Bridgeport, Conn.* New York: Studia Slovenica, 1971.

Ave Maria Koledar (Lemont, Ill.), 1940–1970.

BITTNER, WILLIAM C. *Frank J. Lausche: a Political Biography.* New York: Studia Slovenica, 1975.

BREZNIK, PAVEL. *V senci nebotičnikov.* Ljubljana: Vodnikova Družba, 1930.

CHESAREK, J. "Bogati trgovec." In *American Family Almanac 1945,* pp. 143–55.

CLISSOLD, JOSEPH. *The Slovenes Want to Live.* New York: The Jugoslav Information Center, 1943(?).

Constitution and By-Laws of the Grand Carniolian Slovenian Catholic Union of the United States. Ustava in pravila Kranjsko-Slovenske Katoliške Jednote v Združenih Državah Ameriških. Joliet, Ill.: G.C.S.G.U., 1947.

ČUJEŠ, RUDOLF, and MAUKO, VLADIMIR V. B., eds. *This Is Slovenia: A Glance at the Land and Its People.* Toronto, Ontario: Slovenian National Federation of Canada, 1958.

FELICIJAN, JOSEPH. *The Genesis of the Contractural Theory and the Installation of the Dukes of Carinthia.* Klagenfurt, Austria: Družba Sv. Mohorja, 1967.

FURLAN, W. P. *In Charity Unfeigned.* Saint Cloud, Minn., 1952.

GOBETZ, GILES EDWARD, and FUGGER, DANIEL. *From Carniola to Carnegie Hall: A Biographical Study of Anton Schubel, Slovenian Immigrant Singer and Musical Pedagogue.* Wickliffe, Ohio: Euram Books, 1968.

HOCEVAR, TOUSSAINT. *Slovenia's Role in Yugoslav Economy.* Columbus, Ohio: Slovenian Research Center, 1964.

————. *The Structure of the Slovenian Economy.* New York: Studia Slovenica, 1965.

HROVAT, P. FLORENTIN. *Franc Pirec, oče umne sadjereje na Kranjskem in apostolski misijonar v Severni Ameriki.* Klagenfurt: Družba Sv. Mohorja, 1887.

INGOLIČ, ANTON. *Pri naših v Ameriki.* Ljubljana: Mladinska Knjiga, 1964.

Izseljenski Zbornik Izeljenske Matice v Ljubljani. Ljubljana: Družba S. Rafaela, 1938.

JAZBEC, F., and PRISLAND, M. *Ameriška Slovenka.* Chicago: Slovenian Women's Union of America, 1928.

JEZERNIK, MAKSIMILIJAN. *Frederick Baraga.* New York: Studia Slovenica, 1968.

KRASNA, ANA PRACEK. *Za lepše dni.* New York: By the author, 1950.

KRISTAN, ANTON. *V Ameriko in po Ameriki.* Ljubljana: Zadružna Zoložba, 1928.

KOVAČIČ, ERIC. "Pater Kapus, prvi slovenski misijonar v Severni Ameriki." *Ave Maria Koledar 1970,* pp. 89–91.

MLAKAR, FRANK. *He, the Father.* New York: Harper, 1950.

MOLEK, IVAN. "Rajska Dolina: odlomek iz zgodovine ameriških Slovencev." In *American Family Almanac 1937,* pp. 123–29.

K.S.K.J. *Jubilejna spominska knjiga izdana povodom tridesetletnice Kranjsko-Slovenske Katoliške Jednote v Združenih Državah Ameriških: Jubilee Souvenir Book Published on the Occasion of the Thirtieth Anniversary of the Carniolian-Slovenian Catholic Union in the United States of America.* Joliet, Ill.: K.S.K.J., 1924.

KUBELKA, VICTOR J. *Angleško-slovenski in slovensko-angleški slovar; English-Slovenian and Slovenian-English Dictionary.* New York: V. J. Kubelka, 1912.

—————. *Slovenian-English Grammar, Interpreter, Letter-Writer and Information on Naturalization. English-Slovenian and Slovenian-English Dictionary.* New York: V. J. Kubelka, 1912.

—————. *Slovensko-angleški razgovori. Slovenian-English Interpreter.* New York: V. J. Kubelka, 1912.

LONČAR, DRAGOTIN. *The Slovenes: A Social History.* Cleveland, Ohio: Jugoslav Printing and Publishing Company, 1939.

MELIK, ANTON. *Amerika in ameriška Slovenija: America and American Slovenia.* Ljubljana: Matica Slovenskih Izseljencev, 1956.

NEIDLE, CECYLE S. "Louis Adamic." In *The New Americans.* New York: Twayne Publishers, 1967, pp. 279–83.

McWILLIAMS, CAREY. *Louis Adamic and Shadow America.* Los Angeles: A. Whipple, 1935.

PRISLAND, MARIE. *From Slovenia to America.* Chicago: The Slovenian Women's Union of America—the Bruce Publishing Company, 1968.

REZEK, A. I. "Mrak, Ignatius." In *The Catholic Encyclopedia,* X, 624–25.

—————. "Vertin, John." In *The Catholic Encyclopedia,* XV, 377–78.

TRUNK, J. M. *Amerika in Amerikanci.* Klagenfurt, Austria: By the author, 1912.

TURK, FRANK J. *Slovenski Pionir: Slovenian Pioneer.* Cleveland, Ohio: "Ameriška Domovina," 1955.

UNION OF SLOVENIAN PARISHES OF AMERICA. *Shall Slovenia Be*

Sovietized: A Rebuttal to Louis Adamic. Cleveland, Ohio: "Ameriška Domovina," 1944.

Vetrinjska Tragedija. Cleveland, Ohio: "Ameriška Domovina," 1960.

ZAITZ, FRANK. "Slovenska kulturna društva v Zedinjenih Državah," *American Family Almanac 1933,* pp. 60–99.

ZAVERTNIK, JOSEPH. *Ameriški Slovenci.* Chicago: Slovene National Benefit Society, 1926.

ZEBOT, CYRIL. *Slovenija včeraj, danes, jutri.* Klagenfurt: By the author and Družba Sv. Mohorja, 1967.

Index